THE ROYAL HORTICULTURAL SOCIETY COLLECTION

THE *kitchen* GARDEN

THE ROYAL HORTICULTURAL SOCIETY COLLECTION

THE *kitchen* GARDEN

ANDI CLEVELY

CONRAN OCTOPUS

First published in 1995 by Conran Octopus Limited
37 Shelton Street, London WC2H 9HN

Text copyright © Andi Clevely 1995

Design and layout copyright © Conran Octopus Limited 1995

A catalogue record for this book is available from the
British Library.

ISBN 1 85029 657 X

Project Editor   Jane O'Shea
Project Art Editor   Ann Burnham
Editor   Helen Ridge
Designer   Lesley Craig
Picture Researcher   Helen Fickling
Editorial Assistant   Caroline Davison
Production   Julia Golding
Illustrator   Vanessa Luff

Typeset by Servis Filmsetting Ltd, England
Printed and bound in Hong Kong

FRONT JACKET *Red currants are dependable and colourful soft fruits for gardens of any size.*

BACK JACKET *Well-ordered vegetable beds yield a steady and varied supply of produce all year round.*

PAGE 1 *Crops such as courgettes, sweet corn, apples and climbing beans blend with summer flowers in the kitchen garden.*

PAGE 2 *Well-planned beds can be used for growing a wide range of fruit, vegetables and herbs.*

RIGHT *In a small garden, trained fruit and tall runner beans are attractive and economize on space.*

CONTENTS

What is a kitchen garden?   7

Planning the kitchen garden   13

Routine husbandry   25

Vegetables from the garden   35

Fruit from the garden   79

Herbs in the kitchen garden   113

Through the seasons   119

Index   124

Acknowledgments   128

WHAT IS A KITCHEN GARDEN?

The kitchen garden is somewhere to grow vegetables of all kinds, culinary herbs, fruit trees and soft fruits. Unlike the rest of the garden it is planned and planted for production rather than for beauty, but that does not mean it is not a place of fascination and delight. There is a deeply satisfying sense of order and inevitability about the progress of a crop from seedbed to harvest. Nowhere else does one feel so closely in harmony with the seasons and the elements. And in the end there is the fresh produce: tender, full of flavour and, above all, raised with your own hands.

A kitchen garden is a constantly changing landscape of vegetables, herbs, fruit and even flowers at various stages in their lives. Here, colourful intersecting paths divide the plot into manageable beds planted with winter brassicas such as brussels sprouts and, in the foreground, an unusual form of hardy kale called chou palmier or palm tree cabbage. Beds are edged with strawberries and a dwarf box hedge in its early stages.

To make the best use of the ground organization is essential. Paths can be used both for access and also to divide the plot into beds of manageable size, within which rows of vegetables are rotated or interplanted as ground becomes vacant – the leeks and winter brassicas seen here growing in the right hand bed, for example. Tall peas supported on twiggy sticks subdivide beds and provide valuable shelter, while vigorous climbers such as runner beans can be trained on arches or similar structural features.

Gardeners have always grown food crops and ever since the first wild plants were domesticated, gardens have been intimately associated with the kitchen. Once people gave up their shifting lifestyle as hunter-gatherers, survival depended on the food that could be grown in a cleared patch of soil, in much the same way as crops are still raised in large areas of the world. Later these vegetable patches were fenced in as private gardens, like the 'yard . . . enclosed all about with sticks, and a dry ditch without' that Chaucer describes in the *Nun's Priest's Tale*.

As estates grew, kitchen gardens developed into large and efficiently organized enterprises, rather like small arable farms, that might be surrounded by high brick walls and elaborate structures such as the 'turrets of lattice fashion' recommended by one sixteenth century writer.

Those who tended these vast estates supplemented their wages by growing their own crops in the small gardens attached to their cottages. The original cottage garden was not a riot of elegant perennial flowers as we like to assume today, but very often a rectangular patch of ground divided into two equal beds by a central path. On one side a cereal such as wheat or barley was grown and vegetables on the other; the following year the two sides were changed over in a simple two-course rotation. A few herbs and flowers were fitted in here and there, while fruit cuttings would be brought home from the estate: soft fruits for planting beside the path and top fruits such as apples for grafting on seedlings grown in the garden's boundary hedges.

Self-sufficiency in basic food crops was taken for granted by the owners of the estates and also by those who looked after them, and the necessary skills were common knowledge. As dependence on home-grown produce decreased and gardens became more emphatically decorative, familiarity with the methods and routines of the kitchen garden declined to the point where now they must be rediscovered by many gardeners who would like to grow their own fresh vegetables and fruit.

ABOVE *The author, Andi Clevely, in his garden in Warwickshire.*

ABOVE RIGHT *Kitchen gardens are planned according to the household's needs. Vast amounts of produce are grown in large estate gardens such as this terrace garden at a château in France.*

RIGHT *Useful quantities of produce can also be raised in relatively small beds. Dwarf box edging here encloses a crop of winter-hardy cabbages in one corner of a potager. Variegated strawberries provide colourful ground cover beneath a trained apple tree.*

Making a start often seems daunting. For many people the term 'kitchen garden' has become firmly associated with the grand walled establishments that we visit on open days, with their vast beds and interminable rows of immaculate vegetables and espaliered fruit trees. They are inspiring places that excite awe and admiration. They are stimulating to work in and some of my happiest days have been spent earthing up potatoes, forcing seakale or pruning grape vines on large estates.

These huge kitchen gardens can also be intimidating and can deter many people from raising a few summer salads or strawberries in a small back garden, perhaps for the first time. Nonetheless, there are many incentives to 'grow your own', not least the current preference for a diet high in fresh foods produced without chemical inputs. But if you are not familiar with modern kitchen garden techniques, the obstacles might seem insurmountable.

For example, there are many competing demands for space in a small garden and you might feel challenged to find enough room for a few vegetables. Fortunately, research has shown that many plants can be grown at closer spacings than was once thought feasible and small compact cultivars are now available to help maximize yields from a limited area of ground. By growing fruit on dwarfing rootstocks and training plants in neat productive shapes it is possible to fit a wide range of types into a pocket handkerchief of a garden. Vegetables such as cucumbers, marrows, climbing beans and peas can be trained to save space. They will grow on fences or walls, on tripods of poles set among other crops or even on arches and similar structures that transform them into decorative features. Other vegetables with attractive leaves or flowers can be grown in flower beds, where they will succeed provided you give them the conditions they enjoy. There is no reason why the kitchen garden should not be dispersed rather than confined to a single site.

Traditional large kitchen gardens used animal manure by the trailer-load to keep soils fertile and sustain heavy crops. When thoroughly decayed this

Provided plants have sufficient light, many odd corners of a garden can be adapted for vegetables, especially popular salad crops such as the lettuce, beetroot, radishes and parsley grown here with maincrop onions. The stone path provides all-weather access, but the grass paths need to be cleanly edged to prevent them from invading the cropping space.

remains one of the best soil conditioners, but it is not always easily available. Garden compost is an acceptable substitute produced by recycling waste materials in a suitable container. If you supply this for the plants that need it most and grow these crops in a different place each year, small amounts of organic material can be used to good effect and will gradually improve the soil over the whole garden.

It is important not to be deterred by apparent difficulties such as limited space or infertile soil. There are ways to make the best of these inadequacies and these are discussed in later pages. Gardening advice these days takes account of the fact that few have the ideal medium loam, a benign local climate or a sufficiently large area of open frost-free ground in which to grow perfect crops. More than ever before, useful ideas and products are available – disease-resistant cultivars, inexpensive cloches, pre-mixed fertilizers and catch-crop methods, for example.

Kitchen gardening has to be a compromise between ambition and experience. It is best to start simply by growing one or two favourite crops, planning their cultivation carefully and keeping records of successes and failures. Above all aim to

grow them well, for it is the excellence of the end product that reinforces confidence most. After a few seasons you will become familiar with the basic routines involved and with landmarks such as the time of year when it is safe to start sowing outdoors, the expected arrival of autumn frosts or when to anticipate dry weather. And with this familiarity will come the instinctive understanding of soils, seasons and crops that all gardeners once possessed.

If tending the kitchen garden seems at first sight a serious business, that is only because quality is crucial, whether in the choice of cultivar, the care of the plants or the final product when it is ready for use. There are many incidental pleasures between sowing and harvest, however, and even the most seasoned gardener greets the start of a new season with anticipation. After years of growing all kinds of crops, I still marvel at the sight of a pear tree in full blossom, the pungent scent of parsnip foliage and the miracle of pruning as fruit branches respond to cuts exactly as intended. These seasonal delights, together with the enjoyment of produce fresher than any that can be bought, make growing for the kitchen the most rewarding kind of gardening.

LEFT *Top fruit such as apples trained on posts and wires economize on space and are easily accessible when used to flank a path. Here, various lettuces at different stages of growth demonstrate that you need not sow a whole row at once, nor confine it to a single cultivar. Lettuce needs successional sowing to ensure continuity of cropping, and fresh rows have been sown here before earlier batches reach maturity.*

RIGHT *Keeping the ground filled with repeated small sowings of popular crops avoids the problems of glut and wasted ground. This kitchen garden, blending comfortably with the adjacent herbaceous border, is packed to capacity with compact blocks of peas and broad beans, together with small sowings of chard and lettuce. Climbing runner beans create decorative screens, while a row of french beans is an ideal dwarf hedge beside the main path. Beyond these are blocks of carrots and bush tomatoes.*

PLANNING THE KITCHEN GARDEN

The aim of kitchen gardening is to achieve the best returns from a particular patch of ground. The site may not seem ideal at first, but even an unfavourable plot can be made productive by adapting its surroundings and improving the quality of the soil. Armed with an overall plan and a basic knowledge of the conditions crop plants prefer, you will find that your initial preparations soon result in a satisfying supply of fresh produce combined with the enjoyment of growing your own.

Although the routine of the kitchen garden depends on orderliness, this need not lead to uniformity or the segregation of vegetables from other plants. The urge to embellish is traditional – here, a sundial and training frame for fruit mark the centre of the garden. The cruciform paths separate four large beds in which space has been left for new sowings to succeed maturing crops and rows of flowers for cutting.

Creating the right environment

Adequate shelter from wind and frost is important if crops are to grow unchecked. Walled gardens are a traditional solution, providing crops such as this loose leaf lettuce with a sheltered microclimate, but even a single wall may prove very beneficial, not only shielding tender vegetables but also encouraging them with reflected warmth.

With the exception of herbs from dry Mediterranean habitats and over-wintering vegetables that must be robust enough to withstand severe weather, most crops succeed when grown fast in lavish conditions. Meeting their routine cultural needs is within our capabilities but most of us have to accept the limitations of the garden – its position, the prevailing climate and the type of soil – and adapt it where possible to meet the requirements of plants.

Providing shelter

In addition to water, crops need warmth, sunlight and shelter to reach perfection. Shelter is particularly important because even light winds reduce yields, while exposure to strong winds, especially when

these are also cold, can result in serious injury. Although walls might seem an obvious means of providing shelter for crops, local turbulence on the leeward side of a wall is destructive, and it is better to filter the wind through a permeable windbreak, which provides gradually decreasing protection over a distance up to ten times its own height.

Hedges make effective natural windbreaks, but take time to establish if planted deliberately, and may cast too much shade or compete with crop roots for water and nutrients. A tall perimeter fence of plastic mesh or timber strips separated by gaps of 2.5cm (1in) provides considerable shelter, and may be supplemented by low internal timber or wire-mesh fences, dividing the garden into beds and supporting trained fruit or climbing crops. Tall jerusalem artichokes or sweet corn can be used to provide seasonal shelter, while temporary screens of woven plastic or sacking will protect new plants until they are established. Check the surroundings for possible draughts between buildings and arrange windbreaks to intercept them.

Protection from frost

A totally enclosed low-lying garden can be a lethal frost-hollow, trapping cold air unless there is a gap on the lowest side for this to drain through. The last frosts in spring and their return in autumn define the length of the growing season. This can be extended by using cloches or frames (see page 23), but it may be necessary to choose hardy or fast-growing vegetables and late-flowering or early maturing fruit cultivars to ensure good crops over a longer period.

Sunlight

Most crops need maximum sunlight and suffer if grown too near large overhanging trees or tall hedges: where possible these should be thinned and pruned back or their height lowered to reduce the amount of shadow they cast, without sacrificing their value as shelter. In summer light shade can be valuable, shielding sensitive crops from hot sunshine and preventing them from bolting quickly to seed.

Sloping ground may be an asset, offering improved drainage in many cases and excluding still, cold air. Steeper ground can be terraced, with regular parallel paths dividing the garden into a series of almost level beds that minimize the risk of soil erosion during heavy rainfall. The timber trelliswork on this boundary wall in the background is ideal for providing trained fruit trees with sturdy support.

SQUARE BED
Crops planted in squares, here edged with boards, are easily accessible from all sides.

NARROW BED
Short transverse rows are easiest to manage and plant intensively with crops such as spinach, carrots and radishes.

RAISED BED
Elevated to a convenient height, strawberries mark the corners and lettuces are edged with parsley.

Aspect

Because crops need light for healthy growth, rows are best arranged to run north to south to prevent plants from shading each other. This is particularly important with tall, densely leaved vegetables such as runner beans, although leaf crops such as spinach and many salads appreciate their shade during the summer months. Make a note of which parts of the garden receive most sunlight at various times of the day and year and plant accordingly: over-wintered vegetables need the warmest parts, while slightly tender plants may be injured by rapid thawing in early morning sunlight. Planting frost-sensitive fruit facing away from the sun can delay flowering until the arrival of warmer weather, while late-ripening cultivars benefit from a sunny wall.

Altitude has an influence on temperatures, which decrease by 0.5°C (1°F) for every 300m (1000ft) above sea level, shortening the growing season and determining the plants that can be grown at high altitudes. Sloping sites also affect crop performance, a sunny slope often proving warmer and less prone to frost than comparable level ground. However, they may be difficult to cultivate unless terraced, which also helps minimize soil erosion by heavy rain. Always plant rows across a slope to reduce this risk.

Although crops are often arranged in long, well-spaced straight rows right across the garden, this is not always the most effective way of growing them. Smaller narrow beds, separated by a network of paths and accessible from both sides without treading on the soil, will support a high density of vegetables grown in short rows or blocks. Plants are then more easily moved around the garden according to a rotation scheme or to find sun or shade, while manure and compost can be concentrated where needed. Beds may be at ground level, mounded either with sloping sides or enclosed by solid timber or brick edges, or raised within brick walls about 60cm (2ft) high to reduce bending.

15

Assessing the soil

The ideal kitchen garden soil is deep, fertile, well-structured and easily worked at most times, has a friable crumbly texture that is free-draining and yet retains moisture, and is neither too acid nor very alkaline. Although few of us have this perfect medium, no soil is beyond redemption and there are ways to correct most deficiencies gradually.

Types of soil

It is useful first of all to identify the type of soil in your garden. Very sandy soils are composed of large mineral particles, making them porous and fast-draining, quick to warm in spring and easy to work. They also dry out quickly and become dusty in summer, while winter rains wash out much of their fertility. A handful of moist sandy soil rolled into a ball will immediately fall apart again. If the ball retains its shape, however, and feels sticky or can be polished with the thumb, the soil is heavy clay, composed of very fine particles which keep it cold and wet, even waterlogged, long into spring; once very dry it sets hard and cracks. Clay soil is heavy to work but potentially very fertile once reduced to a more open crumbly structure, and it will then retain nutrients and water for longer than sandy soil. Silty soils lie somewhere in between these two extremes, but most soils are blends of sand, clay and silt particles in various proportions, and may then be known as a 'sandy loam' or 'clay loam', according to the main constituent.

Humus in soil

A further vital ingredient of good soil is humus, which is dark decaying organic matter, although the term is also used loosely to describe any organic materials dug into the soil. Humus is spongy and water-retentive, reducing the rate at which sandy soils dry out yet forcing apart clay particles to improve drainage and make heavy soils more workable. Bacteria break down humus into simple substances that can be absorbed by plants, although humus-forming materials are not normally rich sources of nutrients (see page 18).

As humus decomposes it disappears from the soil, which is the reason why gardeners must regularly add more manure, compost and other vegetable refuse in the course of cultivation. Soil that contains no humus is virtually useless for growing crops, and all kinds benefit from the addition of organic materials, dug into clay in the autumn and sandy soils in spring, or spread on the surface as a mulch (see page 30) for turning in annually as a soil improver.

Most humus normally lies in the topsoil, where the majority of bacteria are active. Below this layer is the subsoil, usually paler and less fertile, and with a poorer texture. It should not be brought to the surface above the topsoil as its quality is difficult to improve, but organic materials can be worked in during the course of deep digging to aid drainage and encourage plants to root more deeply.

Drainage

Waterlogged soil prevents plant roots from functioning, often causing them to rot, and also denies soil bacteria the air they need to continue breaking down humus and improving fertility. Where the ground remains wet for long periods, perhaps with pools of rainwater lying on the surface, or if plants and weeds regularly fail to germinate or grow, you should suspect poor drainage.

The cause may simply be surface compaction, or there may be an impervious buried layer or 'pan' that can be broken up by deep digging. Heavy, unimproved clay drains slowly but this may be improved gradually by adding lime and coarse organic materials, or by digging drainage trenches or installing a system of buried drain-pipes. A hard, rocky subsoil or naturally high water table are difficult problems to remedy, except by constructing raised beds to increase the depth of usable soil.

Coping with poor soil

Improving an infertile or 'difficult' soil can be a daunting task unless you concentrate on digging small areas as deeply as possible, remedying any drainage inadequacies, and adding all the available

GREEN MANURE

Growing green manure crops in vacant ground protects the surface and structure of bare soil, and improves its fertility when dug in. They can help reclaim poor soil, make use of intervals between successive vegetable crops, and productively occupy ground over winter. Choose green manure species according to the type of soil and time of year.

- Bitter lupin: tender annual sown from spring onwards; dig in after 3 months to add nitrogen.
- Fenugreek: tender annual with vigorous taproot for poor subsoils; sow from spring onwards and dig in after 3 months.
- Lucerne (alfalfa): hardy perennial for sowing in spring or autumn, with long taproot for hard subsoils; dig in after 12 months to add nitrogen.
- Mustard: fast, lush and smothers weeds; sow any time in ground vacant for 6 weeks or more; shares brassica pests and diseases.
- Winter (field) beans: sown in autumn for digging in during spring to add nitrogen.

organic material to create individual fertile beds in which to grow your first crops. For fruit trees and bushes, though, improve a larger area of clay than you need for their roots, otherwise water from the surrounding ground will drain into planting holes and turn them into sumps. Lime is a valuable aid to improving clay because it binds the fine particles together, a process known as flocculation, to produce a more manageable crumbly structure.

Potatoes are a useful pioneer crop in the kitchen garden, their cultivation and harvest involving operations that can help improve soil structure. Sowing an appropriate green manure (see Green manure, left) on vacant ground is always beneficial, raising humus levels after being dug in, while the deep taproots of some species open drainage and air channels in the subsoil. Mulching will help stabilize improved soil and supplement its fertility.

You might have to limit crops initially to those likely to succeed in extreme conditions, brassicas in clay or chalky soils, for example, or roots in very sandy ground. If the topsoil is shallow, choose short varieties of root crops, and start seedlings under glass wherever soils are wet or slow to warm in spring.

ABOVE LEFT *Decomposing organic materials such as garden compost are indispensable ingredients of fertile, well-structured soils. Tree leaves are best kept separate and left to decay gradually in a simple enclosure, such as this coarse wire netting container, before being added to the compost or used as a soil conditioner.*

LEFT *To sustain its high density of healthy plants the soil fertility in this plot needs regular renewal.*

Creating a fertile soil

Fertility depends on a number of factors including the soil's structure (see page 16) and on its available supply of nutrients. A balanced combination of these is necessary, some only in small amounts (see Trace elements, page 29), but larger quantities of several important nutrients are needed to sustain healthy plant life (see page 29).

Nitrogen controls a plant's growth rate and ability to manufacture energy (photosynthesis); a shortage is indicated by stunted growth, pale leaves with yellow tints (chlorosis) and small brightly coloured fruits. Phosphorus, or phosphate, is responsible for healthy root activity and the ripening of fruits; deficiency causes poor root development, blue- or purple-tinted leaves, and low fruit yields. Potassium, or potash, reinforces the work of nitrogen, improves fruit quality and sustains general good health; a shortage causes leaf mottling and small crops of inferior fruits. Magnesium is important for seed germination and the production of chlorophyll, the green pigment present in leaves and stems vital for efficient photosynthesis; a lack causes dead patches between leaf veins, premature orange or red tints and early drop of young leaves. Sulphur helps in chlorophyll production; a shortage results in chlorosis.

The last major element is calcium, which is used by plants to strengthen their cells and help in the uptake of nitrogen and other nutrients. A deficiency

of calcium causes problems such as die back of shoots, apple bitter pit and tomato blossom end rot.

Soil acidity

Levels of calcium also influence soil acidity or alkalinity, which is measured on a pH scale: a pH of 7 is neutral, figures below this are acid, and above, alkaline. Most crops grow well in slightly acid soils of pH 6–6.5, although brassicas prefer slightly alkaline conditions.

As calcium is readily leached from most soils, you should check the pH of the kitchen garden annually with a soil test kit, which will explain how to adjust the pH. You can add calcium to raise the pH (and also improve the structure of clay soils) by spreading lime, which is a rich source of the element, and raking or forking it in at any time of year, but always well in advance of planting and not in combination with manures. Do not add lime without testing soils first, as over-alkalinity leads to serious nutrient deficiencies and is difficult to correct.

Using manures

Nutrients must be dissolved for plants to use them, but this solubility allows rain to continuously leach them from the soil, and they are soon exhausted unless replaced by adding manures and fertilizers. Bulky manure is relatively low in nutrients, but releases them steadily as it decays, at the same time

MANURES AND THEIR USES		
Type of manure or compost	Nutrients provided	How to use
Farmyard manure	Small amounts of most nutrients; usually high straw content; valuable humus producer	Mulch or dig in when well-rotted but stack or compost fresh supplies until ready (for 2 years if shavings are included)
Poultry, rabbit manure	High in nitrogen and phosphates; best as a compost activator or for making liquid fertilizer	Add sparingly to the soil, about 220g per sq m (0.5lb per sq yd)
Spent mushroom compost	Usually sterilized and mainly composted straw; contains lime and may also contain chemical pesticide residues	Use as a mulch but not on highly alkaline soils; its high chalk content helps clay break down
Garden compost	Variable quality, depending on how well-made it is, but a valuable home-made source of humus-forming material	Best dug in as surviving seeds may germinate in mulches
Sewage sludge	Recycled waste, sometimes composted; often high in nitrogen but first check that it is free from all traces of heavy metals	Add to the compost heap or mix with straw and stack for a few months before digging in

LEFT *Attention to fertility is particularly important where the roots of other plants such as trees, shrubs or hedges are likely to be competing for nutrients. The good health of these broad beans, carrots and lettuces depends on good feeding and keeping the trees pruned to allow enough light to penetrate.*

RIGHT *A wide range of major and minor nutrients is essential for balanced healthy growth. Each crop has its own preferred diet of the various elements and to support the dense cosmopolitan community of herbs and vegetables growing here, high levels of nutrients should be maintained over the whole area with a combination of manures and fertilizers.*

MAKING COMPOST

The best quality compost is made in a large sturdy timber container, or a proprietary plastic bin, sited on bare soil to allow access for worms. Lay a 5cm (2in) depth of coarse stems or prunings in the bottom, collect enough mixed moist vegetable, animal and household waste to complete a layer about 15–20cm (6–8in) deep; avoid perennial weed roots and diseased or seeding plants. Gradually fill the container with similar layers, adding to autumn and winter heaps a stimulant, such as poultry manure, or a proprietary activator or sulphate of ammonia. Cover with perforated plastic and an insulating layer of sacking or old mats, and cap with a rainproof lid. If possible empty and remix the contents once or twice to accelerate decay. Small amounts of waste can be sealed in black plastic bags, but may take a year or more to rot down.

improving soil structure and water retention, whereas fertilizers provide nutrients without other benefits. Try to add regularly as much manure or compost as possible, mulched 8–10cm (3–4in) deep in autumn for forking in during spring, and worked in when digging to disperse it throughout the soil.

Non-chemical methods

Many gardeners prefer to grow crops by 'organic' methods, decreasing their reliance on chemical fertilizers and treatments. They concentrate instead on raising fertility by careful cultivation and the use of animal or vegetable manures or fertilizers (organic in its strict sense) and natural minerals, and on controlling pests and diseases by mechanical or preventive measures. Since it is often difficult to produce or buy enough compost and manure, and problems have a habit of getting out of control, abandoning inorganic fertilizers and chemical remedies altogether may be unwise, at least initially. However, both soil and plants do benefit from an essentially 'organic' approach.

Deciding what to grow

Decide at an early stage which crops you want to grow, and where. Complete self-sufficiency requires a large area of ground, as well as plenty of time and energy. On the other hand, you might prefer to limit yourself to a few favourite crops, perhaps ones that are unobtainable from shops or superior if fresh, and these can often be fitted here and there into an existing small garden. Most herbs are decorative, many kinds of fruit can be trained in ornamental forms, and small numbers of vegetables may be grown in patches or as edges in flower beds. Many crops can be grown in containers.

Larger quantities are best raised in a separate plot, whose size and shape will be determined by the garden as a whole. It is easier to organize crops if the plot is divided into several beds, separated by paths that permit easy access. Identify main paths and make these as wide as possible, allowing perhaps for the passage of a wheelbarrow; other paths may be temporary or permanent depending on the arrangement of beds, and whether these are fixed or marked out each year as divisions of a larger area. Make sure all beds are within easy reach of water.

Allow room for compost heaps, nursery beds for sowing and raising your own plants, and space for perennial crops such as rhubarb, asparagus and globe artichokes if you wish. Annual herbs may be intercropped with vegetables, but perennials should be grown in a bed to themselves, at the edge of the kitchen garden or near the house. Most fruits, too, need permanent sites, either grouped together, perhaps inside a fruit cage, or dispersed in suitable sites around the garden, trained beside paths, for example, or as internal divisions.

Crop rotation

Traditionally crops are moved in sequence around a number of beds so that the same type of plant is not grown for successive years in a piece of ground. This is mainly to prevent a build-up in the soil of pests and disease organisms, whose life-cycles can be broken by growing other unrelated crops, and to avoid the depletion of particular nutrients.

For this purpose crops with similar requirements and susceptibilities are grouped together, each group moving on to the next plot the following year. A classic 4–year rotation might be potatoes, followed by root crops, then legumes and finally brassicas, with the soil being prepared each year according to the crop to be grown. There are many variations, however: potatoes can be omitted or combined with brassicas in a 3–year sequence, onions may be grown

An example of crop rotation

As explained above, crop rotation schemes involve moving groups of plants that have similar needs or susceptibilities to fresh soil each year. In the example shown here, crops are grouped together and moved annually around three beds, returning to their original positions in the fourth year. Before growing the crops in group 1, the soil should be dug and manured well; the next year the bed for group 2 should be manured and limed, and in the third year the soil should be forked over and fertilizer added for group 3.

A SELECTION OF CROPS FOR GROWING
IN A THREE-YEAR ROTATION

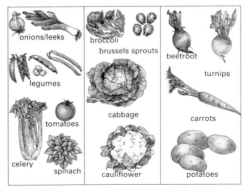

onions/leeks	broccoli	beetroot
legumes	brussels sprouts	turnips
tomatoes	cabbage	carrots
celery / spinach	cauliflower	potatoes

Group 1   *Group 2*   *Group 3*

YEAR 1

Bed A   Bed B   Bed C

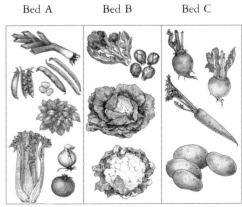

Group 1   *Group 2*   *Group 3*

Uniform spacing ensures rapid consistent growth. Sparse sowing and early thinning of seedlings is one way to ensure this; transplanting at optimum distances is another precondition for growing high quality crops. Choice of spacing is determined both by the type of crop and the need to keep the soil weed-free, as here.

Spacing crops

When drawing up plans, remember that every crop has its individual space requirements for optimum development. Generous distances between fruit plants are important to ensure good health and maximum yield but efficient pruning often admits enough light for some vegetables or herbs to succeed in the intervening spaces. Traditional distances for vegetables are based on the need to walk through rows to cultivate, but unless intercrops are grown this arrangement may be wasteful in small gardens where spacing plants equidistant apart in every direction is more economical.

Distances are usually calculated to give the maximum yield from a given area. Increasing the plant density may still provide a good crop, but of smaller plants, and where this is preferable (see, for example, Growing mini-cauliflowers, page 50) closer planting can be worthwhile. Crops such as lettuces and cabbages can be grown at twice the recommended density if alternate plants are used while they are still young, leaving the others to grow on to maturity. Growing a dwarf or compact variety at closer spacing is another way to economize on space, yielding greater numbers of plants, although there will not be a significant gain in total crop weight.

with legumes, have a year to themselves or remain in a permanent bed, or a further fallow year can be added for green manuring.

In practice limited space makes a rigid system difficult to follow. Some vegetables, especially winter crops, overlap with others, while there are numerous miscellaneous vegetables that do not fit in comfortably. Nor will the usual rotation defeat all pathogens, some of which survive in the soil for many years. The principle of separating groups is sound, however, and where possible you should avoid growing a group or individual crop in the same place in two consecutive years.

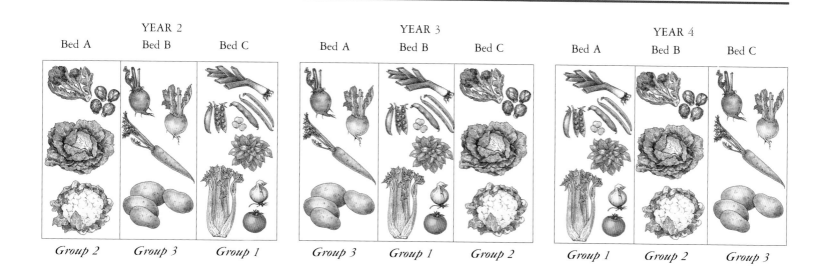

YEAR 2

Bed A   Bed B   Bed C

Group 2   *Group 3*   *Group 1*

YEAR 3

Bed A   Bed B   Bed C

Group 3   *Group 1*   *Group 2*

YEAR 4

Bed A   Bed B   Bed C

Group 1   *Group 2*   *Group 3*

Successional sowing

Some vegetable crops mature and stand in good condition for many weeks, whereas others deteriorate quickly or run to seed and need using immediately. Unless you can freeze or otherwise preserve any surplus, it is better to sow in succession several small batches of crops such as radishes, early carrots, peas, lettuce and summer spinach. By sowing soon after seedlings of the previous batch have emerged, it should be possible to avoid gaps in supplies.

Ground that has been prepared for a particular vegetable may be used again for the same purposes that season, provided the soil is replenished with a top-dressing of fertilizer and no pest or disease problems have occurred. Early calabrese and cabbage cultivars developed for year-round production may be grown in this way, the follow-on crop having been started in a seedbed so that it is ready to transplant when the earlier crop is exhausted.

It is often tempting to plant up a whole area with a wide variety of crops in one go, leaving insufficient space for later sowings to carry supplies through to the end of the season and beyond. With a combination of experience and careful planning, however, you will be able to visualize early in the season how much room to leave vacant, or plant with catch crops or green manure until needed at a later date. Three successive batches of lettuce are here planted near each other. Keep the ground free from weeds even when not being cropped, hoeing between rows or handweeding where the hoe cannot reach.

Continuous cropping

Bearing in mind the need for flexibility if poor weather or some other factor intervenes, drawing up a month-by-month vegetable cropping plan for the year helps make the most of available space and time. Crops vary in the amount of time they need to mature and the area of ground they will occupy. Try to avoid leaving ground empty for any length of time: often, young plants may be kept growing in a nursery bed in readiness for transplanting as soon as another crop is finished, or a quick 'catch crop' of lettuce, radishes or green manure may be fitted in before the next maincrop is sown.

For as unbroken a succession of produce as possible, estimate when crops should be ready and spread out sowings to avoid periods of over- or under-supply. Vegetables that mature in late winter and spring – the 'hungry gap' – are especially welcome. As different cultivars of the same crop often mature at different times, growing two or three kinds of peas, potatoes or leeks, for example, can give a long, uninterrupted season of supply. Remember that surplus vegetables, herbs and fruit may be preserved in a variety of ways, but distinguish between crops and cultivars intended for immediate use and those that store well.

Intercropping

Where a slow-growing vegetable crop is sown or planted at full spacings, there is often room between rows and plants for a different crop or even a fast maturing cultivar of the same vegetable to be grown for clearing before the maincrop fills the spaces. Brassicas need a lot of room, but a row of summer cabbages may fit between winter cultivars if they are cleared while young. Seedlings of a follow-on crop can be transplanted between the rows of its predecessor as it matures, or sown there for moving on later. Fast growing small lettuces can be interplanted with iceberg types that are slow to head, or loose-leaf kinds may be sown around heading lettuces to continue after the latter are cleared.

Different vegetable crops may be grown together in the same bed if their needs can be matched. In good soil, sweet corn plants, for example, are strong enough to support climbing beans sown beside them, while an undercrop of trailing marrows may be planted as ground cover, preventing the soil from drying out and making full use of the intervening spaces. However, fertility must be high for this intensive arrangement to work, and full distances should be allowed between plants to avoid problems of shade and overcrowding.

USING CLOCHES

Cloches are glass or plastic covers that protect early and late crops in low temperatures. Glass is the best material but heavy, expensive and easily broken, whereas plastic is lighter and must be anchored for stability.

Glass or polycarbonate is used to make rigid structures, two panels joined at the top with clips for simple tent cloches or four secured with wires to make taller barn cloches. Polythene sheeting is also stretched over special tubular frames to form larger rigid barn cloches.

Tunnel cloches can be bought or home-made to cover beds of various sizes. Polythene sheeting is stretched over evenly spaced wire hoops, and gathered and tied to stakes at each end; further hoops of wire or string over the plastic keep it taut. The sheeting, which can last for 2–3 seasons, is raised at the sides for watering or ventilation.

Glass or plastic hand-lights are available as mobile frames for placing over individual plants. Many gardeners use bottomless plastic containers as emergency cloches for tender crops after planting out.

Glass barn cloches are ideal for protecting early sowings – taller than tent cloches, they provide greater headroom and more frost-protection. Make the best use of the covered area by growing rows at close spacing or combining two or more crops that do not compete for space, in this case spring onions and carrots. Seal the ends of cloches with a pane of glass to prevent them from becoming wind tunnels.

Extending the season

You can often extend the natural growing season by two to three weeks at the beginning of the season, and likewise at the end, by using a cold frame or portable cloches to protect plants from wind and raise the soil and air temperature. Their use also makes the cultivation of tender crops such as outdoor cucumbers feasible in cooler gardens.

A cold frame is used to raise early seedlings and for hardening off plants raised initially in warmth (see page 43), but where the frame has a soil base early crops may be grown to maturity there, while seedlings can be transplanted to the frame in autumn for late protected cropping. If fitted with heating cables or portable enough to be positioned on a warm compost or manure stack, very early crops such as salads and carrots may be raised in winter.

Use cloches or a portable frame in late winter or early spring to force strawberries or to warm and dry soil before sowing early vegetables, and leave in place until the crops are cleared or can be gradually exposed to outdoor conditions. Make sure the soil is fertile and grow the crops at high density, intercropping if possible, to make maximum use of space, but remember to irrigate, and ventilate often to reduce the risk of fungal diseases.

You can avoid carrying cloches around the garden and the possibility of breaking glass by planning a sequence of adjacent crops ('strip-cropping') for covering at appropriate times, so that the cloches need only be transferred from one row to the next. Carrots and lettuces sown in late winter, for example, can be covered until mid-spring when the cloches are moved over sweet corn and left there until early summer. They can then be used to protect peppers or melons sown earlier under glass. When these are cleared in early autumn, the cloches are moved on to late summer-sown radishes, carrots and spring onions, or may be used to finish ripening bush tomatoes and perpetual strawberries.

Crop covers ('floating mulches') made from woven or perforated film or fleece are an alternative to cloches; with care they can be used for more than one season to raise early vegetables and protect late crops. They are not recommended for use in windy gardens, however, nor where frequent weeding may be necessary. The covers warm the soil for early sowing, are replaced immediately after sowing and removed once the plants are growing well; lighter types of cover can be left in place for the lifetime of crops such as carrots and cabbages, which lift the material as they develop and remain protected from insect pests.

ROUTINE HUSBANDRY

Seedlings and young plants seem full of vitality and promise, but from the moment they start to grow they have to work hard. Their roots must search constantly for water and nutrients, they face competition from opportunist and sometimes invasive weeds, and they may have to pit their natural resilience against pests and diseases. Our role as gardeners is to offer them the best possible soil environment, and then by sensitive husbandry to encourage and intervene where appropriate to help them grow to maturity and eventual harvest.

With good organization and management a varied succession of fresh produce such as leeks, marrows, french beans, artichokes and carrots can be raised in a small plot. Red cabbages and ruby chard add further colour to an already attractive kitchen garden, while flowering groups of onions and red lettuce will soon be cleared to make way for later sowing and planting.

Preparing the ground

Not everyone has the good fortune to start out with clean ground, and you might be faced with an overgrown weedy plot to clear. This can be done using mechanical cultivation, herbicides or a combination of both, depending on the time available and the method you favour. If you prefer not to use herbicides, cut down the weeds and remove any large obstacles and debris, then mow the growth very short with a rotary mower. Finally, dig or rotavate the ground, picking out roots of perennial weeds as you go or raking them off afterwards. If you have all summer at your disposal, repeated rotavation at fortnightly intervals in dry weather, followed by the thorough removal of exposed fragments, should eventually destroy most weed roots, although this is a drastic measure that temporarily damages the soil structure. Black polythene sheeting or old carpets laid over the soil surface for a whole season is another way to kill all but the most tenacious weeds.

Ground cleared in the autumn can be left roughly dug until the spring, when surviving weeds will reappear and then may be forked out or sprayed with a systemic weedkiller such as glyphosate, following the manufacturer's instructions for use carefully. Herbicides can also be used for the initial clearance: spray the whole patch and wait until the topgrowth

has died before cutting it down; some tougher perennials will survive and need spraying again. A more effective method, however, is to cut down the weeds first, and then spray the young regrowth that appears a few weeks later as this is more susceptible than older vegetation to the action of herbicides.

There are compelling arguments for and against digging, but even a 'no-dig' vegetable plot needs thorough preliminary cultivation to ensure good drainage, improve aeration for plant roots and beneficial soil organisms, and to incorporate manures and fertilizers. It is not always necessary, however, to dig the plot every year, and this may in fact be harmful, destroying soil structure and encouraging light soils to dry out rapidly. Heavy and compacted ground, however, does benefit from being opened up to the air and the pulverizing action of frost. If you dig deeply in the first place, it may be sufficient to maintain this improvement by forking or digging the top spit annually, repeating the deep cultivation only when decreasing yields or poor drainage indicate that it is needed.

The best time to dig clay soils is in the autumn, leaving the surface rough and lumpy to expose the greatest area to frost and to prevent compaction from winter rains. Many gardeners only dig sandy soils in

How to double dig

Digging a vegetable bed two spits deep breaks up and aerates compacted soil and allows roots to explore further for water and nutrients. These benefits are long-lasting and double digging is only necessary every few years. Where plenty of compost or manure is available, some of this can be mixed into the lower spit, although loosening the subsoil with a fork is more important, and organic material is best reserved for the topsoil where it is more easily available to plants. Take care to leave the subsoil in the lower spit.

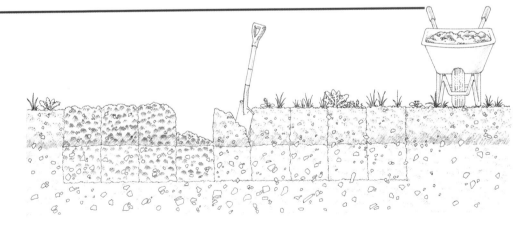

Digging progresses here from left to right, with topsoil from the first trench loaded into the wheelbarrow, ready for filling in the final trench at the end of the plot.

Cultivating ground as soon as it is cleared leaves it in a state of readiness for seedbeds or planting sites for follow-on crops. It is always advisable to break up soil compacted by treading, as here between rows of seedlings and lettuce, since this can impede aeration and drainage. Take the opportunity when forking over bare ground to remove stones and all perennial weeds.

the spring, preferring to protect its light structure from heavy rain with a winter mulch or a green manure crop which is dug in at the beginning of spring. Never dig when the ground is frozen or very wet, as you may seriously damage the soil structure.

Double digging

Double digging, or trenching, involves working the soil to at least two spades or 'spits' deep. This is ideal for deep initial cultivation and periodic renovation; traditional kitchen gardens were divided into four quarters, which were double dug in rotation, one every autumn (see How to double dig, left).

The simplest way is to dig out a trench one spit deep, and take this excavated topsoil to the far end of the plot. Then loosen the subsoil in the bottom of the trench (the second spit) with a fork, at the same time working in plenty of decayed manure or garden compost, before covering it with the topsoil from the next row to produce a new trench. When you reach the end of the bed, fill the last trench with the heap of soil removed at the start of digging. Turf or a matted layer of annual weeds can be skimmed off with the spade and buried at the bottom of each trench, but perennial weeds should be removed as you encounter them. Larger beds seem less daunting

if divided lengthways into two halves; by digging down one half and back up the other, soil from the first trench needs to be moved only a short distance across the bed to the end of the second half.

Single digging

Digging one spit deep is adequate for most purposes, especially if the ground was deeply dug in recent years or if fertility and drainage are adequate. It is used for incorporating manure or compost, and for turning in annual weeds and green manure crops. Excavate a trench one spit deep, as for double digging, and invert topsoil from the next trench into the first and then fork organic material liberally into this disturbed topsoil. In confined spaces or where digging a straight trench is impractical, simply invert each spadeful back into its original position.

Forking

Single digging with a garden fork opens and aerates the soil, and breaks down larger clods into a form suitable for raking when preparing a seedbed (see page 37). A fork is also used to turn in mulches and annual dressings of manure or compost. To 'prick over' a soil crust formed after rain or to loosen weeds, it is inserted to about half its depth.

Watering and feeding

Large amounts of water are naturally stored in the ground for much of the year, but quantities vary according to the nature of the soil: the water in sandy soils is quickly exhausted compared with that in clay, which may hold three times as much.

You can delay the time when supplementary watering must start by adding organic matter to the soil to raise its levels of humus, which is spongy and can hold a lot of water. Mulching shields the surface from heat and wind, reducing the amount of water lost by evaporation, but natural levels will soon fall to the point when irrigation becomes necessary.

When to water

First signs of the need to water are subtle: stems and leaves feel less resilient when gently bent, leaves lose their natural lustre and become dull or dusty, and plant growth loses its normal impetus. Delaying irrigation until plants wilt or stop flowering is unwise, as growth may not recover. Watering too soon can be as harmful, leaching soluble nutrients from the soil, diluting flavour and stimulating leaf growth at the expense of the crop.

There are certain plants, sites and stages in the development of various crops for which timely watering is critical. Germinating seeds, seedlings,

leaf vegetables and plants that have recently been moved or planted should never be allowed to dry out. All fruits need water during flowering and when the fruit is swelling; root crops prefer consistently moist soil in the early stages and heavier applications as the roots develop. Plants growing at the foot of walls or exposed to wind may need watering more often.

Seedlings and very young plants need watering little and often, but otherwise a thorough soaking is more beneficial than light sprinklings. You should aim to give plants about 5 litres per sq metre (1 gal per sq yd) during routine watering, and 23 litres per sq metre (5 gal per sq yd) at critical times, every 8–10 days on light soils and fortnightly on clay. Try to water in still, dull weather or in the evening in order to limit wastage from evaporation.

Individual plants are best watered with a watering can, together with a fine rose for small seedlings. For large areas a hose fitted with a rose spray is suitable but tedious, and often results in less than adequate amounts being delivered. Oscillating sprinklers cover large areas, but waste water unless accurately adjustable and often damage the soil surface. Seep hoses and perforated tubing laid between rows are the most efficient means of concentrating water on particular crops (see Watering crops, below).

Watering crops

Adequate available water is essential for consistent growth but it is also a precious resource that should not be wasted. Plants should be watered either individually with a can or with some form of irrigation hose that controls the supply of water and directs it only where it is needed. Seep hoses are flexible with numerous fine holes that allow water to trickle out gently into the soil, while perforated spray lines apply a band of spray over adjacent plants. They can be moved round the garden or left *in situ*.

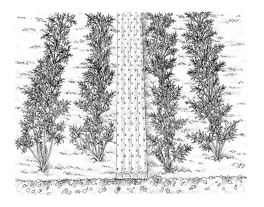

Spray lines are an efficient and adjustable method of watering crops in straight rows.

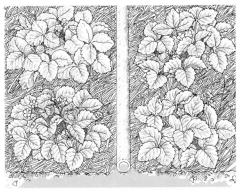

Use a seep hose where foliage or fruit must be kept dry or where plants are not in rows.

When to feed

If the soil is well cultivated and replenished regularly with manure or compost to sustain its fertility, crops will often mature without extra feeding. Gardeners expect a lot from their plants, however, and on poorer soils or at the end of winter when rains have impoverished light soils, fertilizers can make the difference between success and disappointment.

The main nutrients needed by plants are nitrogen, phosphorus and potassium, or potash (see also page 18), usually listed in that order and abbreviated to their chemical symbols – N, P and K, respectively. All fertilizers are rated by their NPK value. Fertilizers may be fast acting or slow-release, chemical or organic, straight (supplying one main nutrient, for example rock potash which has an NPK ratio of 0:0:10) or compound (a balanced mixture for general purposes, such as Growmore which has an NPK ratio of 7:7:7).

Fertilizers are applied as base dressings (powders or granules raked into the soil before sowing or planting), as top-dressings sprinkled around growing plants and hoed or watered in, or as foliar feeds (solutions sprayed on plant foliage for fast effect). They should be used as supplements to reinforce a basic good level of fertility created by adding organic

Whereas crops such as potatoes can be watered with a can or hosepipe, leafy vegetables and others needing plenty of water are best irrigated with spray lines that are left in position.

materials during cultivation. Base dressings of compound fertilizers such as blood, fish and bone at sowing or planting time help to fuel strong early growth, maintained by later top-dressings, as appropriate. However, fertilizers add nothing to soil structure and long-term fertility. Use them with discretion, for over-application may be harmful, excess amounts often leaching into water supplies or blocking the uptake of other elements.

Amounts to apply vary according to the type of plant (see individual crop entries in the following chapters on vegetables and fruit), its stage of growth and the time of year, and also the reason for feeding. Nitrogen, for example, which controls the rate of growth, is constantly leached from the soil and is often added as a spring tonic; phosphorus, which helps develop healthy roots and ripe fruits, and potassium or potash, which is essential for good fruit quality and general good health, are applied at any time, but often in autumn. Lack of these, and other minor nutrients or 'trace elements', leads to various disorders (see right), although these are unlikely to occur in well-tended soils.

TRACE ELEMENTS

In addition to the major nutrients, small quantities of other elements are vital. Their deficiency causes various symptoms.
- Boron: rough patches on fruits and leaves, brown hearts in vegetables; treat with borax.
- Copper: wilt and death of young leaves and shoots; feed with fertilizer containing trace elements.
- Iron: pale foliage, especially on chalky soils; apply sequestered iron and check the soil pH.
- Manganese: pale leaf patches between bright green veins and some leaf rolling; avoid over-liming and spray with manganese sulphate.
- Molybdenum: distorted leaves and shoot tips, and cauliflower whiptail on acid soils; check pH, add lime.
- Zinc: distorted leaves and shoots, and brown buds, often on light soils; avoid over-liming and treat as for copper.

COMMON FERTILIZERS		
Type of fertilizer	NPK ratio	Uses
Bonemeal	3:20:0	Organic source of phosphates and slow-release nitrogen
Dried blood	12:2:1	Organic source of nitrogen, very quickly released
Hoof and horn	14:1:0	Slow-acting organic source of nitrogen
Nitrate of soda	16:0:0	Soluble fast chemical source of nitrogen
Nitrate of potash	15:0:36	Fast-acting nitrogen and potassium
Nitrochalk	20:0:0	Quick chemical source of nitrogen and lime
Rock potash	0:0:10	Supplies slow-release organic potash
Rock phosphate	26:0:0	Long-term source of organic phosphates
Sulphate of ammonia	20.5:0:0	Potent, rapid chemical supply of nitrogen
Sulphate of potash	0:0:48	Fairly fast chemical potash source
Superphosphate of lime	0:15:0	Chemical phosphates but no available lime
Wood ashes	0:1:5	Variable source of soluble potash; best used fresh

Mulching the soil

A much is a protective top-dressing or covering for the soil, intended to insulate it from exteme weather conditions and to suppress weeds. Hot sunshine, frost, wind or heavy rain cause the temperature and moistness of bare ground to fluctuate widely, whereas a mulch moderates these influences and thus stabilizes soil conditions.

Traditional mulches are composed of organic materials such as decayed manure, garden compost, straw, bracken, lawn mowings, mushroom compost or used hops. As well as reducing surface evaporation and denying light to annual weed seeds, they supply plants with nutrients, encourage earthworm activity and gradually improve soil texture. They also absorb a lot of water, sometimes preventing light rainfall from reaching the ground below, so it is important always to spread materials over moist soil and to soak the mulched plants whenever watering. Since they reduce temperature changes, they are best applied before the soil cools in autumn, to protect vulnerable plants from frost and to shield the ground from heavy rain, or in spring after the ground has started to warm up, to conserve moisture and reduce weeds.

Annual weeds that do appear are easily pulled up, but perennials are rarely deterred by an organic mulch. As it settles, organic matter becomes more impervious and less effective as an insulator, and long-term mulches should be loosened with a fork occasionally to improve their efficiency.

Most plants benefit from mulching, but where supplies of organic materials are limited concentrate on leaf and stem crops, which grow best in consistently moist soil, and vegetables such as peas, beans and carrots that are difficult to weed as they develop. Take care only to use fully or partly decayed materials, or those that add nitrogen to the soil: a wood-based mulch such as uncomposted bark may 'rob' nitrogen from the soil as it rots, and depress plant growth.

Mulches can be used to help clear weedy ground, using less penetrable materials such as cardboard, old carpets or plastic film, left in place for at least a complete season before starting to cultivate (see also pages 26–7). Plastic film is also an extremely effective mulch for growing crops, which can be planted through slits in a sheet stretched across a prepared bed and secured at the edges. Potatoes grown under black plastic do not need earthing up, white film reflects sunlight on to ripening fruit, and clear film helps warm soils in spring.

Leafy crops like spinach soon show signs of stress in hot weather if they are not kept growing in consistently moist soil. A thick mulch of organic material such as straw can reduce violent fluctuations and stabilize soil moisture. Make sure slugs, snails and other pests do not shelter under the mulch.

Clearing weeds

WEEDS AS SOIL INDICATORS

Prevalent weeds are often useful for identifying the nature of the soil. Solitary specimens are not reliable indicators, but if some of the following weeds commonly occur in mixed communities, this may be a symptom of soil type.

- Acid soils: black bindweed, cinquefoil, corn marigold, daisy, foxglove, fumitory, horsetail, mercury, shepherd's cress, small nettle, sorrel, spurrey, wild pansy.
- Chalky soils: bellflowers, black medick, cat's ear, greater hawkbit, knapweed, lamb's lettuce, oxeye daisy, pennycress, stonecrop, tansy, valerian, white mustard.
- Neutral medium loam: coltsfoot, creeping thistle, curled dock, forget-me-not, goosegrass, mayweed, sow-thistle, sun spurge, yarrow.

A mixed population of vigorous weeds is usually a sign of fertile soil, but is likely also to be a menace to cultivated plants. Weeds compete with these for available light, space, water and nutrients, and as alternative hosts may also spread pests and diseases; controlling them in the kitchen garden is therefore very important.

It is impossible to eliminate them altogether, however. As weed seeds survive for many years in the soil at various depths, cultivation regularly brings more to the surface where they then germinate. Seeds dispersed by wind or birds are continually arriving in the garden, and many quickly grow and shed their own seeds to recolonize clean ground, occasionally several times in a single season.

Reducing weed populations to manageable levels depends on both prevention and treatment. Annual weeds grow from seed, and are easily dealt with, whereas perennials survive and spread in other ways, usually by means of creeping stems or roots, or by deep inaccessible taproots, all of which can regenerate from small fragments. For this reason perennials should not be added to compost heaps, unlike annuals which may safely be composted if they have not set seed.

Clear perennial weeds before planting (see page 26), and hoe, uproot or 'spot' spray with systemic weedkiller any survivors that reappear. Persistence will eventually control them, as it will annual weeds, even in badly infested soil. Hoeing while they are still small prevents weeds from flowering and seeding, and exposes other buried seeds; these will inevitably germinate, but in dwindling numbers if shallow hoeing is carried out regularly.

Once you have reduced weed populations, keep them at acceptable levels by hoeing between crops at frequent intervals, before seedlings and very young plants can be overwhelmed, uprooting larger weeds before they seed, or by using a herbicide. In smaller gardens, spraying or watering weeds with herbicides is a practical option only when clearing whole plots of ground, as the risk of accidental splashes or spray drift is high in confined spaces.

Where weed seeds are a problem, it is worth preparing a bed well before it is needed. After watering the bed in dry weather, wait 2–3 weeks for weed seedlings to germinate and spray or hoe them off before sowing. Cultivate shallowly once or twice again during the following month, before mulching between plants to suppress further germination.

Inert materials, such as horticultural paper or the plastic sheeting used here, are perfect for keeping crops moist and weed-free. Strawberries, in particular, benefit from a black plastic mulch which covers the soil, keeping the fruit clean. Hold these materials in place by wedging the sides into the soil with a spade or by weighting down the edges with soil, stones or bricks.

31

Pests and diseases

Kitchen garden crops are susceptible in varying degrees to a number of common pests and diseases, and these need to be recognized. As with weeds, however, reducing their incidence to an acceptably low level is more realistic than hoping to avoid or eradicate them altogether. Vigorous well-tended plants are less likely to succumb than weaker specimens under some kind of stress, or if affected they will often survive a disorder, and the best prevention is to encourage the positive health of your plants.

Preventing pests

Do not assume everything that moves in the garden is hostile, for many creatures are the gardener's allies and should be distinguished from pests. Only certain pests are major threats, while others cause superficial damage: asparagus beetles, for example, can dramatically reduce crop yields, whereas froghoppers ('cuckoo spit') are merely a cosmetic nuisance.

A number of preventive measures can reduce the impact of serious pests. Keeping the soil clean and well-cultivated discourages soil pests such as wire-

worms and leatherjackets or exposes them to birds and other predators, while maintaining fertility and effective drainage strengthens plants against attack. Clear weeds and plant debris to limit the hiding places of slugs and other pests, and use physical barriers such as fencing or netting to exclude cats, dogs and birds, or spun fibre 'floating mulches' or low screens to deter carrot root flies (see page 23).

Choosing tolerant or resistant cultivars is one effective defence against both pests and diseases, crop rotation another (see page 20). Intercropping and dispersing crops amongst other unrelated plants can reduce the scale of any attack, while regular inspection often reveals early arrivals that can be dealt with before their numbers increase. Attract insectivorous birds by feeding them when food is in short supply, and recognize predators that feed on insect pests. Centipedes and rove beetles are valuable allies at soil level, while above ground ladybirds, lacewings and hoverflies can be encouraged by growing nearby favourite flowers such as asters, chrysanthemums, limnanthes, marigolds and sedum, and by using insecticides only in emergencies.

Despite all precautions, major infestations do occur. Countermeasures include introducing specific parasites, predators or pathogens. Known as biological control, this method is particularly successful under glass, or you may decide to spray with an insecticide. These are selective (affecting only specific pests) or non-selective; some kill on contact and are then rendered ineffective, while systemic or translocated insecticides are persistent substances absorbed by the plants and remaining active for a number of days.

Many gardeners dislike using systemic chemicals on edible crops because of the delay in absorption and fear of residues, and prefer to use a contact insecticide, often of organic origin such as derris and pyrethrum. Always follow instructions for use carefully, never exceeding the most appropriate dilution and only spraying in the evening when pollinating insects are not active, for they are as susceptible as pests to most insecticides.

RIGHT *One method of keeping crops safe from pests and diseases is to install mechanical barriers – a particularly effective example of this is an enclosure of netting or plastic film to prevent carrot flies from laying their eggs on the developing roots.*

BELOW LEFT *An interesting approach to pest control, but one which needs further research, is companion planting. Some gardeners find that certain plants such as mauve catmint help keep crops – here carrots – free from pests.*

Preventing diseases

These often seem more threatening than pests because disease organisms are usually invisible and less responsive to emergency treatment. By the time symptoms of infection are obvious, it may be too late for a cure, especially since many pathogens have developed resistance to common fungicides. Consequently, it is better to counter disease by good hygiene and cultivation than to trust in remedies.

Stress of some kind is a common precondition for infection, which often strikes plants already suffering from drought, starvation, overcrowding or a poor soil environment, factors that also cause physiological disorders easily corrected by improved management. Clear away dead plants and decaying leaves as these are frequent sites of disease. Regularly check the acidity and free drainage of your soil (see page 16), rotate crops where possible, and avoid overfeeding as well as deficiencies in nutrients and trace elements (see pages 18 and 29).

Vigilance is essential, for diseases are infectious and culling a solitary victim can save the rest of a crop; burn diseased plants, and never add them to the compost heap where spores may survive. Spraying with systemic fungicides may limit the spread of local disorders or prevent initial infection. Cultivars that resist or tolerate certain diseases are widely available for crops such as blackcurrants, gooseberries and strawberries, leeks, lettuce, parsnips and potatoes, and should be grown wherever possible.

Always confirm the health status of new plants, many of which are subject to official inspection and certification, especially for freedom from viruses. These incurable disorders, with symptoms that include mottled leaves and stunted growth, are transmitted by insect pests or contact with infected hands and tools. Although some viruses are relatively harmless, they often cause depressed yields or the death of plants, and affected plants should be dug up and burned.

COMMON DISEASES
Specific diseases and how to treat them are discussed on pages 76–7 (vegetables) and 110–11 (fruit), but the following are some of the more common ones.
● Cankers: these cause bark and tissue death on woody plants such as fruit trees, leaving wounds that may eventually girdle a shoot and kill it.
● Mildews: powdery mildew produces greyish dusty deposit on foliage, and is encouraged by poor air circulation in hot dry weather, while downy mildew occurs in prolonged damp conditions.
● Rots: a diverse group of fungi and bacteria generally causing the decay of plant tissues. Examples include damping off disease of seedlings and white rot of onions and leeks.
● Rusts: fungal diseases producing typical black, yellow or brown spots on plant tissues.
● Scabs: rough crusty disfigurations on fruits and roots, often superficial but sometimes admitting other disease organisms.
● Wilts: soil diseases encouraged by poor drainage and cold wet weather, resulting in the collapse of plants such as tomatoes and cucumbers.

VEGETABLES FROM THE GARDEN

Growing fresh vegetables is an annual creative adventure. You can decide whether to explore gourmet crops rarely available elsewhere, raise a few favourites in quantities large enough to fill a freezer for year-round availability, or grow a little of everything for varied seasonal supplies. And at every stage, from selecting the seeds until you harvest the produce in peak condition for immediate enjoyment or storage, you can choose how to grow your vegetables and control their quality.

Cottage gardeners have always grown a few vegetables wherever there is room, often planting only a few favourite kinds, such as these onions, carrots and parsnips, for fresh harvest as required. Crops flourish in well-tilled soil, especially when provided with an open aspect and sheltered from cold winds by surrounding plants and fences.

Selecting seeds

High quality seeds that are fresh or have been stored under good conditions are more likely to germinate evenly, with few gaps in the rows. Although sparse, even sowing will help reduce the risk of congestion, rows usually need thinning once or twice to leave seedlings at regular distances apart, with room for later development.

Even though their quality is regulated by legal standards of purity and germination, vegetable seeds should be selected with care from a reputable supplier and are best bought in vacuum-sealed packets to ensure freshness and viability.

F_1 hybrids are bred by crossing two known parents to produce seedlings with reliable qualities of vigour, consistency, high yields or disease resistance and are usually worth their higher cost. Open-pollinated seeds are produced at random by self-fertilization or uncontrolled cross-fertilization, and plants raised from these are usually more variable than F_1 hybrids. Uniformity and predictability are important characteristics, but do not overlook the older 'heritage' kinds that have stood the test of time and possess outstanding virtues of their own. New

cultivars are regularly trialled and assessed and any approved by the National Institute of Agricultural Botany (NIAB) or the Royal Horticultural Society in Britain, for example, may be chosen with confidence, although this does not imply that others are necessarily inferior.

Check that cultivars suit your soil and climate and are the right type for your needs: early or maincrop, tall or dwarf, hardy, self-blanching and so on. Many seeds are sold in varied quantities and where appropriate individual crop entries later in this chapter indicate how much to sow and the anticipated yield. Some seeds have been dressed with chemical fungicides to protect them from diseases during germination. Pelleted seeds have been individually encased in clay for easier handling, while pre-germinated or 'chitted' seeds are ready for sowing immediately.

The seeds of some vegetables – marrows and melons, for example – remain viable for several years, whereas others, such as parsnips, germinate erratically, if at all, the next season. Intact plastic or foil seed packets should keep for several seasons, but once a packet is opened and the seeds are exposed to dampness, air and heat, they start to age. Store opened packets in screw-topped jars containing a sachet of silica gel to absorb any moisture, and keep in a cool, dry, dark place. Test a sample of doubtful seeds by sprinkling them on a damp cloth or tissue, and keeping them in a warm place; if a large proportion germinates, the seeds should be viable.

Many gardeners save their own seeds from superior plants. Collecting seeds from F_1 hybrids is not recommended as resulting plants can be unpredictable and may reproduce unwelcome characteristics, whereas open-pollinated kinds, especially peas, beans, onions and notably hardy survivors after a severe winter, are often worth saving, and over the years it is possible to develop a selection adapted to your particular garden. Let the best plants flower and before they are quite ripe enclose the dry seedheads in plastic bags. When ripe, shake the seeds free in the bags, clean them of all debris and carefully store them in labelled packets.

Sowing outdoors

Seeds may be sown outdoors *in situ* where the crops will grow to maturity, or in a separate nursery bed from which young plants are transplanted to permanent positions when large enough. In both cases a seedbed suitable for germination must be prepared with a fine level surface for small seeds or a rougher finish for larger seeds such as peas and beans.

Sowing in a seedbed

When the soil is still moist but crumbles readily, break it down with a fork to a fine 'tilth' (a loose texture free from lumps), and rake level, removing any large clods and stones (see Preparing a seedbed, below). Water dry soils before starting work; in wet conditions cover the area for a few days with cloches until dry enough to work, and stand on a board while working to avoid compacting the soil.

Sowing in drills

Most vegetables are sown in the bottom of straight parallel furrows known as drills at various distances apart according to the crop; rows in a seedbed for later transplanting may be fairly close, about 15–20cm (6–8in) apart (see Preparing a seed drill, page 38). Using a taut garden line or the edge of a board as a guide, draw out a shallow, level V-shaped

RIGHT *Vegetables such as carrots need to be sown* in situ, *whereas lettuces, onions and similar crops can be started elsewhere – in a separate seedbed or under glass – for transplanting to growing positions when large enough. Young onions grow slowly at first and do not form a canopy, making it possible to secure a catch crop of lettuces interplanted at the same time and cleared several weeks later.*

Preparing a seedbed

Seedbeds need to be firm, level and crumbled to a fine tilth to provide the best conditions for germination. When the soil is moist, but not too wet, use a fork or tined cultivator to break down larger clods. Remove weeds and large stones, and roughly rake the bed level. Before sowing a row or patch of seeds, consolidate the area with the head of a rake (treading is permissible on very loose, light soils) and again level the soil. This stage may need repeating several times to produce a tilth suitable for the size of seeds to be sown.

Break down clods with a hand cultivator.

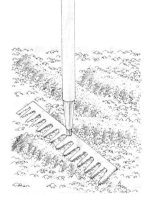

Tamp and crumble the soil with a rake.

Rake the soil surface to produce a fine, level tilth.

drill with a stick, the tip of a trowel or the corner of a hoe or rake. For short rows some gardeners simply press a rake handle into the soil. Uniform depth is important for consistent germination, and varies according to the size of seed, ranging from 1cm (½in) deep for the smallest seeds, to 5cm (2in) for the largest ones, such as broad beans.

Large or pelleted seeds can be spaced at the required distance apart, smaller ones such as parsnips can be sown in groups or 'stations' of 4–5 seeds at measured intervals or in a thin continuous line along the drill. To reduce overcrowding and the amount of thinning needed later, sow continuous rows sparingly with a seed dispenser or by tapping seeds from the packet, or by gently tipping a quantity into your hand and taking a pinch at a time, trickling them into the drill. Cover the seeds after sowing by drawing soil back over them with a hoe or rake (or use your hand), gently firm level and label the row. Do not water immediately after sowing. Protect sown rows from birds or cats with panels of netting or strands of black cotton attached to short sticks.

Sowing can also be done in a wide drill, made with a draw hoe, which saves room by accommodating the equivalent of several single rows in its flat bottom. Large seeds such as peas and beans can be spaced out evenly, while small seeds such as carrots, radishes and loose-leaf lettuce can be thinly broadcast in the bottom of the drill. Small seeds may also be sown

Preparing a seed drill

Most seeds need to be buried to provide them with the ideal conditions required for germination. Short drills can be scribed in the soil with a stick or trowel along the edge of a board, but longer drills should be marked out using a taut garden line and the corner of a hoe or rake. Aim for a consistent depth according to the type of crop: if the seeds are sown too deeply, they exhaust food reserves before emerging, while shallow sowing risks premature drying out. Make sure the soil is moist before sowing and label rows clearly.

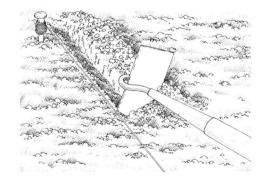

Many crops are sown in single V-shaped drills, prepared at the appropriate depth. Remove large stones exposed as you go.

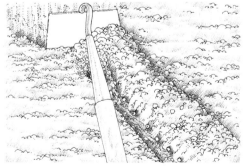

Flood drills in dry weather and sow the seeds as thinly as possible before covering them with the excavated soil and levelling.

Tender crops such as sweet corn need particular care in cooler regions where late frosts are a threat and reduce the length of the growing season. Seeds may be sown in pots under glass to gain a head start, or alternatively sown in situ under cloches. Two or three seeds are sown at each station, the seedlings later being singled to leave the strongest to grow on (when grown at wider spacings than here, multiple sowings can be left unthinned). Make sure sweetcorn and similarly tall crops do not shade sun-loving neighbours such as the shallots and onions growing nearby.

broadcast in patches or wide drills on the surface of a moist clean seedbed, then lightly buried by raking first in one direction and again at right angles.

When sowing in a nursery seedbed for later transplanting, seeds are sown in drills as above, although the rows may be as close as 15–20cm (6–8in) apart. In narrow beds it is usually more convenient to sow several short parallel rows running from one side of·the bed to the other, in drills drawn with a trowel along the side of a flat board or marked out by pressing a rake handle into the soil.

Where space is limited or the soil is seriously in need of improvement, many vegetables can be grown in containers such as growbags or large pots filled with good potting compost. According to the crop, seeds may be sown direct at stations or broadcast, or you can start plants in modules for transplanting. Remember container crops may need watering more frequently than those in the open ground, perhaps once or twice daily in a hot summer, and regular feeding after about 6 weeks is also advisable.

Coping with difficulties

Germination takes place only when soil temperatures are above critical levels (see under individual crop entries), so sowing in cold soils is often a waste of time. Cloches or plastic film can be used to warm the site for a week or two before sowing as well as to cover sowings until seedlings emerge.

Soil moisture levels need to be right, too. In wet conditions drills may be opened up and covered with cloches for a few days to help them dry out; covering the seeds with dry soil or seed compost after sowing also helps counter excess dampness. Dry seedbeds are best watered before sowing, or individual drills can be flooded first with water and allowed to drain.

Keep drills evenly moist after sowing, watering them gently with a can and rose whenever they start to dry out. This is particularly important for crops which can be injured by drought during their slow germination, such as parsley and parsnips, and for pelleted seeds, which need constant moisture to break down the seed coat.

Thinning seedlings

No matter how sparsely sown, most seedlings will need thinning to leave them enough space to develop without undue competition. Start thinning when seedlings are still small, making sure that the leaves of those left do not touch each other. Either hoe or pinch off superfluous seedlings at soil level to avoid disturbing the roots of those that remain, or carefully transplant them elsewhere. Thin several times, leaving seedlings at progressively greater distances apart until the plants are at recommended spacings. Compost unwanted thinnings, as these may attract pests and diseases if left on the soil, and firm or water the disturbed drills afterwards.

Wider drills for peas, beans or broad bands of other crops can be made with a draw hoe or by shovelling out soil with a spade.

Check that the bottom of the wide drill is level and at the right depth. Sow the seeds thinly or at regular spacings, and backfill.

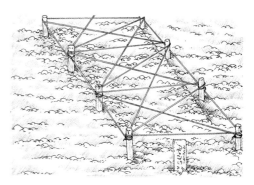

To avoid disturbance by birds or pets, protect drills after sowing with strips of netting or black cotton threaded between sticks.

Planting and transplanting

SELECTING A
HEALTHY PLANT
*The following points
should be helpful when
buying vegetable plants.
Illustrated here is a
healthy tomato plant.*
- *Check that the leaf
colour is true – an
indication of good
cultivation and vigour.*
- *Avoid plants that
have speckled leaves and
any other symptoms of
pests and disease.*
- *Check that the stems
are short-jointed and
that there are seed
leaves on tomato
plants; brassicas should
not have twisting or
woody stems.*
- *Plants are best
bought growing in
containers – either pots
or strips.*
- *Ensure the compost
is free from moss, dead
leaves and other signs
of neglect.*

It is possible to sow all crops *in situ* and so avoid any transplanting, but this greatly limits the number of vegetables that can be grown and their season of use. Starting early sowings under glass (see page 42) for planting out when conditions improve or transplanting late summer sowings to frames for protection extends the season. Sowing successional crops in a nursery bed or between existing rows for transplanting as soon as open ground becomes available allows a quick turn-over and greater variety of produce from a limited space. To avoid serious stress, all plants are best moved while still young and with the least possible disturbance to their roots.

Winter brassicas seem to benefit from being transplanted and are sometimes moved twice, first from seedbed to nursery bed and again 4–6 weeks later to their cropping positions, producing strong fibrous root systems as a result. But transplanting does not suit all crops, however, and root crops, in particular, seldom transplant successfully once their taproots have started to develop. Bare-root lettuce seedlings transplanted in hot summers rarely grow as well as those left *in situ* or planted out in soil blocks, degradable pots, or from modules (see page 43), whereas if transplanted in spring, they move easily from one part of the garden to another.

As transplanting checks growth, you must wait until conditions are ideal – cold or very wet soils, frost or hot dry weather can all prove lethal. Tender crops must be fully hardened off (see page 43) before being planted out after any serious risk of frost is past. In summer plant or transplant on a dull or showery day, or in the evening, to prevent wilting; in hot weather it often helps to cover leafy transplants by day with upturned pots until they recover.

If the soil is relatively clean and in good heart, lightly pricking over the surface and removing any obvious weeds may be sufficient preparation for planting, especially for crops such as brassicas and onions that prefer firm ground. Otherwise fork the site more deeply a week or two beforehand and leave to settle; just before planting, spread a base dressing of compound fertilizer where recommended or if the soil is not fertile enough and rake this in, leaving the surface roughly level but not as fine as for a seedbed. Make sure the soil is moist, and water the plants a few hours before they are to be transplanted.

Using a trowel or hand fork, dig up individual plants with as much soil on their roots as possible; hold them by their leaves or stems, and carry them in a seedtray to prevent loss of soil. Spare seedlings thinned from crops such as lettuce and onions should be forked up from the rows without disturbing the seedlings that remain. Only lift and plant a few at a time to reduce the risk of roots drying out and use a marked stick to measure planting distances.

Make a hole for each plant, large enough to take the roots without doubling or cramping them; with the exception of leeks, always use a trowel rather than a dibber. Holding the plant in one hand, replace the soil around the roots and then firm round the stem with your fingers. In dry weather you will need to water and mulch after planting; on light dry soils in summer 'puddle' plants in by flooding them in position before refilling the holes with soil.

Heeling in

If immediate planting must be delayed, bought plants will stay in good condition if heeled in temporarily in a sheltered piece of spare ground. Although mainly used for fruit, this is a useful technique for brassicas and other vegetable plants. Dig out a trench deep enough to accommodate the roots, lean the plants against one side of the trench and just touching each other. Refill the trench with moist soil and lightly firm.

Spacing vegetables

Planting vegetables quite closely together in widely spaced rows is not the most economical nor necessarily the most productive arrangement. Research suggests that the same population of plants in a given area can be arranged symmetrically to make better use of available water and nutrients in the soil, suppress weeds and allow plants to develop without undue competition from each other.

METHODS OF SPACING

Equidistant spacing makes efficient use of ground and each plant develops unhindered.

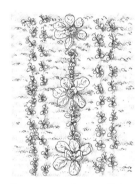

Fast-maturing radishes followed by peas will be cleared before brussels sprouts need more room.

Where the soil has been thoroughly cultivated in advance and kept clear of weeds, as here, you can sow or plant with little further preparation. For transplants to grow away without any check, it is best to choose a dull or showery day, and make sure both the transplants and the planting site are moist. Use a garden line to mark out longer rows and expose the roots to the air for as short a time as possible.

Weed and thin crops sown broadcast to leave seedlings at regular spacings for even, consistent growth.

In most cases, the best method is to arrange plants equidistantly from each other, staggered in adjacent parallel rows so that each plant has an equal circle of space in which to develop. The distance apart determines the final size of each plant as well as the yield from the area. For example, summer cabbages spaced at 35 × 35cm (14 × 14in) give a heavy crop of small heads, while at 45 × 45cm (18 × 18in) a third fewer plants give the same total yield, but individual heads are larger with more solid hearts.

In the USA many gardeners grow crops such as carrots, spinach, beetroot and loose-leaf lettuce in broad bands up to 90cm (3ft) wide, broadcasting the seeds over the whole area and then roughly thinning the seedlings by 'combing' through the row with a wire-tined rake to leave plants a few centimetres apart. It is difficult to estimate or measure optimum plant densities with this method, but the principle is ideal for leaf lettuce and mixed salad leaf crops, sown in several parallel rows 10cm (4in) apart with the seedlings thinned to about 2.5cm (1in) apart.

Weeding is important in the early stages with any arrangement, using a narrow onion hoe or hand weeding between closely spaced plants. Most closely spaced plants soon reach the stage where their spreading leaves suppress any further weed growth, whereas conventional rows of plants will be too far apart to affect the growth of weeds in the ground. Competition from weeds between rows is more serious than from those growing among plants within a row so hoeing must continue for most of the life of widely spaced crops.

Growing crops at close symmetrical spacing is ideal for narrow beds tended from parallel paths, with no need to walk between plants, but you might prefer to follow conventional planting arrangements, hoeing between rows to eliminate weeds and perhaps exploiting the more generous spacing to grow inter-crops. Which system to use depends on your arrangement of beds and how much routine cultivation you enjoy doing. Optimum distances for both systems are given in individual crop entries.

Sowing under glass

Starting vegetables in a greenhouse or on a window sill allows you to make early progress while temperatures outdoors are still too low for germination. Timing is important, though. As a rough guide to the best time to sow under glass, count back from the date when the last spring frosts normally occur in your locality, allowing several weeks' growth from sowing – this varies according to the climate and the crop (see individual crop entries later in this chapter) – plus a further fortnight for hardening off (see page 43). Chitted or pre-germinated seeds need less time to reach the planting stage.

How to sow

The traditional method is to sow seeds in pots or trays of sterile seed compost, sometimes in a propagator with additional warmth, for pricking out into trays of more fertile, coarser potting compost.

Fill containers loosely with moist, fresh seed compost and level the top with a strip of wood. Gently press down soil-based compost to give an even surface for sowing; give containers of soilless compost a sharp tap to settle their contents. Sow the seeds thinly and evenly over the surface, cover with a thin layer of sieved compost and stand in a propagator or warm place. Keep the compost moist by covering containers with sheets of glass or clear plastic film; turn or wipe this daily to remove any condensation and remove altogether after germination. When seedlings emerge, move containers into good light but shield them from bright sunshine. If the compost dries out, stand them in a little water until damp patches start to appear on the surface.

Pricking out seedlings

As soon as the seedlings are large enough to handle, water and then prick them out into trays of potting compost where they have more room to develop (see How to prick out, below). Use a table fork, small dibber or seed label to ease out a clump of seedlings and carefully separate them, handling them only by the leaves as their stems are very fragile. Transfer each seedling to a dibber hole in the new compost large enough to take the roots and stem of the seedling so that it sits with its leaves just above the surface; gently firm into place, then water the tray with a can fitted with a fine rose. Seedlings should be pricked out about 2.5–5cm (1–2in) apart in rows: a standard seedtray will take between 24 (arranged 6 × 4) and 40 (8 × 5) according to the eventual size of the young plants. Templates can be bought or made to press all the holes at once.

How to prick out

If seedlings are to develop quickly and healthily, they must be transferred to seed trays or modules before they become overcrowded and drawn or leggy. Use clean sterilized trays and fresh compost, gently firmed if soil-based but otherwise levelled and settled by tapping. Prick out the sturdiest seedlings, rejecting any that are thin or misshaped, and plant immediately. Grow the seedlings at a lower temperature than during germination, in good light but shaded from bright sunshine for the first few days.

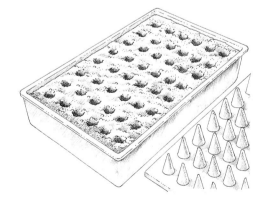

Either mark out transplanting distances freehand or use an appropriate template.

Handle seedlings by their leaves and gently firm in place. Water with a fine rose.

Except for soil blocks, modules use ordinary potting compost, which contains enough fertilizer to sustain growth almost to planting out stage. Seeds may be sown initially in pots or trays to save space, the seedlings then being pricked out into modules; alternatively seeds are sown singly or in small groups in the units, surplus seedlings being pinched off at surface level to leave the strongest.

Hardening off

Plants raised in warmth need to be acclimatized gradually to outdoor conditions before they can be fully exposed without harm. Move the plants first to the coolest part of the greenhouse for 2–3 days before transferring them to a cold frame, kept closed initially and protected with mats or sacking if frost occurs. Ventilate the frame for longer periods each day, until after about a fortnight the plants are left completely uncovered. Plants under cloches need similar preparation before being fully exposed. If you have no cold frame, stand plants in a sheltered position outdoors on mild days, at first returning them to the greenhouse in the evening, but eventually leaving them outside for a few nights before planting out. Where planting is delayed, feed trays occasionally to keep plants in peak condition.

To ensure unforced and healthy growth, prick out seedlings far enough apart to allow them to grow without competition from each other. Always use clean sterilized trays and fresh compost.

Using modules

You can avoid pricking out by sowing in small pots, trays divided into separate cells, or in variously sized soil blocks of compressed blocking compost which you can make yourself with a special tool, thus avoiding the risks of root disturbance at planting time (see Sowing in modules, below). Large seeds such as beans and sweet corn are often sown individually in small pots where they grow until planted out; plants in biodegradable pots made of peat or paper can be planted out intact, the pots gradually decaying in the soil.

Sowing in modules

Modules, such as divided cell trays or separate compressed soil blocks, keep root disturbance to a minimum and thus reduce the check to growth when transplanting outdoors. Seeds can be sown individually or in clusters in units, or seedlings may be pricked out singly into cells after germination in seed trays. Keep the seedlings consistently moist during growth and do not leave them too long in their modules after reaching planting size. Harden off early sowings and water modules just before planting in moist soil.

With a template make holes in the potting compost before sowing.

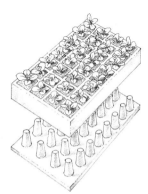

Press the tray on the template to release cells ready for planting.

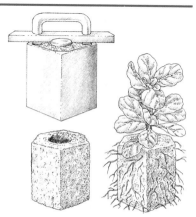

Insert a seed or cutting into the soil block and plant out when roots appear through the sides.

Growing vegetables

Related crops tend to have similar cultural needs and also share common pests and diseases. Vegetables are grouped together according to these affinities when planning rotation schemes, and this arrangement is followed here, starting with the three largest groups – legumes (peas and beans), brassicas (members of the cabbage family) and root crops.

French beans

While some gardeners regard this annual crop as supreme, sowing seeds in succession to crop throughout the season, others grow them only for early use until runner beans are ready (see right). Numerous cultivars have been developed from early Central American ancestors, many of them now endangered heritage kinds. Cultivars have white, pink, mauve or red flowers followed by round or flat pods that may be green, yellow, red or purple, some flecked with other colours. Most are dwarf ('bush beans') and early to crop, but climbing cultivars ('pole beans') are more prolific and may be used as an alternative to runner beans. They are grown for their immature pods and for the seeds, either fresh (flageolets) or dried (haricots).

Sites (see Growing legumes, left)

French bean plants are tender with fragile leaves so prefer warm sunny positions that are sheltered from the wind, and light rich soils; heavy clay is not suitable, nor are cold poorly drained soils which are often lethal to plants.

Dig the ground well before planting and add plenty of well-rotted manure or compost. Prepare the seedbed a fortnight before sowing or planting and apply a base dressing of compound fertilizer. In cold areas warm the soil with cloches before sowing, and use dressed seed as a precaution against soil-borne diseases. A seed or soil inoculant can be used to introduce nitrogen-fixing bacteria; some gardeners achieve this by transferring a little soil from a previous site, but there is the drawback that this may also spread disease and defeat the purpose of rotation.

GROWING LEGUMES

Legumes (peas and beans) are susceptible to soil-borne diseases, and so need rotating around the garden. They are hosts to nitrifying bacteria that live in swellings (nodules) on the roots where they make nitrogen available to the plants. Provided that soils are reasonably fertile, crops need little extra nitrogen fertilizer beyond an initial base dressing. As the bacteria need a slightly alkaline environment, soils should be tested for acidity and dressed with lime if necessary, raked in before sowing and planting or dusted on the surface afterwards. After cropping, cut down topgrowth and dig in, with the roots, as green manure.

Cultivation

Do not risk outdoor sowings too early; either sow 4–5cm (1½–2in) deep in pre-warmed soil under cloches or plastic film in mid- to late spring or start seeds in pots or soil blocks under glass 3–4 weeks before the last frosts. For succession make 2–3 further sowings at intervals until mid-summer, the last for covering with cloches in early autumn.

Earth up and mulch plants once established and support their stems with twigs to keep crops clean. Keep soils consistently moist and water liberally when flowering starts, up to 22 litres per sq m (4gal per sq yd) every 7–10 days in a dry season.

The flowers are self-fertile and seldom have problems setting crops. Start picking beans while they are still young (when pods snap cleanly in half and the seeds are not yet prominent), and repeat every 2–3 days for the 6–8 week lifespan of the crop. Leave pods for drying until they turn brown, pull up the plants and suspend in a dry well-ventilated place until brittle, when the seeds are shelled for storage.

Crop details Seed count: 2–3 per g, 50–70 per 25g (1oz); 12.5g (0.5oz) per 10ft row. Germination: 10–14 days at 12°C (54°F) minimum. Life of seeds: 2 years. Height: 30–45cm (1–1½ft); climbing cultivars 1.8–2.5m (6–8ft). Spacing: 10cm (4in) in rows 45cm (18in) apart, or 23cm (9in) apart each way in staggered rows; climbers as for runner beans. Sowing to harvest: 8–12 weeks. Average yield: 112–225g (4–8oz) per plant, double for climbing beans.

Recommended cultivars Green: 'Deuil Fin Precoce', 'Montano', 'Sunray', 'Tendergreen', 'The Prince'. Coloured: 'Kinghorn Wax' (yellow), 'Mont D'Or' (yellow), 'Purple Queen', 'Royal Burgundy'/'Royalty'. Climbing: 'Borlotto' (red striped pods), 'Climbing Blue Lake', 'Hunter', 'Purple-Podded'. For drying: 'Blue Lake', 'Chevriet Vert', 'Climbing Blue Lake', 'Dutch Brown'.

Pests and diseases Bean seed flies, black bean aphids, root aphids, slugs; anthracnose, foot and root rots, halo blight, viruses (see pages 76–7).

Runner beans

Prolific in moist fertile soils and usually grown as a tender annual in cool climates, this popular bean is highly decorative, with lush handsome foliage and red, white, pink or bicoloured red-and-white flowers, followed by long fat pods, sometimes stringless. Some cultivars are naturally dwarf but most are vigorous twining climbers that need sturdy support; a few such as 'Kelvedon Marvel' and 'Sunset' are often pinched out to make bushy self-supporting plants with early crops (but lower yields).

Sites (see Growing legumes, left)

Runner beans need a warm sheltered position where their shade will not discourage other plants; they may be grown against fences and walls or as decorative screens. As the plants root deeply, they seldom crop well on hungry or badly drained soils; dig the site the previous autumn at least one-spit deep, working in plenty of compost or decayed manure. Lime acid soils and rake in a base dressing of general fertilizer a week or so prior to sowing or planting. Climbing beans need strong supports, using 2.5m (8ft) canes or poles set firmly in position before planting (see Supporting climbing beans, below).

Cultivation

Sow in the open 5cm (2in) deep in late spring or early summer when serious danger of frosts is past; in cold gardens sowing should take place about a month before the last frosts, outdoors under cloches or polythene tunnels, or indoors in pots, hardening off seedlings thoroughly before fully exposing them to the open air. Sow a few extra seeds at the end of rows to fill any gaps that may occur later. Mulch after germination or planting.

Water regularly, especially when the flower buds start to form and again when the first flowers open. Thereafter, water twice weekly at a rate of about 5–11 litres per sq m (1–2gal per sq yd); this usually helps the flowers to set in dry weather. Arranging plants in blocks of short rows to shelter pollinating insects, growing white-flowered cultivars or pinching out plants to keep them dwarf are other ways to encourage efficient setting where this is a problem.

Climbing plants may need securing loosely to supports until they twine naturally; pinch out their growing tips when they reach the tops of canes. For dwarf climbing cultivars, pinch growing tips when stems are 23–30cm (9–12in) tall and pinch sideshoots at weekly intervals; support the stems on twiggy sticks to keep pods clear of the soil.

Supporting climbing beans

As climbing beans quickly develop heavy canopies of lush foliage, sturdy support is essential. Stout 2.5m (8ft) tall poles or thick bamboo canes erected firmly in the ground before planting are tied together at the tops for stability. Arrange these in groups as wigwams, or in long continuous rows joined by horizontal canes. For further reinforcement erect strong posts every 2.5–3m (8–10ft), with cross-pieces at top and bottom to which taut wires are attached and used to keep vertical canes securely in place.

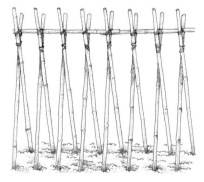
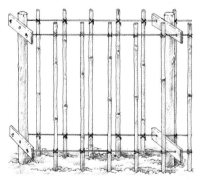

For continuous rows cross the supports and brace with horizontal canes or support rows of vertical canes with sturdy posts and *wires. Small groups of beans can be grown on wigwams, but in windy gardens a more substantial structure is advisable.*

Harvesting should begin when the pods are 15–20cm (6–8in) in length; regular picking every 2–3 days prevents the pods from becoming tough and stringy and helps prolong the crop until the first frosts. Surplus pods may be frozen or preserved in layers of salt and mature beans can be dried.

Crop details Seed count: 1 per g, 25–30 per 25g (1oz); 25g (1oz) per 3m (10ft) double row. Germination: 7–10 days at 12°C (54°F) minimum. Life of seeds: 2 years. Height: 2.5–3.7m (8–12ft), dwarf cultivars 45cm (18in). Spacing: 15cm (6in), in double rows 60cm (2ft) apart. Sowing to harvest: 12–16 weeks. Average yield: 1–1.3kg (2–3lb) per plant.

Recommended cultivars Standard: 'Enorma', 'Kelvedon Marvel' (early), 'Painted Lady' (red-and-white bicoloured flowers), 'Streamline', 'Sunset' (pink flowers). Stringless: 'Butler', 'Desirée' (white flowers and seeds), 'Lady Di', 'Polestar', 'Red Knight'. Dwarf: 'Gulliver', 'Hammond's Dwarf', 'Pickwick'.

Pests and diseases As for french beans.

Tall broad bean cultivars are vigorous plants that often need strong support in exposed gardens. Pinching out the tops of stems when their first pods have set reduces the risk of wind damage as well as deterring aphids. Water during flowering and when pods are swelling to produce the best yields. After harvest many gardeners cut down and feed plants to encourage a light crop on resulting sideshoots.

Broad beans

Broad beans are a prolific and very nutritious crop, grown mainly for the seeds, although many people eat the young pods and also the leafy tips. The green, white or red seeds are used while immature when they are delicately flavoured; large ripe beans, too strong for many tastes, may be used in soups, or saved for sowing as a green manure crop.

Cultivars are variously classified, but for most gardeners the important distinction is between 'Longpods', with 4–10 medium-sized seeds per pod, and less hardy 'Windsor' types with 2–5 very large seeds. The hardiest kinds tolerate many degrees of frost and all prefer cool conditions, rarely succeeding from summer sowings.

Sites (see Growing legumes, page 44)

An open, fairly sunny position is best for spring sowings; crops sown in late autumn need shelter to protect them from severe winter weather and good drainage to prevent root problems. Most fertile deeply dug soils are suitable, if not too acid or water-logged. Cultivate well in advance, adding decayed manure or compost unless the ground is already enriched from previous crops. Lime and rake in a general fertilizer a few days before sowing.

Cultivation

Main spring sowings begin in late winter or early spring, with two further successional sowings at monthly intervals. For over-wintered crops, sow in mid- to late autumn 5cm (2in) deep, in cold gardens covering rows with cloches until late winter. In very cold districts where over-wintered sowings may not be worthwhile, sow in deep boxes or pots under cool glass or in a frame in mid- to late winter.

Earth up autumn-sown plants and support taller cultivars in exposed positions by enclosing rows or blocks with string attached to stout canes or stakes. Support dwarf plants with twiggy sticks or tuck straw around their stems to keep pods clear of the ground. These plants dislike drought but if spring-sown crops are mulched after soils warm up, there is usually no need to water until they flower, when they should be given 22 litres per sq m (4gal per sq yd)

Garden peas

Fresh garden peas are a crop well worth growing for their supreme quality (raw or cooked) when gathered just before use. Cultivars with wrinkled seeds are sweetest but generally less hardy than round-seeded kinds, which have higher starch levels and are most likely to survive winters outdoors.

Ordinary garden peas are grown for their immature seeds, which are small and outstandingly sweet in 'petits pois' cultivars, whereas the entire pod of 'mangetout' kinds (sugar peas, snow peas) is eaten while seeds are still small. There are many types of these, some flat and others, such as 'sugar snap' peas, producing fat succulent pods that are fibreless while young. All types include tall cultivars that make productive use of space but need strong supports and dwarf kinds with earlier, lighter crops. Even the shortest cultivars benefit from some form of support, although semi-leafless types develop extra tendrils, making them virtually self-supporting.

Depending on the time they take to mature, peas are grouped into early and maincrop cultivars, the latter sometimes subdivided to give a second early (early maincrop) group. Early peas can be sown in succession throughout the season, but it is a fallacy to assume they are best for small gardens; if shade-tolerant crops are grown nearby, tall high-yielding peas make excellent screens, the plants occupying no more ground than early dwarf cultivars.

Sites (see Growing legumes, page 44)

Early and late crops prefer a position in full sun and mid-summer crops prefer light shade. Peas need deep, cool rooting conditions and free drainage, so dig the ground deeply and work in plenty of compost or decayed manure to prevent roots from drying out. Lime the soil if it is acid and rake in a base dressing of compound fertilizer at one-third the recommended rate before sowing on poor soils.

Cultivation

Peas resent cold soils, so make the first sowings, 2.5–5cm (1–2in) deep, under cloches in late winter or early spring in a warm position, using an early or round-seeded cultivar and seeds that have been

Apart from their obvious popularity as a fresh vegetable, peas have great design potential when planning kitchen garden beds. Most kinds, even very dwarf cultivars, benefit from some kind of support such as twiggy sticks, as here, and this transforms plants into simple screens, divisions and even temporary windbreaks (although peas cannot withstand very high winds). Taller kinds may be grown as wigwams or on strings or wide-mesh netting attached to canes and arranged, as for runner beans, in rows.

every week in dry weather. When plants are flowering well and the first beans form, pinch off the tops of main stems to encourage early maturity and help deter aphids. Start picking pods when they are 5–8cm (2–3in) long for cooking whole, but leave enough to plump up for shelling. Young surplus pods and beans can be frozen while mature beans can be dried for winter use.

Crop details Seed count: 15 per 25g (1oz), 600 per kilo, 200 per pint; 50g (2oz) per 3m (10ft) double row. Germination: 10–14 days at temperatures below 15°C (60°F). Life of seeds: 2–3 years. Height: 1.2–1.8m (4–6ft); dwarf cultivars 30–45cm (1–1½ft). Spacing: 20cm (8in) in double rows 23cm (9in) apart and 60cm (2ft) between pairs of rows, or in blocks with plants 25cm (10in) apart each way. Sowing to harvest: spring sown 12–15 weeks; autumn sown 26–30 weeks. Average yield: 225–450g (8–16oz) per plant, more if pods used.

Recommended cultivars Tall: 'Green Windsor', 'Imperial Green Longpod', 'Jubilee Hysor' (Windsor), 'Masterpiece Green Longpod', 'Red Epicure' (red-seeded), 'Witkiem Manita' (early), 'Witkiem Vroma'. Dwarf: 'Bonny Lad', 'The Sutton'. For autumn sowing: 'Aquadulce (Claudia)', 'Bunyard's Exhibition', 'The Sutton'.

Pests and diseases Black bean aphids, birds, mice; chocolate spot, foot and root rots (see pages 76–7).

dressed with fungicide. Further sowings of an early wrinkled-seed kind can be made at 3–4 week intervals from mid-spring onwards. Maincrop, mangetout and petits pois peas are sown in mid- to late spring; for the last peas of the season sow at mid-summer, using an early short-stemmed cultivar such as 'Kelvedon Wonder', or a similar fast growing early cultivar that is resistant to mildew, which usually appears in autumn. In cold or wet gardens, you can save time in early spring by starting peas in 8cm (3in) pots in a cool greenhouse or frame. Sow 4–5 seeds per pot, and when plants are 8–10cm (3–4in) high, harden them off and plant out the pots intact 15cm (6in) apart in single rows.

As peas dislike overcrowding take time to space seeds evenly. Protect sowings from birds with wire netting or strands of black cotton. Support plants when the first tendrils appear, using twigs or netting along the side of single rows, down the centre of wide rows, or arranged to enclose wider blocks. Draw soil up the stems with a hoe to provide additional support, keep the rows weeded, and mulch when plants are about 15cm (6in) high. At first water if necessary in a dry season but when flowering starts irrigate weekly at the rate of 22 litres per sq m (4gal per sq yd) until picking ceases (see Growing garden peas, below).

Begin harvesting garden peas when pods are well filled, but before they are tightly packed and lose their bloom, mangetouts when the seeds are starting to develop, sugar snap peas while the pods still break cleanly. Surplus peas may be frozen, or the pods can be left to ripen fully; pull up plants and suspend in a dry airy place until pods are brittle, when the dried peas may be shelled for storage.

Crop details Seed count: 120 per 25g (1oz), 5000 per kilo, 1500 per pint; 50g (2oz) per 3m (10ft) row 23cm (9in) wide. Germination: 2–3 weeks at 10°C (50°F) minimum. Life of seeds: 2–3 years. Height: 30–150cm (1–5ft) according to cultivar. Spacing: for mass harvest 5cm (2in) each way in rows 23cm (9in) wide; for prolonged picking 10cm (4in) in broad strips, each comprising three single rows 10cm (4in) apart, with 45cm (18in) between strips. Sowing to harvest: early 12–14 weeks, maincrop 14–16 weeks, autumn-sown 30–34 weeks. Average yield: 450g–1kg (1–2lb) per 30cm (1ft) wide row.

Recommended cultivars Round-seeded: 'Feltham First', 'Meteor', 'Pilot'. Early: '(Hurst) Beagle', '(Hurst) Greenshaft', 'Kelvedon Wonder', 'Little Marvel'. Maincrop: 'Alderman','Lynx' (petits pois), 'Markana' (semi-leafless), 'Onward'. Mangetout: 'Carouby de Mousanne' (purple flowers), 'Sugar Snap', 'Sugar Rae'.

Pests and diseases Birds, mice, pea moth, pea thrips; damping off, foot and root rots, Fusarium wilt, mildew, pod spotting (see pages 76–7).

FAR RIGHT *For plants to make good solid hearts, savoy cabbages need a long season of growth, but as one of the more decorative brassicas they blend well with ornamentals and may often be worked in wherever there is space.*

Growing garden peas

Although it takes a little more time to space out pea seeds at regular distances in drills than sowing haphazardly, it does result in healthier and more uniform growth and uses fewer seeds. Sow in a wide drill or several parallel rows close together to economize on space and the need for support. Except for leafless and semi-leafless cultivars, all peas need supporting with twiggy sticks, horizontal strings attached to vertical canes, or panels of wire or plastic netting to keep the pods and foliage clear of the ground.

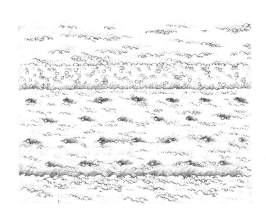

Level the bottom of the drill and space seeds evenly to ensure reliable germination.

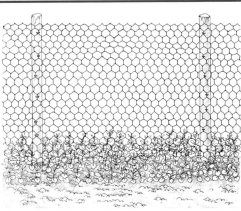

Position netting down the centre of the drill before the plants develop tendrils.

GROWING BRASSICAS

This vast group of cabbage relatives shares the same site preferences, pests and diseases. Brassicas are cool-season vegetables which need an open position, except for summer crops which are grown in light shade. Soils should be moist, rich in humus and firm: tread light soils if recently cultivated or plant in ground undisturbed after previous crops such as legumes have been cleared. They should be rotated to discourage diseases such as clubroot. They also need alkaline conditions (pH7 or higher), so test soils beforehand and lime if acid. Water consistently in dry weather, giving up to 22 litres per sq m (4gal per sq yd) every 7–10 days. Although they seem to be root crops, turnips, swedes and radishes are members of the brassica group and are therefore considered in this section.

Cabbage

A widely varied race of leaf crops, cabbages can be available all year round in the garden, although many gardeners prefer to concentrate on crops that mature from late autumn until spring. Cultivars are normally grouped according to season of use, but there is considerable overlap and some kinds may be grown all year round. You can choose from pointed, spherical and flattened ('drumhead') types, green smooth-leaved cabbages or crinkled savoys (or crosses between these), red and white kinds for fresh use or storage, hearted spring cabbages or leafy 'greens', and Chinese cabbages for cooking or eating raw like a cos lettuce. For general garden use, select cultivars that stand for a long time without deterioration and compact kinds such as 'Minicole' or 'Stonehead' where space is limited. F₁ hybrids are more uniform than long-established cultivars and often display pest- or disease-resistance.

Sites See Growing brassicas, left.

Cultivation

Sow seeds 2–2.5cm (¾–1in) deep *in situ* or in a nursery bed; thin or transplant to 8cm (3in) apart, before planting out in cropping positions when seedlings have 5–6 leaves (about 6 weeks old). Alternatively, sow under glass in modules.

Sow spring cultivars in late summer; summer kinds in early spring (late winter under glass for earliest crops); autumn and winter types in late spring; and chinese cabbages from early summer to early autumn. In cold areas or to advance crops, grow spring cabbages under cloches or perforated film; feed with nitrogenous fertilizer in late winter or early spring. Earth up all over-wintered crops for stability and firm any loosened by wind and frost.

Harvest closely planted spring cabbages as greens, leaving every third plant to heart up. All cabbages are normally pulled up as required, with their roots cut off and discarded, but if you cut spring and summer kinds close to ground level and then inscribe a deep cross in the stumps, a second crop of small cabbages will follow. Red and white cultivars can be cut at ground level in late autumn for storing in straw-lined boxes in a dry cool shed.

Crop details Seed count: 250 per g, 6–7000 per 25g (1oz). Germination: 1–2 weeks at 5°C (41°F) minimum. Life of seeds: up to 8 years in ideal conditions. Height: 25–38cm (10–15in). Spacing: spring cabbage 10–25cm (4–10in) in rows 30cm (1ft) apart, or 25cm (10in) square; summer/autumn cabbage 35cm (14in) square for small heads, to 45cm (18in) each way for large heads; winter cabbage 50cm (20in) square; chinese cabbage 30cm (1ft) square. Sowing to harvest: chinese 10 weeks, summer/autumn/winter 20–35 weeks, spring 20–35 weeks. Average yield: 450g–1.5kg (1–4lb) per plant.

Recommended cultivars Spring cabbage: F₁ 'Duncan', 'Durham Early', 'First Early Market', 'Pixie', F₁ 'Spring Hero', 'Wintergreen'. Summer cabbage: 'Derby Day', F₁ 'Kingspi', F₁ 'Minicole', F₁ 'Ruby Ball' (red), F₁ 'Spitfire'. Autumn cabbage: F₁ 'Castello', F₁ 'Hardora' (red), F₁ 'Novusa' (savoy), F₁ 'Stonehead', F₁ 'Taler' (savoy), 'Winnigstadt'. Winter cabbage: F₁ 'Celtic', 'Christmas Drumhead' 'Ice Queen', 'January King, Hardy Late Stock 3', F₁ 'Polinius' (white), F₁ 'Tundra', F₁ 'Winterton', F₁ 'Wivoy' (savoy). Chinese cabbage: F₁ 'Kasumi', F₁ 'Nagaoka', F₁ 'Tip Top',

Pests and diseases Aphids, birds, cabbage root fly, cabbage white fly, caterpillars, flea beetle, slugs; clubroot, damping off (see pages 76–7).

Cauliflower

This is a fussy crop and perhaps the hardest brassica to grow well, especially on light dry soils deficient in humus, but success can be very satisfying. Cauli-flowers are grown for their solid heads of flower buds ('curds'), which are usually white although purple, creamy yellow and green cultivars are available. Summer-heading cultivars and mini-cauliflowers (see Growing mini-cauliflowers, below) make the best use of space as other kinds, especially over-wintered types ('winter broccoli'), need wider spacing. In mild gardens the latter will produce heads for cutting during winter but elsewhere crops stand all winter to start heading in spring.

Sites (see Growing brassicas, page 49)

All types need deep, fertile soils that retain plenty of moisture at all stages of growth and a pH as high as 7.5 to avoid physiological disorders such as whiptail (narrow leaves and undeveloped heads).

Cultivation

Sow summer kinds 2–2.5cm (¾–1in) deep in autumn in a frame or under cloches; thin to 5–8cm (2–3in) apart and keep well-ventilated and cool (but frost-free) over winter. Alternatively, cauliflowers can be sown in modules or small pots in autumn or under glass at 21°C (70°F) in late winter. Harden off and plant out in early spring, when you can make a further sowing in a frame or a seedbed outdoors for planting out in late spring for succession. Sow late summer/autumn cultivars in mid- to late spring in a seedbed outdoors for planting out in mid-summer. Sow cultivars for winter use in mild areas and over-wintered crops for spring use in a seedbed outdoors in late spring for transplanting in late summer.

Water regularly during growth and especially before and after transplanting, and mulch to keep the soil moist; during dry weather, give 22 litres per sq m (4gal per sq yd) every 10–14 days. On very dry soils, puddle in transplants at a slightly wider spacing, leaving a depression round each plant for flooding with water. When summer or winter heads start to form, break a few surrounding leaves across the curds for protection from sun or frost.

Plants often mature together, so cut the first while the curds are still very tight, and harvest any that start to deteriorate for freezing. To store for up to 3 weeks, pull up plants with their roots and suspend upside down in a well-ventilated cool shed.

Crop details Seed count: 250 per g, 6–7000 per 25g (1oz). Germination: 1–2 weeks at 5°C (41°F) minimum. Life of seeds: up to 6 years. Height: 30–45cm (1–1½ft). Spacing: summer 45cm (18in) in rows 60cm (2ft) apart or 50cm (20in) square; late summer/autumn 60cm (2ft) apart each way; winter

---

Growing mini-cauliflowers

Where space is rationed, try growing cauliflowers at high density to produce small heads 5–8cm (2–3in) in diameter after only 3–4 months' growth. Raise the seedlings in modules and transplant them 15cm (6in) apart each way in blocks, or sow *in situ* in drills, a few seeds at each station, as shown here, and thin. Water in dry weather and clear complete batches as they mature, freezing any surplus. Sowing every 3–4 weeks from mid-spring to mid-summer provides heads through summer and autumn.

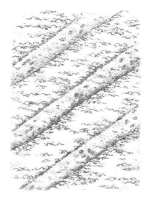

Sow the seeds in parallel drills 15cm (6in apart).

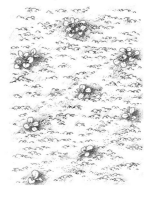

Thin seedlings to leave one per station.

Mature heads 5–8cm (2–3in) in diameter.

Hybrid calabrese cultivars grown for their large main head of buds are very uniform in growth rate and appearance. Whether planted out in rows or squares they are neat, decorative plants. Here, a block of fast growing plants is being cropped within a surrounding hedge of purple sage.

75cm (30in) apart each way; for mini-cauliflowers, see below left. Sowing to harvest: summer/autumn 16–20 weeks; winter 40–50 weeks. Average yield: 450g–1kg (1–2lb) per plant (lower yield for mini-cauliflowers).

Recommended cultivars Summer: 'Aubade', 'Alpha Paloma', 'Dominant', F_1 'Montano', 'Snowball', F_1 'Snow Crown'. Late summer/autumn: 'Barrier Reef', 'Canberra', 'Dok (Elgon)', F_1 'Plana', 'Snowcap', 'Violet Queen' (purple), 'Wallaby', 'White Rock'. Winter: 'English Winter – Vilna', 'Maystar', 'Purple Cape' (purple), 'Walcheren Winter – Armado April', 'Walcheren Winter – Markanta'.
Pests and diseases As for cabbage, page 49.

Calabrese

There is some confusion over the term 'broccoli', still used by many gardeners to refer to winter-heading cauliflowers. Originally, broccoli was an Italian description of any tender young brassica shoots, but is now generally confined to sprouting broccoli (see page 52) and large-heading cultivars, better known as calabrese and often sold as 'broccoli spears'.

Most calabrese cultivars grown today are F_1 hybrids, which quickly develop a large central head of blue-green buds, followed in many cases by smaller secondary spears on sideshoots. Some cultivars are better at this than others, while the older

'Green Sprouting' produces small spears only, but prolifically over a long season. Hybrids planted at closer spacings yield smaller heads that mature simultaneously for freezing. Cultivars head at different rates – 'Mercedes' for example can take only 10–11 weeks and is therefore ideal for successional sowing, whereas 'Shogun' needs a few more weeks to produce heavier heads.

Sites (see Growing brassicas, page 49)
Calabrese tolerates less fertile soils than other crops in the brassica group.

Cultivation

Transplanting from the open ground is not recommended, but seeds may be sown in modules or small pots 6–8 weeks before the last frosts for early crops; plant out in mid-spring, under cloches if necessary. Later sowings are made *in situ*, 2–2.5cm (1–2in) deep, in small pinches at stations the required distance apart, with clusters of seedlings later singled to leave the strongest. Make the last outdoor sowings in early summer. An early maturing cultivar can be sown in modules in late summer for transplanting outdoors in mild regions, elsewhere in a frame, to crop in early spring.

Water regularly and mulch to retain moisture. In a dry season give 11–22 litres per sq m (2–4gal per sq yd) every fortnight according to the type of soil. Harvest the main head while still firm and before the flower buds open, and then top-dress plants with a nitrogenous fertilizer to encourage sideshoots; cut these when 10–13cm (4–5in) long.

Crop details Seed count: 200 per g, 5–6000 per 25g (1oz). Germination: 1–2 weeks at 5°C (41°F) minimum. Life of seeds: up to 6 years. Height: 38–60cm (15–24in). Spacing: 15cm (6in) in rows 30cm (1ft) apart, or 23cm (9in) apart each way. Sowing to harvest: 10–14 weeks. Average yield: 450g–1kg (1–2lb) per plant.
Recommended cultivars F_1 'Corvet', F_1 'Emperor', F_1 'Green Comet', 'Green Sprouting/Italian Sprouting', F_1 'Mercedes', 'Romanesco' (yellow-green heads), F_1 'Shogun'.
Pests and diseases As for cabbage, page 49.

Sprouting broccoli

Sown one spring to crop the next, sprouting broccoli cultivars are biennial plants that occupy the ground for almost a whole year. They are quite hardy and provide large pickings of young flowering shoots from late winter until late spring when other vegetables tend to be scarce.

Many gardeners, however, feel that modern seed selections are unreliable, so like to save their own seeds from the strongest survivors after a cold winter. You can do this by leaving a few shoots on outstanding plants, which will flower in late spring and set ripe seeds by mid-summer; gather these for drying and storage until the following spring. By repeating the process over several seasons it is possible to develop your own selection of seed, with improved quality and hardiness. 'Red Arrow' is an early heading F_1 hybrid with a more consistent performance than traditional kinds.

Early and late cultivars are available in both white and purple-flowered forms. The latter are slightly hardier and more prolific, but some people prefer the milder flavour of white sprouting.

Perennial sprouting broccoli, sometimes called the perennial cauliflower, can grow up to 1.5m (5ft) tall and 90cm (3ft) across. It is well suited for a sunny corner of the kitchen garden where annually in mid- and late spring it will produce 8–10 creamy-white, small cauliflower-like heads.

Sites (see Growing brassicas, page 49)
Choose a position where the tall top-heavy plants are sheltered from winter winds. The ground should be very firm and fairly rich in organic matter to sustain the long season of growth.

Cultivation
Sow 2–2.5cm (¾–1in) deep in a seedbed outdoors from mid- to late spring, starting with the early kinds to give them as long a growing season as possible; in cold areas make the first sowings in pots or modules in a frame. Thin outdoor seedlings to 8cm (3in) apart and transfer to cropping positions in early summer, planting firmly and deeply so that the lowest leaves are at soil level.

Water during dry weather to maintain steady growth and mulch. In early autumn earth up the stems, stake plants in exposed positions, and protect them with netting wherever wood pigeons are a problem. Harvest the young flowering shoots as soon as they are in bud and approximately 10–15cm (4–6in) long, cutting or snapping them off with a few young leaves. Additional sideshoots will follow for up to two months if plants are cropped regularly to prevent flowering and top-dressed with general fertilizer after the first cut.

For perennial sprouting broccoli sow a few seeds in modules in spring and plant out 90cm (3ft) apart each way in fertile soil. The first heads will appear the following spring. Mulch with compost or decayed manure each spring, or top-dress with a general fertilizer. It is important not to let heads run to flower, and trim back long shoots after harvest. When plants begin to decline, pull off young shoots 10–15cm (4–6in) long and root them as cuttings in a cold frame for replacements.

Crop details Seed count: 200 per g, 5–6000 per 25g (1oz). Germination: 1–2 weeks at 5°C (41°F) minimum. Life of seeds: up to 6 years. Height: 90–120cm (3–4ft). Spacing: 60–75cm (2–2½ft) apart each way. Sowing to harvest: 40 weeks. Average yield: 450g–1kg (1–2lb) per plant.
Recommended cultivars 'Early Purple', 'Early White', 'Late Purple', 'Late White', F_1 'Red Arrow'; perennial: 'Nine Star Perennial'.
Pests and diseases As for cabbage, page 49.

Brussels sprouts

This is the crop that once gave allotment and vegetable gardens a bad name, the tall gaunt stems of older cultivars suggesting dereliction with their yellowing leaves and stems leaning at all angles. The development of F_1 hybrids has changed the image of brussels sprouts, for these produce sturdier plants with strong roots which are able to withstand high winds (except on loose light soils – see Sites, right). Contrary to popular opinion, hybrid brussels sprouts do not all mature at the same time, although this is possible if you want to harvest crops wholesale for freezing: to achieve this plant early cultivars at close spacings and remove their leafy tops when the lowest sprouts are about half-formed.

Cultivars mature at different times, earlies from late summer to mid-autumn, maincrop (mid-season) kinds from mid-autumn to early winter, and lates from mid-winter to early spring. Both the sprouts that form at the base of leaves and the leafy tops are eaten ('Ormavon' has a particularly large head resembling a small cabbage). Plants are very hardy, but are extremely difficult to grow in hot climates, where early autumn sowings for harvesting in winter are likely to be the most successful.

Sites (see Growing brassicas, page 49)

The soil needs to be very firm to support the tall leafy plants, and fairly fertile; rich soils, however, cause loose-hearted sprouts.

Cultivation

For very early crops sow in late winter in a cool greenhouse and prick out into trays, or sow in a frame late the previous summer and thin seedlings to 8cm (3in) apart. Harden off and plant out in spring, after raking a base dressing of general fertilizer into the cropping site; set plants deep with their lowest leaves at soil level.

Sow early, maincrop and late cultivars in succession in a seedbed from early to mid-spring, and about a fortnight apart. Either sow very sparsely or thin seedlings to 8cm (3in) apart to avoid weak spindly growth. When seedlings are 10–15cm (4–6in) high (about 6 weeks after sowing), transplant as for very early crops.

Water in a dry season until plants are established and growing freely, after which little irrigation is needed. About mid-summer top-dress with a nitrogenous fertilizer, and on windy sites earth up tall cultivars for stability. You may need to support tall plants with individual stakes or an enclosure of canes and string. Pick off any yellow, dead or diseased leaves as they appear and inspect regularly for signs of insect pests.

Start harvesting when the lowest sprouts are large enough, snapping them cleanly with a downwards pull; do not leave any blown or misshaped sprouts

and remove all leaves up to the level picked. Continue gathering sprouts as they mature, finally using the leafy top as 'greens'. In severe winters complete stems can be dug up and suspended upside down in a cool airy shed, where they will remain usable for several weeks. Exhausted stems should be pulled up and burnt. Alternatively, they may be crushed with a hammer or the back of a spade and then used as the base layer in a compost heap, or passed through a shredder.

Crop details Seed count: 250 per g, 6–7000 per 25g (1oz). Germination: 1–2 weeks at 5°C (41°F) minimum. Life of seeds: up to 8 years. Height: 45–120cm (1½–4ft). Spacing: 60cm (2ft) apart each way, 50cm (20in) for freezing. Sowing to harvest: 20–36 weeks according to season. Average yield: 1–1.3kg (2–3lb) per plant.

Recommended cultivars Early: 'Evesham Special', F_1 'Oliver', F_1 'Peer Gynt'. Maincrop: 'Bedford Darkmar 21', F_1 'Montgomery', F_1 'Ormavon', F_1 'Rampart', F_1 'Roger', F_1 'Welland'. Late: F_1 'Fortress', F_1 'Troika', F_1 'Wellington'.

Pests and diseases As for cabbage, page 49.

Brussels sprouts are particularly prone to most of the pests and diseases that affect brassicas, so maintaining their good health is important. As most cultivars persist over winter, there is a risk of carrying over brassica problems from one season to the next unless yellow leaves, such as the one shown here, are removed as picking progresses, with all stems and plant debris being promptly cleared.

Radishes

Radishes come in many shapes and sizes. Small ('summer') kinds are round, oval or long-rooted, with red, white or bicoloured skins. Japanese or mooli radishes are heavier, with long white roots. Hardy winter cultivars are very large, round or oval in shape, with red or black skins. Special cultivars tolerant of low temperatures are used for cropping under glass in winter.

Sites (see Growing brassicas, page 49)

A sunny open position is best although summer sowings do better in light shade, as catch crops between other vegetables for example. Prepare seedbeds as for carrots (see page 56).

Cultivation

Sow low-temperature cultivars in a cool greenhouse or frost-free frame between mid-autumn and late winter at approximately 4–6 week intervals. Sow ordinary radishes 1cm (½in) deep, thinly and in small quantities every 2 weeks for succession; start under cloches in late winter, continue outdoors from spring to late summer and then sow again under cover in early autumn. Mooli radishes are sown in mid- and late summer, winter kinds in late summer outdoors or in frames in early autumn.

Thin seedlings at an early stage as they cannot tolerate competition. Keep weed-free and water regularly to sustain fast even growth, giving up to 11 litres per sq m (2gal per sq yd) every week in dry weather. Take care not to overwater low-temperature radishes under glass, especially in cold dull weather.

Harvest small radishes as soon as they are large enough, using up sowings before roots become hollow and woody. Mooli radishes can be pulled after about 10 weeks, when roots should be 15cm (6in) long or more. Use winter radishes as required and either leave in the ground over winter (those in frames will be safe) or lift in late autumn and store in the same way as maincrop carrots (see page 56).

Crop details Seed count: 100–150 per g, 3000 per 25g (1oz). Germination: 3–7 days at 5°C (41°F). Life of seeds: 8–10 years. Height: 10–15cm (4–6in), up to 60cm (24in) for winter types. Spacing: small 2.5cm (1in) in rows 15cm (6in) apart or 2.5cm (1in) apart broadcast; under cover 5cm (2in) apart each way; mooli and winter 15–23cm (6–9in) in rows 23cm (9in) apart or 20cm (8in) each way. Sowing to harvest: small, 3–4 weeks, others 8–12 weeks. Average yield: 225g (8oz) per 30cm (12in) row, at least double for winter kinds.

Recommended cultivars 'Cherry Belle', 'French Breakfast', 'Long White Icicle', 'Parat', 'Red Prince'/ 'Prinz Rotin', 'Sparkler'. Low temperature: 'Ribella', 'Robino', Saxa'. Winter: 'Black Spanish Round', 'Black Spanish Long', 'China Rose'. Mooli: F₁ 'April Cross', F₁ 'Minowase Summer'.

Pests and diseases Cabbage root fly, flea beetle, slugs (see page 76).

Turnips

Turnips, useful and popular root brassicas, may be long, round or flattened, with white, red, pink or yellow skins, and white or yellow flesh. Hardy maincrop cultivars are grown for winter use and quick-maturing ('early') kinds are often sown as catch crops for continuous harvest during the season. The fastest early cultivar, 'Tokyo Cross', is sometimes ready for pulling after only 35 days, but often bolts if sown before the longest day.

Sites (see Growing brassicas, page 49)

Turnips like moist fertile soil and rarely succeed if checked by dryness at the roots, starvation or poor drainage. Grow in an open warm position, although summer sowings should be made in light shade.

Cultivation

Sow earliest crops 2cm (¾in) deep in late winter in a frame or under cloches. Start outdoor sowings of fast cultivars a month later, continuing at 3–4 week intervals for succession until early in mid-summer. Sow maincrops in mid- and late summer for winter use fresh or from store. 'Tokyo Cross' may be sown at intervals until early autumn for late crops of small turnips. A hardy cultivar sown in late summer or early autumn will produce tops the following spring (see Turnip tops, right).

TURNIP TOPS
Hardy turnip cultivars are often sown late for leaving in the ground over winter to provide leafy 'turnip tops' in spring. For subsequent crops sow any cultivar under cover in early spring and outdoors in spring. Grow in rows at closer spacings than for root production and leave the seedlings unthinned. Cut turnip tops when 10–15cm (4–6in) high, leaving a short stump of stems for regrowth, and repeat until plants bolt to flower. Some gardeners earth up turnips with 15cm (6in) high soil ridges in mid-winter to force and blanch early leaf growth.

Thin seedlings (except those for tops) while still small, repeating this until plants are at required spacings. Keep plants growing steadily by weeding, mulching, and watering little and often. In a very dry spell, give up to 11 litres per sq m (2gal per sq yd), but do not soak dry soil suddenly when roots are near harvest or they might split, and never water too generously as this increases the weight of crop at the expense of flavour.

Pull up fast cultivars while their roots are still less than 5cm (2in) across. Maincrop turnips can be harvested as soon as roots are usable; dig them up with a fork as required. Winter crops are usually left in the ground, but in cold or wet gardens they may be lifted in late autumn: twist off the tops and store between layers of sand in boxes in a cool place, or spread on a straw bed on the floor and cover with straw or sacking.

Crop details Seed count: 400 per g, 10,000 per 25g (1oz). Germination: 6–10 days at 5°C (41°F) minimum. Life of seeds: 6–8 years. Height: 23–25cm (9–10in). Spacing: early 10cm (4in) in rows 23cm (9in) apart; maincrop 15cm (6in) in rows 30cm (1ft) apart; turnip tops unthinned in rows 15cm (6in) apart. Sowing to harvest: 6–12 weeks. Average yield: 450–1000g (1–2lb) per 30cm (12in) row.
Recommended cultivars Fast-maturing: 'Purple Top Milan', 'Snowball', F₁ 'Tokyo Cross'. Maincrop: 'Golden Ball' (yellow-flesh), 'Manchester Market'.
Pests and diseases As for cabbage, page 49.

Swede

Often dismissed by gardeners as a commercial field crop, swedes are hardier than maincrop turnips and frequently yield more heavily. Modern cultivars are vigorous and robust, 'Lizzy', for example, being resistant to bolting and cracking, 'Marian' to clubroot and mildew. The roots of swede are cream or purple skinned, sometimes both, and the flesh is usually yellow and sweet flavoured.

Sites
Swedes like the same conditions as turnips, but prefer an open sunny position.

Cultivation
Sow *in situ*, 2cm (¾in) deep, in late spring or very early summer, thinning seedlings several times from an early stage until the required distance apart. Weed, mulch and water in the same way as turnips.

Roots may be lifted in autumn as soon as they reach a usable size, leaving others to continue developing. Swedes will usually survive the winter unharmed if left in the ground, especially if covered with a thick layer of straw, but it may be more convenient to lift the remaining crop in early winter, twist off the leaves and store in layers in boxes of sand in a cool shed. Spare roots left in the ground may be forced and blanched in the same way as turnips (see Turnip tops, left).

Crop details Seed count: 400 per g, 10,000 per 25g (1oz). Germination: 6–10 days at 5°C (41°F) minimum. Life of seeds: 6–8 years. Height: 23–25cm (9–10in). Spacing: 23cm (9in) in rows 38cm (15in) apart. Sowing to harvest: 20–26 weeks. Average yield: 1.3kg (3lb) per 30cm (1ft) row.
Recommended cultivars 'Acme Purple Top', 'Best of All', 'Lizzy', 'Marian'.
Pests and diseases As for cabbage, page 49. Mildew may be a problem on non-resistant swedes.

Leaving radish seedlings unthinned often results in disappointing crops – roots such as these well-filled 'French Breakfast' and 'Ribella' only swell to usable size when allowed to grow unhampered. 'Ribella' is one of the valuable recent cultivars that will both tolerate low temperatures under glass in winter and also grow successfully as a maincrop sown outdoors at regular intervals for continuous supplies throughout summer and autumn.

Carrots

GROWING ROOT CROPS

Root crops need open, cultivated soils with fairly high fertility, but not fresh manure. You can provide this by rotating roots after a well-manured crop so that they benefit from the earlier cultivation and nutrient residues, but before a crop that needs liming, as most roots prefer slightly acid conditions. With the exception of sowings in modules, root crops are grown *in situ* because transplanting injures or stunts their taproots. Prepare seedbeds with a deep fine tilth free from large stones, a fortnight before sowing if possible, to allow weeds to germinate first as most root crops are difficult to keep weed-free.

There are numerous carrot cultivars, producing either sweet slender 'finger' carrots or large maincrop roots which have a distinctly different flavour. Most kinds have orange or red roots, although purple, yellow and white carrots are also grown in some parts of the world, but sorting out their pedigrees, shapes and uses is often very bewildering.

Carrots can be divided into two groups. Fast maturing early carrots are used for both early and successional sowings; they include cultivars prefixed with the names 'Amsterdam Forcing', 'Nantes' and 'Early French Frame', the last of which is round-rooted and ideal for sowing in modules (see under beetroot, page 59) or for growing in shallow soils.

Maincrop kinds are larger and take longer to mature; types include 'Autumn King', 'Berlicum' and 'Chantenay', together with their improved selections. They are productive and valuable for winter use; however, many gardeners prefer to concentrate on raising a continuous supply of early carrots, which can be extended well into winter if late crops are grown in frames or a cool greenhouse.

Sites (see Growing root crops, left)

Light, friable well-drained soils with a pH of 6.5–7.5 are best and with plenty of organic matter worked in the previous year. On heavy or stony soils grow shorter-rooted types such as 'Amsterdam Forcing', 'Nantes' and 'Chantenay' (maincrop) cultivars, or grow in raised beds. Choose warm sites for early sowings, open sunny positions for others.

Cultivation

Sow very thinly *in situ*, 1–2cm (½–¾in) deep. Make the earliest sowings under cloches or in a frame in early spring, follow with successional sowings of an early cultivar every 2–3 weeks outdoors from spring to mid-summer, and again in a frame or cool greenhouse in early and mid-autumn for winter and spring use. Where carrot fly is a problem, you can sometimes prevent serious attacks by sowing outdoors in mid-spring and again in mid-summer when fly populations are low. Sow maincrop cultivars in late spring.

Keep the soil consistently moist but not too wet; in a dry season give 16–23 litres per sq m (3–5gal per sq yd) every 2–3 weeks. Thin seedlings in stages, pinching off the surplus at ground level to avoid disturbing the soil, and destroy the thinnings. Weed seedlings carefully until they make 2–3 true leaves and then mulch to conserve moisture and help suppress further weed growth.

Start harvesting as soon as roots are usable, pulling them or easing them out with a fork. Lift maincrops in mid-autumn with a fork, cut or twist off their tops and clean the roots ready for storing between layers of sand in boxes in a cool place indoors. Alternatively leave roots in the ground, allow the foliage to die down and then cover with a 15cm (6in) blanket of leaves or straw, held in place with wire netting or a layer of soil.

Crop details Seed count: 1000 per g, 25,000 per 25g (1oz). Germination: 2–3 weeks at 7°C (45°F) minimum. Life of seeds: up to 6 years. Height: 23–38cm (9–15in). Spacing: early 8–10cm (3–4in), maincrop 5–8cm (2–3in), in rows 15cm (6in) apart. Sowing to harvest: early 7–10 weeks, maincrop 10–16 weeks. Average yield: 225–450g (8–16oz) per 30cm (1ft) row.

Recommended cultivars Early: 'Amsterdam Sweetheart', 'Early French Frame – Lisa' (round), F_1 'Nandor', 'Parmex' (round), 'Sytan', F_1 'Tamino', 'Tiptop'. Maincrop: 'Autumn King – Vita Longa', 'Berlicum – Berjo', 'Camberley', 'Chantenay – Redca', 'Favourite'.

Pests and diseases Aphids, carrot fly ('Sytan' shows partial resistance); viruses (see pages 76–7).

Parsnips

Provided you choose a cultivar to match your soil, this traditional winter root crop can be worthwhile and productive. Those with long roots ('Tender and True', for example) need 23–30cm (9–12in) of friable stone-free soil to develop satisfactorily, whereas the shortest (such as 'Avonresister') will grow in about 10cm (4in) of topsoil. Canker is a serious disfiguring disease on some soils, but the cultivars here all have varying degrees of resistance.

A few of the more popular and productive rootcrops. These carrots, beetroot, turnip and potatoes in the process of being dug are all vegetables worth growing in gardens in well-broken soil.

Sites (see Growing root crops, left)

Choose an open position on well-broken soil that has been deeply cultivated and manured for a previous crop, and limed if below pH6.5.

Cultivation

Sow *in situ*, as early as possible for very large roots, but not while the soil is cold and wet. In mild gardens you can start in late winter or early spring, under cloches if necessary; seeds may also be sown in modules under cool glass, but should be planted out before the taproots develop, which is usually 3–4 weeks after sowing. Otherwise sowing should be delayed until mid- to late spring, when emergence is faster and more consistent.

Choose a still day, as the seeds are light and papery, and sow 2cm (¾in) deep, either continuously or dropping a few seeds at each station the recommended distance apart. You can sow radishes between stations to mark rows – they will be cleared before the parsnips need the space. Thin seedlings to leave single plants at required spacings. Weed, mulch and water as for carrots (see page 56).

Start lifting roots with a fork as required from autumn onwards. Parsnips can remain safely in the ground over winter, but remember to mark the rows of hidden roots with canes. Lift a supply in advance of severe frost or cover part of a row with straw for easier digging. Roots left at the end of winter can be dug up and heeled in elsewhere if the space is needed for other crops.

Crop details Seed count: 300 per g, 7–8000 per 25g (1oz). Germination: 2–4 weeks at 7°C (45°F) minimum. Life of seeds: 2 years. Height: 38–45cm (15–18in). Spacing: 15cm (6in) in rows 30cm (12in) apart for largest roots, down to 10cm (4in) in rows 20cm (8in) apart or 12–15cm (5–6in) square for small roots. Sowing to harvest: 20–35 weeks according to size. Average yield: 450g (1lb) per 30cm (12in) row

Recommended cultivars 'Avonresister', 'Bayonet', 'Cobham Improved Marrow', F$_1$ 'Gladiator', 'Tender and True', 'White Gem', 'White King'.

Pests and diseases Carrot fly, celery fly, root aphids; canker (see pages 76–7).

Potatoes

A very fast growing and maturing potato cultivar such as 'Concorde' is ideal for the smaller garden. Its neat compact foliage demands little space, and its early clearance means that other crops can be sown or transplanted before the season has progressed too far.

Early cultivars are the kind most gardeners prefer to grow, even a few plants providing a worthwhile crop of 'new' potatoes in summer. The same kinds can be planted again in mid-summer for late crops. 'Salad' types are popular because of their high quality and relative unavailability in shops. Maincrop potatoes need more room, but in larger gardens are a profitable vegetable for winter storage.

Potatoes are easy to grow and most soils will produce a crop, but yields improve dramatically with any soil improvement you can make. The two main areas of concern are the plants' frost-tenderness (delay planting if in doubt), and their susceptibility to pests and diseases. Starting with clean, certified (disease-free) seed tubers is an important precaution, as is familiarity with cultivars: 'Estima', for example, is fairly blight-resistant, slugs rarely trouble 'Pentland Squire', while 'Desirée' has often proved highly tolerant of dry soils and seasonal drought.

Sites

Choose an open, sunny and frost-free position, ideally with fertile, well-drained, slightly acid soil (avoid recently limed ground). Potatoes succeed on most soils, however, and are a useful pioneer crop for poor or uncultivated ground. Dig and work in plenty of decayed manure or compost well before planting. Rotate each season, leaving at least 3 years between successive crops.

Cultivation

Obtain certified seed tubers ('sets') at least 6 weeks before planting, and arrange them with their buds ('eyes') uppermost in trays in a light frost-free place to chit, that is to produce young shoots about 2.5cm (1in) long and so extend the growing season. Leave these intact, or if large early potatoes are required, rub off all but 2–3.

Plant 10–15cm (4–6in) deep (the greater depth on light soils) in drills, or make individual holes with a dibber; start with early cultivars in early spring or when serious frost risks are past, continuing with other cultivars in mid- and late spring. Set the tubers with their shoots uppermost and cover with soil. Early rows may be covered with cloches or plastic film to protect and advance crops; alternatively they can be planted through black polythene sheeting to avoid later earthing up.

If frost threatens, it is important to cover the young leaves with straw or newspapers or draw a little soil over them. Start earthing up plants when their topgrowth is about 23cm (9in) high to prevent the tubers from turning green near the light; use a draw hoe to pull up loose soil on both sides of the row to produce a uniform ridge about 15cm (6in) high.

Potatoes need constant moisture, so water in dry weather, earlies every fortnight at a rate of 16 litres per sq m (3gal per sq yd), other crops once only, at 23 litres per sq m (5gal per sq yd) when plants start to flower. Guard against the temptation to water more often: too much water can cause lush topgrowth to develop at the expense of tuber production, while overwatering main crops may affect their quality and reduce storage life.

Start harvesting earlies when their flowers are full open and continue lifting with a fork as required. Cut down the stems of maincrops to about 5cm (2in) high in autumn when they start to turn brown, and wait for a fortnight before digging the tubers on a warm dry day. Leave them on the surface to dry for 2–3 hours and then pack in wooden boxes or paper sacks, and store in a dark frost-free shed.

Crop details Tubers: 20–30 per kilo (2.2lb). Soil temperature: 7°C (45°F) minimum. Height: 45–90cm (18–36in). Spacing: early 30cm (12in) in rows 45cm (18in) apart, second early and maincrop 38cm (15in) in rows 75cm (30in) apart. Planting to harvest: early 13–14 weeks, second early 15–18 weeks, maincrop 18–22 weeks. Average yield: up to 1.3kg (3lb) per plant.

Recommended cultivars Early: 'Arran Pilot', 'Concorde', 'Dunluce', 'Foremost', 'Pentland Javelin'. Second early: 'Belle de Fontenay' (salad), 'Estima', 'Marfona', 'Wilja'. Maincrop: 'Cara', 'Charlotte' (salad), 'Desirée', 'Kondor', 'Maris Piper', 'Pentland Squire', 'Romano', 'Sante'.

Pests and diseases Cutworms, eelworms, slugs, wireworms; common scab, potato blight, viruses (see pages 76–7).

Beetroot

The roots of beetroot may be round, flat, barrel-shaped or tapering, with red, yellow or white flesh. Round, bolt-resistant cultivars are usually chosen for early fresh use and for pickling, often as catch crops, whereas longer kinds are traditionally treated as maincrops, producing large roots for winter storage.

The 'seeds' are in fact capsules that contain several seeds, all or many of which will germinate and therefore need thinning, but monogerm cultivars (usually with 'Mono' in their names) have been bred with single-seeded capsules.

Some cultivars are bred for the production of small 'baby' beetroot and others for large maincrop production. Many kinds, though, may be grown for both purposes, using later thinnings as small roots and leaving the rest to mature for storage.

Sites

As for carrots but rake in a base dressing of compound fertilizer before sowing seeds.

Cultivation

In dry weather, flood seed drills before sowing or soak seeds first in tepid water for an hour to hasten germination. A month before the last spring frosts, sow a bolt-resistant round type under cloches or in modules (see Sowing beetroot in clusters, below) for earliest crops. Further sowings of the same cultivar can be made outdoors, 2cm (¾in) deep, at monthly intervals from mid-spring to mid-summer. Sow maincrops for storing 12–14 weeks before the autumn frosts.

Protect seedlings from birds with netting or strands of black cotton and thin to the required distance when about 2.5cm (1in) high. Weed until plants are large enough to mulch and make sure that the soil is kept consistently moist, applying up to 11 litres per sq m (2gal per sq yd) every 2–3 weeks in dry weather. Top-dress with general fertilizer as soon as the roots start to swell.

Harvest early roots and those for pickling when about 5cm (2in) across; maincrops can be dug up and stored or left outdoors as for maincrop carrots (see page 56). Twist rather than cut the foliage off roots for store, leaving about 5cm (2in) of stems.

Crop details Seed count: 70 per g, 2000 per 25g (1oz). Germination: 2 weeks at 7°C (45°F) minimum. Life of seeds: 3 years. Height: 15–30cm (6–12in). Spacing: early 10cm (4in) in rows 23cm (9in) apart; maincrop 10cm (4in) in rows 30cm (12in) apart or 15cm (6in) square; pickling 8cm (3in) square. Sowing to harvest: 8–16 weeks according to type. Average yield: 450g (1lb) per 30cm (12in) row.

Recommended cultivars 'Bikores', 'Boltardy', 'Burpees Golden', 'Cheltenham Mono', 'Cylindra', 'Detroit – Little Ball', 'Forono', 'Monodet', 'Monopoly'.

Pests and diseases Aphids, birds, cutworms; damping off, leaf spots (see pages 76–7).

Sowing beetroot in clusters

When starting early crops under glass, you can economize on time and materials by sowing crops such as beetroot, leeks, round carrots, turnips, salad and maincrop onions in small groups. Use home-made soil blocks, divided cell trays or small pots and sow 2–3 seeds (6–8 for carrots and onions) per unit. Germinate the seeds in a warm greenhouse and then move to a cooler place to grow on until hardened off and large enough to plant out. Allow wider spacing than usual, leaving room for the unthinned clusters to develop.

Sow 2–3 seeds per cell in moist compost.

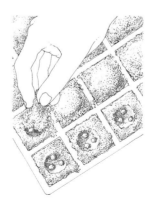

Cover seeds with sieved compost or sharp sand.

Plant out clusters before seedlings are overcrowded.

GROWING ONIONS

All onion crops like fertile conditions, produced by digging in large amounts of organic material several months beforehand; this allows soils to settle and provides the firm root run onions enjoy. They prefer light or medium ground to heavy clay and resent acid soils. Grow bulbing onions in open, sunny positions, and rotate all kinds, either as a separate group or together with legumes (which share similar needs); at least three years should elapse between crops, preferably longer, as a precaution against white rot disease. Weeding is an essential routine throughout the life of crops, because the slim leaves of onions have little effect in suppressing the growth of weeds.

Bulbing onions

For the kitchen, small to medium onions are preferable, which can be achieved by growing plants close together. Wider spacings and early sowing (sometimes soon after the shortest day), can result in enormous bulbs for exhibition or sheer bravado.

Bulb onions are spherical, flattened or elongated ('torpedo' shaped), with yellow, red or white skins, and may be grown from seed, or from immature 'sets' (prepared bulbs) which often avoid attacks from onion flies. Many gardeners prefer to use sets as these are the result of several weeks' growth and therefore have a head start over seeds; they avoid the need for pricking out or transplanting, tolerate poorer soils and often mature earlier. Cultivars started in spring begin ripening after mid-summer for autumn harvest and storage, whereas over-wintered kinds, sown or planted late in the season, are for use the following summer and do not store for long.

Sites (see Growing onions, left)

Although some enthusiasts grow onions in the same bed year after year with success, the pest and disease risks make rotation advisable for general garden cultivation. Dig the ground well in advance, if possible the previous autumn for spring-sown crops, and work in plenty of compost or rotted manure. Lime acid soils to bring them above pH6.5. Prepare a fine seedbed and rake in a base dressing of general fertilizer; tread very light soils firm and then rake again to leave an even tilth.

Cultivation

For large bulbs or where the growing season is short, sow under glass in late winter at 10°C (50°F) or a little warmer. Sow in trays for pricking out, singly in modules, or as clusters of 6–8 seeds in modules for planting out unthinned at twice the recommended distances. Harden off when seedlings have two strong true leaves and plant out in spring.

Crops are started outdoors in early spring, under cloches in a late season. Sow seeds sparingly 1cm (½in) deep and thin 2–3 times until seedlings are the full distance apart; destroy all thinnings to deter onion flies. Plant sets at final spacings in drills deep enough to just cover their tips; choose sets of intermediate size – the smallest rarely grow well, while large ones have a tendency to run to flower – and be sure not to push them into the ground as this may cause damage to their base.

Sow seeds of traditional over-wintered cultivars in late summer, thin once in autumn and then again to final spacings in spring; thinnings may be transplanted with care. Japanese cultivars are sown at the same time. Precise dates vary according to latitude, the aim being to raise seedlings large enough to survive the winter but not so large that they flower in spring: 15cm (6in) is an ideal height. Plant sets for over-wintering in early to mid-autumn, in well-drained ground. Although very hardy, these sets are more susceptible to prolonged wet conditions. Do not attempt to use autumn sets for spring planting, as their requirements differ and they are unlikely to be successful without a winter period of exposure to low temperatures.

Weeds can seriously check growth so hoe initially and handweed once plants are established (onions are shallow-rooted and easily damaged by careless hoeing). On well-prepared soils watering is usually unnecessary, except for over-wintering crops which may need water after sowing or planting in a dry season. Plants may be mulched but the material should be pulled away from bulbs once they start to ripen. Do not water or feed spring-sown onions after mid-summer, as this may impair the quality; over-wintered onions may be top-dressed with a nitrogenous fertilizer in spring. Break or cut off any flower stems that appear and use these bulbs first.

Bulbs can be harvested any time as soon as they are large enough. For storage wait until the tops bend over of their own accord and begin to die down. Ease bulbs from the soil with a fork (never pull them out) and spread out to dry in the sun on sacks or netting raised above the ground, or under glass in a wet season. When their skins are dry and papery, perfect bulbs can be stored in nets or tied to strings, or laid out carefully in boxes. Keep in a cool, frost-free place. Storage life depends on the cultivar and the quality of the bulb: split, thick-necked or damaged bulbs should be used immediately, Japanese kinds within a month or two of harvest.

Maincrop onions need to be started as early in the season as possible to ensure maximum growth before mid-summer, after which plants concentrate on producing and ripening their bulbs. The size and quality of these is directly linked with the vigour and leaf development of the plants, together with the amount of light and warmth that reaches the bulbs.

Bulbing onions grown at close spacings may be pulled while immature for use as spring onions. True spring onion cultivars eventually form small bulbs, but are grown primarily for their slim white stems and green leaves for use as a salad vegetable. Successional sowings will ensure supplies from spring right the way through to autumn. Prepare sites in the same way as for bulbing onions.

For onions ready in spring, sow a winter-hardy cultivar in late summer; protect the young plants with cloches in severe winter conditions, or sow in a cold frame and keep covered in very cold weather. Sow sparingly, thinning where necessary (after serious frosts are past) to 2.5cm (1in) apart; use the thinnings in salads. For a follow-on crop, sow a

normal cultivar in mid- to late winter in modules under glass, a few seeds per unit, and harden off for planting out in early spring. Sow outdoors from late winter in mild areas or early spring, every 3–4 weeks until mid-summer. Water in dry weather.

Crop details Seed count: 250 per g, 6–7000 per 25g (1oz), sets 120–150 per kilo (2.2lb). Germination: 2–3 weeks at 7°C (45°F) minimum – 21°C (70°F) maximum. Life of seeds: 2–3 years. Height: 45–60cm (18–24in). Spacing: medium bulbs, 4cm (1½in), large bulbs, 8cm (3in), in rows 30cm (12in) apart; spring onions, thinly in single rows 10cm (4in) apart, or 8cm (3in) wide bands 15cm (6in) apart. Sowing to harvest: spring-sown 16–22 weeks, autumn-sown 40–46 weeks; spring onions 8 weeks or 30–36 weeks over winter. Average yield: 450g (1lb) per 30cm (12in) row for bulb onions.

Recommended cultivars Autumn bulbs: F_1 'Albion' (white-skinned), F_1 'Buffalo', 'Giant Fen Globe', F_1 'Hygro', F_1 'Norstar', 'Robusta', 'Southport Red Globe' (red), 'Sturon' (sets), 'Stuttgart Giant', 'Turbo' (sets). Over-wintered bulbs: F_1 'Buffalo', F_1 'Express Harvest Yellow', 'Imai Early Yellow', 'Marshall's Autumn Gold' (sets), 'Reliance', 'Senshyu Semi-Globe', 'Senshyu Yellow', 'Southport Red Globe' (red). Spring onions: 'White Lisbon', 'White Lisbon – Winter Hardy', 'Winterover', 'Winter White Bunching'.

Pests and diseases Eelworms, onion fly; downy mildew, viruses, white rot (see pages 76–7).

Garlic

Usually very hardy, garlic is a pungent underground bulb with a white or pink papery skin enclosing numerous 'cloves', each of which can be planted to produce a new bulb that keeps for nearly a year. Only plant firm plump cloves over 1cm (½in) across; four bulbs provide enough cloves for a 3m (10ft) row.

To grow well, garlic needs several weeks' exposure in winter to low temperatures in the range 0–10°C (32–50°F), and planting in autumn allows for this. In very cold regions or where soils are cold and wet during winter, cloves can be started in pots for planting out when conditions improve.

The efficient ripening of all types of onion is critical for long trouble-free storage. These garlic bulbs, dug up when their leaves first began to turn colour, are suspended on the supports of raspberry wires to expose them to sunlight until the skins are quite dry.

Garlic plants often flower, especially the large related form known as 'elephant garlic', but this reduces only the size of bulbs and not their usefulness or keeping qualities, which depend on thorough ripening and good storage conditions.

Sites (see Growing onions, page 60)

Light soils and moderate fertility are best, together with efficient drainage. Where the soil is heavy, open up the planting area by working in grit, coarse sand or spent potting compost, or grow the crop in a small, specially prepared raised bed (an empty soil-based cold frame is ideal for this purpose).

Cultivation

Plant cloves outdoors, point uppermost and flattened end downwards, in mid-autumn in holes 5–10cm (2–4in) deep, the higher figure for the lightest soils, and cover to soil level. Alternatively plant individually in 11cm (4¼in) pots and stand these in a cold frame or sheltered place outdoors until the ground is suitable for transplanting in spring. Keep plants free from weeds and water occasionally in dry weather.

Lift bulbs carefully with a fork when the leaf tips turn yellow at or after mid-summer; do not wait until topgrowth has died down completely. Suspend in bunches in the sun or spread plants out to dry in the same way as for bulbing onions (see page 60) When the skins are papery and the dead foliage dry, plait or tie in bundles, or spread the intact bulbs on trays, and store in perfectly dry conditions at a temperature of 5–10°C (41–50°F).

Crop details Height: 60cm (2ft). Spacing: 10cm (4in) in rows 30cm (12in) apart, or 15–20cm (6–8in) square. Planting to harvest: 24–36 weeks. Yield: one bulb per clove planted.

Recommended cultivars None. There are numerous variants and selections, but these need to be suitable for the region and climate. Some are infected with virus disease, but any kind listed in seed catalogues is likely to be virus-free and worth growing. Good cloves may be saved from a healthy crop for replanting.

Pests and diseases Virus is usually the only threat (see page 77).

Shallots

Easily grown and with a unique flavour, shallots are multiplier onions, each planted bulb splitting to form a cluster of similar bulbs that can be stored for up to a year. They have a distinctive flavour as a vegetable, and are often used as a substitute for pickling onions. Modern cultivars are an improvement on older types, producing larger bulbs with enhanced keeping qualities. Shallot seeds are sometimes available, and these can be sown in the same way as bulbing onions (see page 60). Choose smaller bulbs, about 2cm (¾in) across, for planting, as larger ones often bolt or split into masses of small bulbs, and make sure bought supplies are virus-free. During the growing season a few of the fresh leaves may be cut and used for garnishing or flavouring.

Sites See Growing onions, page 60.

Cultivation

Shallots need a long growing season, and are traditionally planted on the shortest day for harvest after the longest. Where conditions prevent an early start, plant in late winter or early spring instead. Take out a drill 2.5cm (1in) deep or plant bulbs individually with a trowel, burying them upright so that they are just covered to hide them from birds. Water if necessary after planting and keep free from weeds.

When the leaves die down in mid-summer, carefully fork up the clusters but do not separate at this stage. Leave on the surface or move under cover in a wet season, until the foliage is quite withered and the skins of bulbs dry and papery; the clusters should then fall apart easily. Store the shallots in the same way as for onions (see page 60), reserving healthy bulbs of suitable size for replanting.

Crop details Height: 38cm (15in). Spacing: 15cm (6in) in rows 23cm (9in) apart, or 20cm (8in) square. Planting to harvest: up to 26 weeks. Yield: 8–12 bulbs per bulb planted.

Recommended cultivars 'Atlantic' (red-brown), 'Delicato' (red), 'Hative de Niort' (brown), 'Pikant' (red-brown), 'Topper' (yellow).

Pests and diseases As for onions, page 61.

Hardier leek cultivars, such as those shown here, are ornamental plants with their dark strap-like leaves often marked with blue or purple tints.

Leeks

Less demanding than bulbing onions, leeks are a reliable hardy crop available in cool climates for 6–8 months of the year. They are also remarkably versatile – they can be transplanted in holes for blanching (the best way), earthed up on the surface or left to develop a natural blanch. You can control size by manipulating spacing and the length of growing season; unthinned seedlings may be used like salad onions; and stately spherical flowerheads on surplus plants the following year generate envy in a flower arranger's heart.

Although show enthusiasts concentrate on fat, short-stemmed types known as pot leeks, for kitchen use gardeners normally grow cultivars with long white stems or 'shanks'. These are grouped into early, mid-season and late-maturing kinds, but there is considerable overlap between them; some mid-season leeks, for example, mature sooner from early sowings or last well into spring if the winter is mild. Early cultivars have paler foliage and are less hardy than dark-leaved later kinds.

Sites (see Growing onions, page 60)
Unlike other onion crops, leeks do not need firm ground, and the site can be dug and manured shortly before planting. Level and water to encourage weed seeds to germinate, and hoe these off first as later cultivation will be easier in a weed-free bed.

Cultivation
For good-size early leeks, sow an early cultivar under glass in late winter, in trays for pricking out, or in modules, either singly or in pinches of 3–4 seeds for planting out unthinned 23cm (9in) each way.

Make main sowings of all kinds for transplanting outdoors in drills 1–2cm (½–¾in) deep in a separate seedbed in early or mid-spring, the earliest under cloches in a cold season. These may also be sown *in situ* for thinning to final distances apart; if they are watered beforehand and handled with care, thinnings may be transplanted elsewhere in the garden. For a crop late the following spring, you can sow a late cultivar in early summer *in situ* or for transplanting a month later.

Harden off sowings started under glass so that they are ready for planting out in late spring. Thin outdoor sowings for transplanting to 4cm (1½in) apart and leave until they have 2–3 strong leaves or have reached 20cm (8in) tall. Water the seedlings and rake a dressing of nitrogenous fertilizer into the planting site. The next day fork up the seedlings and separate them carefully. Use a dibber to make vertical holes 15cm (6in) deep at the required distance apart and drop a seedling into each, making sure the roots reach the bottom. Gently fill the holes with water, but not deliberately with soil as the shanks will eventually fill this space.

Keep plants weed-free, either by hoeing carefully or by mulching to avoid damaging the shanks. Both buried leeks and those grown on the surface can be further blanched by drawing soil with a hoe up around the stems as they develop. Do this in gradual stages, never piling the soil so high that it falls between the leaves, and finish earthing up in early autumn. Water occasionally in a very dry season. Early leeks may be fed with liquid nitrogenous fertilizer if necessary, but do not feed over-wintering crops after late summer.

Harvest leeks as soon as they are large enough, using a fork to ease them from the ground, and clear early crops before severe frosts arrive. Late cultivars often last in good condition for several months, and may be dug up for heeling in elsewhere if they are in the way of spring cultivation.

Crop details Seed count: 400 per g, 10,000 per 25g (1oz). Germination: 2–3 weeks at 7°C (45°F) minimum. Life of seeds: 3 years. Height: 30–45cm (12–18in). Spacing: at least 15cm (6in) in rows 30cm (12in) apart for large shafts, down to 8cm (3in) in rows 20cm (8in) apart for slender stems. Sowing to harvest: 26–40 weeks according to season. Average yield: 450g (1lb) per 30cm (12in) row.

Recommended cultivars Early: 'Albinstar', 'Gennevilliers – Splendid', 'King Richard'. Mid-season: 'Autumn Mammoth – Argenta', 'Autumn Mammoth – Goliath', 'Snowstar'. Late: 'Alaska', 'Cortina', 'Giant Winter – Wila'.

Pests and diseases As for onions, page 61. Leek rust may occasionally be troublesome (see page 77).

OTHER POPULAR CROPS

There are many other crops whose cultivation sets them apart from the major crops such as brassicas and legumes. They might share some of the soil preferences of one vegetable and the susceptibility to pests and diseases of another, or they may be unique in the type of attention they require. Those listed here are some of the most popular with gardeners. Individual entries specify if a crop should be rotated (tomatoes for example); others, such as lettuce, can be grown wherever there is space, perhaps as a catch crop, or between rows of other vegetables. Where possible, though, avoid growing any crop in the same place in successive seasons as an insurance against soil pests or nutrient deficiency.

Spinach

Several leaf crops are grown for use as spinach, each with its particular virtues. Modern cultivars of true spinach are slow to bolt and can be sown in succession to give supplies from spring to autumn; they will even survive the winter with a little protection, although older types with prickly seeds are hardier for this purpose in cool districts.

Choose cultivars such as F_1 'Triade' for summer and autumn use, autumn-sown F_1 'Triathlon' and 'Bergola' for spring use, 'Broad Leaf Prickly' for winter use only, or 'Monnopa' (low in oxalic acid, high levels of which may cause digestive ailments) for year-round crops.

Soils should be fairly rich, and high in humus to maintain moisture levels. Summer crops prefer light shade and make ideal catch crops between taller vegetables, but winter spinach is best grown in a sunny position, sheltered from winds or where rows can be covered with cloches.

For summer and autumn crops, sow every 3–4 weeks from late winter or early spring (under cloches in cool districts) until early summer. Sow winter and spring crops in late summer and again a month later, the second sowing in a frame or cool greenhouse where winters are cold. Sow 2.5cm (1in) deep in rows 30cm (12in) apart, and thin seedlings to 8cm (3in) apart initially; when large enough pull up alternate plants for use, leaving the others at 15cm (6in) spacings for repeated cropping. Sowings may also be left unthinned to provide several small cuts while still young.

Water freely in dry weather, especially during summer when drought and high temperatures may cause early bolting. Harvest by cutting individual leaves when large enough, or cut complete plants down to 2.5cm (1in) high. The only problems with spinach are likely to be birds attacking the seedlings and mildew (see page 77) in unthinned crops.

Perpetual spinach

Perpetual spinach (leaf or spinach beet) is hardy and prolific, making robust plants usable all the year round especially on light soils. No distinct cultivars are normally offered.

Most soils are suitable for perpetual spinach, but working in plenty of organic material will repay dividends as moist fertile conditions produce larger and leafier plants. Choose a lightly shaded position if possible where plants can remain for up to a year.

Sow 2.5cm (1in) deep in rows 38–45cm (15–18in) apart in early or mid-spring and thin seedlings to 23cm (9in) apart. In good soils these can remain productive until the following spring, but where there is space make a further sowing in late summer for winter and spring cutting, clearing the first crop when the later batch starts yielding. Thinnings from this later sowing can be transplanted while still young to a frame for protection in a cold winter. Water occasionally in dry weather, especially on poorer soils. Harvest as above.

Sweet corn

Since the sugar in sweet corn cobs starts changing to starch soon after picking, connoisseurs insist they should be cooked within minutes of harvest, a very sound reason for growing your own. The plants are handsome annual grasses, with male tassels at their tips and female flowers in the 'silks' at the ends of cobs. They are wind-pollinated, which explains why crops are grown in blocks rather than long rows. Plants are decorative and dwarf cultivars crop successfully in small groups in flower borders.

Choose an early cultivar for cool climates with shorter seasons to make sure the cobs have enough time to ripen. Maincrop cultivars are for warmer gardens with at least 15–16 frost-free weeks, although all kinds can be started under glass to extend the growing season. Supersweet and sugar-enhanced cultivars have a higher sugar content but must be grown on their own because cross-pollination with ordinary kinds destroys this quality.

Sites

Sweet corn plants need a warm sunny position that is sheltered from cold winds, with well-drained fertile soil, preferably manured for a previous crop and slightly acid. Fork over poorer soils, adding compost or raking in a base dressing of general fertilizer just before sowing or planting.

The 'tassels' or female flowers at the tip of sweet corn cobs give the first indication of approaching ripeness, drying gradually from pale green to a dark brown, crinkled texture that indicates it is time to test the grains themselves.

Cultivation

Sow in pots or modules (seedlings dislike root disturbance) under glass 5–6 weeks before the last frosts and harden off before transplanting. Sow outdoors when the risk of frost is past, 2–3 seeds per station and 2.5cm (1in) deep; in cool climates use seeds dressed with fungicide and cover stations with cloches or jam jars until plants have 4–5 leaves. Seeds may also be sown under plastic sheeting – holes will need to be cut in the sheeting once the seedlings have germinated.

Hand weed plants or hoe shallowly: the roots are only 2.5–4cm (1–1½in) below the surface. At wider spacings plants may be undercropped with marrows or dwarf beans. In exposed areas earth up stems for support. Water plants in a dry season, first when flowers appear and again while the cobs are swelling, at a rate of 23 litres per sq m (5gal per sq yd). Feed with nitrogenous fertilizer if necessary, when plants are 20–25cm (8–10in) high and again when in flower. Plants sometimes produce side shoots at the base, and these are best stopped by pinching off the end when they are almost 15cm (6in) long.

Harvest miniature cobs (baby corn) when they are about 15cm (6in) long. Ordinary kinds are ready when the silks turn brown; test by peeling back the husk and pressing a thumbnail into a grain – the contents should still be liquid, but milky rather than watery. Colour is also a guide, the grains ripening from ivory-white to creamy yellow. Stems may be cut up and composted when the crop is finished.

Crop details Seed count: 5–6 per g, 120–150 per 25g (1oz). Germination: 10–14 days at 10°C (50°F) minimum. Life of seeds: 2–3 years. Height: 90cm–2.5m (3–8ft). Spacing: 30cm (12in) square, if underplanted 60cm (2ft) square; for miniature cobs 15cm (6in) square. Sowing to harvest: 10–14 weeks. Average yield: 1–2 cobs per plant.

Recommended cultivars Early: F_1 'Dawn', 'Earliking', F_1 'Honeycomb', 'Kelvedon Sweetheart', F_1 'Sunrise'. Maincrop: F_1 'Minisweet' (baby corn), F_1 'Minor' (baby corn), F_1 'Reward', F_1 'Sweet Season', F_1 'Sweet 77'.

Pests and diseases Birds, mice, slugs, frit fly (see page 76).

Lettuce

With a little care and the choice of appropriate cultivars, it is possible to harvest lettuce and other salad crops all the year round, even in winter except in the coldest gardens. You might be confused, however, by the huge range of lettuce cultivars available, with more being introduced each year, perhaps with new colour variation or greater resistance to pests and diseases.

The basic division in lettuces is between hearted or 'heading' lettuces, and loose-leaf (unhearted) lettuces. Heading kinds include the soft butterheads (Bibb lettuce); tall, upright cos (romaine) and the smaller semi-cos types, hardier than most others; and crunchy, densely hearted crispheads, sometimes known as Webbs after one of the best known cultivars ('Webbs Wonderful') or as icebergs when sold without their green outer leaves. Loose-leaf kinds have masses of small, often very decorative leaves, that can be harvested over a long period without risk of bolting.

Lettuces are not demanding plants, providing they are grown in moist, and preferably cool, conditions. Crispheads tolerate the most heat, but even they will quickly bolt on hot dry soils. Although they will germinate in fairly cold soils, lettuce seeds have a habit of becoming dormant above about 25°C (77°F), crispheads above 29°C (85°F), and summer sowings sometimes fail for this reason. Avoid this by sowing in the afternoon when temperatures are about to fall, covering seed drills with damp newspaper for 24 hours after sowing and keeping pots or modules in a cool shaded place.

Sites

Consistent moisture at the roots is the first priority, together with free-drainage and a fair level of fertility near the surface to feed the shallow roots. Dig or fork the soil well before planting, deeply if drainage is suspect and work in plenty of compost. Lime very acid soils to an ideal level of pH6.5. Crops need rotating to avoid build up of disease problems, but may be fitted in with any group, often as a catch or inter-crop. Grow summer lettuce in light shade, other crops in an open sunny position.

RIGHT *The choice of lettuce cultivars is extensive, as this varied block of healthy plants shows. Green and red forms of hearted and loose-leaf lettuce grow at ideal spacings among other seasonal salads and maincrop onions, with strawberries in the foreground.*

Cultivation

For sowing sequence, see below. Make early sowings in trays or modules. Make main sowings outdoors 1cm (½in) deep, preferably *in situ* as seedlings dislike being transplanted except in spring and while still small. Sow little and often for continuity, starting each batch when the previous one has emerged. Thin in stages until plants are the required distance apart. Summer sowings can also be made under cool glass, in modules for planting out without disturbance.

Plant out seedlings when they have 4–5 leaves in moist soil, with the leaves just above surface level (deeper planting can be lethal), and shade for a few days in sunny weather until they stop wilting. Crops under cloches should be kept slightly dry and well-ventilated; outdoor plants are watered as necessary, in dry weather up to 23 litres per sq m (5gal per sq yd), especially when plants are near maturity. Keep weed-free at all times and mulch plants on hot dry soils. On poorer ground, give a nitrogenous feed 2–3 times during growth.

Harvest heading types when they are large enough to use; do not wait until maturity, as whole sowings usually head up together and might bolt soon afterwards. Loose-leaf kinds are often ready first, and a few leaves may be picked from each plant over a long season; larger ones can be cut down to a stump 2.5cm (1in) high for regrowth.

Crop details Seed count: 800 per g, 20,000 per 25g (1oz). Germination: 1–2 weeks at 10–25°C

By the selective choice of cultivars and sowing times it is possible to have a year-round succession of lettuce crops either outdoors or under cover in the cold garden.

(50–77°F). Life of seeds: 3 years. Height: up to 25cm (10in). Spacing: 15–30cm (6–12in), each way. Sowing to harvest: 8–12 weeks.

Recommended cultivars Butterhead: 'Avon-defiance', 'Marvel of Four Seasons', 'Musette'. Crisp-head: 'Beatrice', 'Lakeland', 'Saladin', 'Webbs Wonderful'. Cos: 'Little Gem', 'Lobjoits Green Cos', 'Winter Density'. Unhearted: 'Lollo Green', 'Lollo Rosso', 'Oakleaf', 'Salad Bowl', 'Salad Bowl Red'.

Pests and diseases Aphids, birds, cutworms, leatherjackets, slugs; downy mildew, grey mould, viruses (see pages 76–7). Many modern cultivars have some resistance to common ailments.

Leaf lettuce

Cos lettuces or bought mixtures, sometimes called mesclun (try mixing your own from the seeds of left-over lettuce, especially cos, loose-leaf kinds and chicory) can be sown in patches for cutting several times at the large seedling stage. Soils should be the same as for ordinary lettuce and preferably clean as crops are difficult to weed. Sow sparingly in parallel rows 10cm (4in) apart; thin seedlings if necessary to 2.5cm (1in) apart. Sow in late spring for summer crops, late summer for autumn, and early mid-autumn and late winter in a frame for winter and spring cutting. Cut leaves 2.5cm (1in) above the ground when 8cm (3in) tall, harvesting gradually across the patch to leave stumps cut earlier to revive.

LETTUCE SOWING TIMES FOR YEAR-ROUND CROPPING			
Type	**Sow**	**Harvest**	**Comments**
Early summer, e.g. 'Little Gem', 'Winter Density', 'Salad Bowl'	Late winter and early spring	Late spring to early summer	Sow under cloches, or in frames or modules for transplanting
Maincrop, e.g. 'Musette', 'Saladin', 'Webbs Wonderful'	Early spring to mid-summer at 2–4 week intervals	Early summer to late autumn	Sow *in situ* or in modules; cloche late sowings in early autumn
Winter crops under cover, e.g. 'Salad Bowl', 'Lollo' types, 'Marvel of Four Seasons', leaf lettuce	Late summer to mid-autumn	Late autumn to late winter	Sow in modules, transplant to frames or greenhouse
'Over-wintered outdoors, e.g 'Winter Density', 'Avondefiance', 'Lobjoits Green Cos', leaf lettuce	Late summer and early autumn	Early to late spring	Sow *in situ*; cloche during winter and thin in early spring

Chicory

There are several kinds of chicory, all with slightly bitter but refreshing crisp leaves. Red chicory or radicchio and sugar loaf chicory, which is hearted rather like a cos lettuce, are both grown in the same type of soil as lettuce. They may be sown in spring and summer like leaf lettuce, or in early summer at 20cm (10in) spacings for outdoor crops and again in mid-summer for covering with cloches or transplanting to frames for late cutting.

Witloof or belgian chicory is grown for forcing (see Forcing chicory, below); sow outdoors in late spring, in rows 30cm (12in) apart, and thin seedlings to 20cm (8in). Leave the seedlings *in situ* for forcing in winter under ridges of soil, or dig them up in autumn, trim the leaves back to 2.5cm (1in) and store the roots between layers of sand in a cool place if not needed for immediate indoor forcing.

Corn salad

Also known as lamb's lettuce, this hardy salad crop with mildly flavoured leaves is normally used in winter and early spring from mid- to late summer sowings, either outdoors or in frames. Sow in moist soil in rows 15cm (6in) apart and thin seedlings to 10cm (4in). This plant self-seeds freely, producing seedlings that can be transplanted.

Land cress

Producing salad leaves that are very similar to watercress, this hardy crop, sometimes called american cress, is easily grown in moist shade. Grow plants 15cm (6in) apart, either sowing *in situ* or in trays under cover for pricking out and transplanting. Crops sown in spring will mature in summer, while mid- or late summer sowings crop from autumn to spring, prolifically if covered with cloches or grown in a frame in cool gardens. Pick leaves as required or cut whole plants just above soil level. This plant self-seeds, producing seedlings that can be transplanted.

Although best known as a reliable winter crop, especially useful under glass or in cold gardens, corn salad may also be sown outdoors from early spring to mid-summer for cutting like leaf lettuce or for harvesting when mature. A few leaves may be used at a time or whole plants can be uprooted.

Forcing chicory

The best chicons (fat, conical buds of crisp, white leaves) are produced by roots measuring about 5cm (2in) thick across at the top. Trim the roots to 15–20cm (6–8in) long and plant several upright in a large pot of moist soil, with their stumps at surface level. Cover with an inverted pot, with the drainage holes covered, to ensure total darkness and keep in a warm place, with a minimum temperature of 10°C (50°F). Growth is brisker at higher temperatures and at 18°C (65°F) chicons will be ready for cutting in 3–4 weeks.

Plant the roots upright in moist soil, with the crowns showing just above the soil.

Cut the creamy-white chicons close to the soil surface and use immediately.

Tomatoes

With the exception of cultivars bred exclusively for greenhouse cultivation, most tomatoes can be grown in the kitchen garden, but they are very sensitive to cold and must not be grown outdoors until after the last frosts. They grow best at temperatures of 21°C (70°F) or a little more, and where summers are cool they need sowing under glass for a head start, followed by the protection of a warm wall or a sheltered sunny position when planted out.

Cultivars may be tall (indeterminate), bush or dwarf (both determinate) in habit. Tall kinds are usually restricted to a single stem or cordon (but see below), and continue growing until the top is pinched out; semi-determinate kinds are grown as cordons, like tall cultivars, but stop themselves at about 120cm (4ft). Stems of determinates tend to set a truss of fruit and then stop growing, sending out new sideshoots instead. Small dwarf cultivars are ideal for growing in pots or as edgings beside paths.

Tomato cultivars display a wide range of shapes (round, plum or ribbed, for example), colours (red, yellow, striped) and sizes (from large 'Marmande' kinds to cherry or bite-size fruit). Flavour depends more on cultivation than cultivar, although several cherry types are markedly sweeter than larger tomatoes. Excessive watering and feeding, and lack of sun are main causes of diminished flavour.

Sites

A sunny sheltered position is essential, on well-drained soils that are fairly fertile but not too rich; dig the ground at least a spit deep and add plenty of compost or thoroughly decayed manure. Rake in a base dressing of fertilizer that is high in phosphates before sowing or planting. Crops should be rotated, preferably with root vegetables. However, note that tomatoes and potatoes are related and have several ailments in common.

Cultivation

For a long growing season, sow about 8 weeks before the last frosts, indoors in a temperature of 18°C (65°F), in seedtrays or pots for transplanting individually into 11cm (4¼in) pots, and grow on in good light. Harden off for planting out, normally when the first flower truss is showing colour; if the weather is still cold, delay planting or protect transplants with cloches or plastic film.

Wait for about 6 weeks for the sun to warm the soil after planting, and then mulch heavily, adding a layer of straw under the branches of determinate kinds to protect their fruit; alternatively support their branches with twigs or string tied to a central stake. Train tall kinds as cordons by tying the main stem to a stout post and pinching out all sideshoots as they appear. Pinch out the growing tips of cordons in late summer when they have set 3–5 trusses.

Training tomatoes as fans

Tall or indeterminate cultivars are usually grown as single cordons with all sideshoots removed as they appear, but plants may also be trained as fans against a wall to increase yields by leaving one or more pairs of low sideshoots to develop and bear fruit. Treat each branch in the same way as the main stem, tying the stems securely to its support and pinching out unwanted sideshoots, together with the growing tip, after three or four trusses have developed. Mulch plants generously, and water and feed regularly.

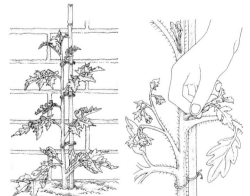

Leave the lowest sideshoots to grow but pinch out all others as they appear.

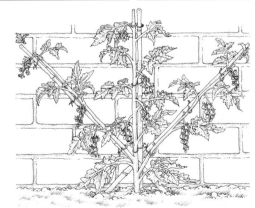

Train branches on canes or wires, fanning them out to admit air and light.

Tomatoes are universally popular, whether grown in the garden or as a greenhouse crop.

Hot peppers need a longer growing season than sweet cultivars if they are to develop maximum flavour and pungency.

Water plants in dry weather as soon as flowering starts, at a weekly rate of 11 litres per sq m (2gal per sq yd). Extra feeding will be unnecessary provided that the soil has been well prepared.

Gather fruits as they ripen. In autumn cover bush kinds with cloches and untie cordon plants, laying them down on a bed of straw and covering with cloches to hasten ripening. Before the first frosts, pull up plants and hang in a greenhouse to continue ripening or pick the green fruits and bring indoors to finish colouring up.

Crop details Seed count: 300 per g, 7–8000 per 25g (1oz). Germination: 1–2 weeks at 15°C (60°F) minimum. Life of seeds: up to 10 years. Height: tall, 1.2–1.8m (4–6ft); bush, 45–60cm (18–24in); dwarf, 30–38cm (12–15in). Spacing: cordons, 38–45cm (15–18in) in rows 45cm (18in) apart; bush, 53cm (21in) each way; dwarf, 25cm (10in) each way. Sowing to harvest: 16 (bush) to 20 weeks (tall). Average yield: up to 4.5kg (10lb) for tall plants.

Recommended cultivars Tall: 'Alicante', F$_1$ 'Mirabell' (yellow cherry), 'Outdoor Girl', 'San Marzano' (plum), F$_1$ 'Sungold' (yellow), 'Super Marmande' (large), F$_1$ 'Sweet 100' (cherry), 'Tigerella' (striped). Bush: F$_1$ 'Alfresco', 'Golden Sunrise' (yellow), F$_1$ 'Pixie', F$_1$ 'Red Alert', F$_1$ 'Tornado'. Dwarf: 'Minibel', F$_1$ 'Phyra' (cherry), F$_1$ 'Totem', F$_1$ 'Tumbler' (cherry).

Pests and diseases Birds, potato cyst eelworm, slugs; grey mould, potato blight, stem rot, viruses (see pages 76–7).

Sweet and hot peppers

Peppers need similar conditions to tomatoes, but prefer higher temperatures, need watering more often and like slightly acid soils – some gardeners sprinkle a pinch of sulphur under each plant at planting time to ensure local acidity.

Sweet peppers (*Capsicum annuum*) come in several forms, including wrinkled peppers, paprikas and chillies, as well as the large hollow sweet peppers with variously coloured fruits. Hot peppers (*Capsicum frutescens*) may be grown as perennials above 21°C (70°F); forms include bird chillies and cayenne peppers, pungent fruits that take longer to reach maturity but otherwise can be grown in the same way as sweet peppers. They are all decorative plants which in cool climates may be grown outdoors in large containers, for moving under cover in autumn to finish ripening.

Sites

As for tomatoes. In cool districts, grow at the foot of a sunny wall or fence, in a soil-based frame or include as part of a cloching sequence for covering from late summer or early autumn onwards.

Cultivation

Raise plants under glass in spring, in the same way as for tomatoes. Plant out after all risk of frost has passed, when the first flowers are visible. Water freely in dry weather, up to 9 litres (2gal) per plant every fortnight, and mulch thickly; feed every 2–3 weeks with a high-potash fertilizer, starting when the first flowers are fully open. Stake taller cultivars, pinch out the growing tip if plants are reluctant to make sideshoots, and also stop the ends of sideshoots once these have set fruit. Harvest sweet peppers when they are green or wait until they turn colour, about 12 weeks after planting out. Hot peppers should be left until ripe – 14–16 weeks after planting. When autumn frosts threaten, pull up plants and hang them in a sunny place under glass, where fruits will continue to ripen.

Crop details Seed count: 300 per g, 7–8000 per 25g (1oz). Germination: 14–21 days at 18°C (65°F) minimum. Life of seeds: 6–8 years. Height: 38–120cm (15in-4ft). Spacing: 50cm (20in) square; dwarf, 30cm (12in) square. Sowing to harvest: sweet, 20 weeks; hot, 22–24 weeks. Average yield: 1kg (2.2lb) per plant.

Recommended cultivars Sweet peppers: 'Bell Boy', 'Delphin', 'Eagle', 'Early Prolific', 'Gypsy', 'New Ace', 'Redskin' (all F$_1$ hybrids). Hot peppers: F$_1$ 'Apache', 'Hungarian Wax', 'Jalapeno', F$_1$ 'Super Cayenne'.

Pests and diseases Aphids, cutworms, slugs; viruses (see pages 76–7).

Outdoor cucumbers

In cold climates, the long slim cucumbers bought in shops must be grown under cool or heated glass. These greenhouse or 'frame' cultivars need high temperatures and humidity, unlike outdoor or 'ridge' cucumbers which crop satisfactorily at 15°C (60°F) or higher.

Traditional ridge cultivars have short, fat rough-skinned fruits about 15cm (6in) long, while gherkins for pickling are similar but only half the size; Japanese and some hybrid cucumbers are more like greenhouse kinds in appearance. A group of round-fruited cultivars, for example 'Crystal Apple', has a reputation for flavour and quality.

A few bush forms are available, but most are vining cucumbers, producing long stems that trail on the ground or are trained vertically on nets, trellis or tripods of long poles. Unlike greenhouse types, outdoor cucumbers do not become bitter if fertilized and so there is no need to remove the male flowers.

Sites

Plants cannot tolerate temperatures below 10°C (50°F), and prefer much warmer positions, sheltered from wind, on fertile, well-drained ground that is nevertheless high in humus. Soils should be neutral or slightly acid.

Cucumbers are traditionally grown on mounds or 'hills' to ensure good drainage, each position having been prepared a fortnight before planting or sowing. This is done by digging out a planting pocket, 30–45cm (12–18in) deep and wide, then refilling with a rich mixture of equal parts compost or rotted manure and soil.

Cultivation

Sow indoors 4–5 weeks before the last frost, sowing two seeds on edge 1cm (½in) deep in each 8cm (3in) pot. Germinate at 21–26°C (70–80°F), remove the weaker seedling, then grow on at 15°C (60°F) minimum, until ready to harden off and plant out with the least possible root disturbance. Plant seedlings no deeper than they were growing before and water thoroughly afterwards. Alternatively sow *in situ* when the risk of frost is past, covering the

stations with cloches or jam jars for extra warmth. Most families will find that 2–3 plants produce sufficient fruits for their general needs.

Bush forms need no training, but the growing tip of vining cultivars should be pinched out after 5–6 true leaves have developed. Strong sideshoots will then appear and these can be left to trail on the ground, or they may be fanned out evenly and tied to supports; they will attach themselves to netting with their tendrils as their stems grow.

Pinch out trained stems when they reach the tops of supports, those on the ground when they have covered their allotted space. Mulch plants with straw or black polythene, especially those cropping on the ground. Water frequently in dry weather, around plants and not directly on top, and give high-potash liquid feeds when fruits start to swell. Sometimes a sideshoot will not show any sign of producing fruits, and where this happens it is best to pinch off the growing tip after 6–7 leaves.

To encourage further cropping, harvest fruits before they reach maximum size, cutting them cleanly with a knife. After picking a fruit from a vining plant, pinch out the tip of that shoot to encourage further branching. Clear before the first autumn frosts, using any very small fruits for pickling; in a cool autumn, plants may develop mildew and should then be pulled up as this is not worth treating with a fungicide. Protect ground-level plants against slugs.

Crop details Seed count: 30 per g, 750 per 25g (1oz). Germination: 1 week at 20°C (68°F) minimum. Life of seeds: 6 years. Height: vining, 3m (10ft), bush, 60cm (2ft). Spacing: climbing, 45cm (18in), trailing and bush, 75cm (30in) apart. Sowing to harvest: 12–14 weeks. Average yield: bush 3–4 fruits, vining 8–12 per plant.

Recommended cultivars Tall: F₁ 'Burpless Tasty Green', 'Crystal Apple', 'Kyoto', 'Perfection', F₁ 'Tokyo Slicer', 'Yamato'. Bush: 'Bush Champion', F₁ 'Bush Crop'. Gherkin/pickling: F₁ 'Bestal', F₁ 'Fanfare'.

Pests and diseases Aphids, cutworms, slugs; foot and root rots, powdery mildew, viruses (see pages 76–7).

When well fed and watered, cucumbers crop prolifically and freely produce such high quality fruits as these. They will not remain in peak condition for long, and should be harvested before they become misshaped or show signs of turning yellow.

Squash

The squash family (strictly speaking, the cucurbit tribe of the gourd family) is a diverse group of fleshy vegetables that likes warm temperatures and lavish growing conditions. Summer squashes, including marrows and courgettes, have soft skins and generally pale flesh. They are eaten fresh and do not keep for very long in store, whereas winter squashes such as pumpkins and turk's cap gourds have well-flavoured yellow or orange flesh, and skins that dry very hard for long storage.

There are bush, trailing and semi-trailing cultivars, the first kind best for small gardens. Trailing kinds tolerate light shade, however, and may be undercropped between vegetables such as sweet corn, or look attractive with their broad lush leaves and large yellow flowers when trained up trelliswork, fences and arches. They may also be planted on the top of compost heaps, where they are well fed and have room to trail freely.

Sites

As for cucumbers. Prepare planting pockets 30cm (12in) deep and 45cm (18in) across.

Cultivation

Soak seeds overnight, and then sow (outdoors or under glass) and plant in the same way as for cucumbers. Do not grow too many plants, as they can be very productive. Mulch heavily, and once growth is vigorous water in dry weather, at the rate of 9 litres (2gal) per plant every week, especially when in flower and while fruits are swelling. Feed if necessary once cropping starts; trailing stems often root where they touch the soil, and pegging these down will help supplement the plants' energies.

Bush cultivars need little attention but it is worth protecting the fruit with a bed of straw tucked all round the plants. Pinch out the tips of shoots on trailing squashes when they are about 60cm (2ft) long, and arrange the resulting sideshoots evenly over the ground or tie them to supports. Courgettes grow on a single stem that is often too weak to remain upright; tying the stems to upright stakes like cordons keeps them tidy and increases air circulation, which helps keep powdery mildew at bay. In cool seasons plants may not set freely, and female flowers (those with a tiny swelling behind the petals) should be fertilized manually. Pick a male flower, carefully peel off its petals and then push it in the centre of the female flower.

Harvest courgettes while small, cutting them with a knife when about 8–10cm (3–4in) long, with the withered flower still attached; any left unused will develop as small usable marrows, but cannot be stored. Cut other summer squash while young. True marrows are gathered when about 20–25 (8–10in) long and while the surface near the stalk is still soft; a few may be left to ripen on the plant for storing before the frosts can damage them – lightly frosted fruits can still be used for immediate consumption but will not keep.

Winter squash and fruits of summer cultivars intended for storage are cut as soon as their stems start to dry, and must be brought safely under cover before autumn frost. Cut each sound fruit with a long piece of stem and harden the skins in warmth, up to 27°C (80°F) for a fortnight in full sunshine or under glass if necessary; turn occasionally for even curing. Store the fruits in an airy place at about 10°C (50°F) on shelves or suspend them in netting to provide efficient air circulation.

Crop details Seed count: F_1 hybrids 5 per g, 120 per 25g (1oz); others twice that rate. Germination: 5–10 days at 15°C (60°F) minimum. Life of seeds: 6 years. Height: trailing 1.8m (6ft) or more; bush 90cm (3ft). Spacing: trailing 1.8m (6ft); bush 90cm (3ft). Sowing to harvest: 8–12 weeks. Average yield: larger squash 3–4, courgettes 12–20, per plant.

Recommended cultivars Marrows: 'Long Green Trailing', F_1 'Tivoli' (spaghetti), F_1 'Zebra Cross' (bush). Courgettes: F_1 'Ambassador', F_1 'Gold Rush' (yellow), F_1 'Moreno', F_1 'Zucchini'. Other summer squash: 'Custard White', 'Jack be Little', F_1 'Sunburst'. Winter squash: 'Atlantic Giant' (pumpkin), F_1 'Butternut', F_1 'Cream of the Crop', F_1 'Crown Prince', 'Hubbard's Golden', 'Mammoth' (pumpkin), F_1 'Table Ace', 'Turk's Turban'.

Pests and diseases Slugs; powdery mildew, viruses (see pages 76–7).

All forms of squash are productive and easily grown on fertile soils. Although strictly one of the summer squashes, marrows have been traditionally grown as a late-season crop, with an emphasis on raising large fruits for autumn use and short-term winter storage. The total yield, however, will be heavier if some are cut as soon as they reach usable medium size, as here, leaving a few later fruits to develop and ripen for store.

Celery

Traditional hardy celery is grown in trenches for winter use (see Growing trench celery, below). Self-blanching and (American) green cultivars are easier to raise, but must be used before frosts arrive, although plants may be grown in frames for covering in autumn to prolong the crop.

Sites

Grow in open sunny positions sheltered from drying winds. Plants prefer very moist, fertile soil, so dig in plenty of compost or decayed manure at least a spit deep, and lime to nearly neutral readings. Rake in a base dressing of general fertilizer before planting. Rotate crops and keep away from parsnips, which also suffer from celery fly.

Cultivation

Sow all types 10 weeks before the last frosts, indoors on the surface of modules, or trays for pricking out into pots. Use seeds dressed with fungicide. Harden off and plant out seedlings with 5–6 true leaves after the last frosts, a little earlier in frames; outdoor transplants may be protected initially with cloches or perforated film.

Plant self-blanching and green kinds on the surface, in blocks so that plants shade each other. If planting is delayed, feed seedlings if their leaves start to turn yellow; well-advanced plants may be cut back to 8cm (3in) high and then grown on until the weather improves. Remove any leaves blistered by celery fly and reject badly disfigured plants.

Water copiously in dry weather, up to 23 litres per sq m (5gal per sq yd) every week, and mulch when plants are established. Feed with nitrogenous fertilizer at mid-summer. Tuck straw between plants when 20–23cm (8–9in) high, especially plants at the edges of blocks, to improve their blanch.

Harvest plants as soon as they are large enough, about 8 weeks after planting, and continue until the frosts; covering remaining plants with polythene sheeting or woven fleece can prolong cutting.

Crop details Seed count: 2000 per g, 50,000 per 25g (1oz). Germination: 3 weeks at 10°C (50°F) minimum. Life of seeds: 6 years. Height: 30–60cm (12–24in). Spacing: self-blanching/green 23cm (9in) each way; trench 30cm (12in) apart. Sowing to harvest: self-blanching/green 12–16 weeks; trench 30–35 weeks. Average yield: up to 450g (1lb) per plant.

Recommended cultivars Self-blanching: 'Celebrity', 'Ivory Tower', 'Lathom'. Green: 'Green Sleeves', 'Green Utah', 'Hopkin's Fenlander'. Trench: 'Giant Pink', 'Giant Red', 'Giant White'.

Pests and diseases Celery fly, slugs; leaf spot (see pages 76–7).

Growing trench celery

Fork plenty of manure or compost into the bottom of the trench before replacing some of the soil to 8cm (3in) below ground level. Rake in a base dressing of fertilizer and then plant, water and feed as above. When about 38cm (15in) high, loop string around the tops of plants and use a draw hoe to surround the stems with soil to about half their height. Repeat again at 3-week intervals until the final earthing up in late autumn. Dig plants as required from early winter onwards, in a hard season protecting those left with straw.

Dig a trench 30cm (1ft) deep by 38cm (15in) wide, and fork in manure.

Grow lettuces or radishes on the ridges, and plant out celery after the frosts.

Final earthing creates a smooth soil ridge sloping to the base of the leaves.

GROWING PERENNIAL CROPS

Several vegetables crop from one year to the next and do not fit comfortably, therefore, into any rotation scheme. These perennial crops can be given a bed to themselves or may, like perennial broccoli, be allocated spare areas of the kitchen garden that suit their particular requirements.

Jerusalem artichokes

As the starch-free tubers of this tall sunflower relative, which grows up to 3m (10ft) high, keep best in the ground, many gardeners leave them in the same place for several years. Unfortunately they spread and are apt to become weedy, so it is often better to treat them as an annual crop, clearing all tubers left in the ground at planting time. Most cultivars are similar, although the tubers of 'Fuseau' are smoother than others, while 'Dwarf Sunray' has shorter stems and large yellow flowers in late summer. Plants are a useful pioneer crop on heavy, poor or new ground, but superior crops are produced on well-drained fertile soils.

Plant small tubers 10–15cm (4–6in) deep and 30cm (12in) apart in spring, as soon as the ground is workable. When stems are 30–45cm (12–18in) tall, earth them up to half their height and mulch to conserve moisture. Water freely in dry weather and in exposed positions support the tall stems with posts and wire. For maximum crops remove flowers as they appear and shorten stems in mid-summer to 1.8m (6ft). Dig tubers as required, clearing a complete plant at a time; in cold areas all tubers may be lifted for storing in damp soil or sand in boxes. Otherwise leave them buried until the following spring, when crops can finally be cleared, reserving some of the smaller ones for replanting.

Globe artichokes

This is a true perennial plant, with deeply cut and silvery-green arching leaves and tall stems up to 1.5m (5ft) high. In summer these bear large, blue thistle flowers if left to bloom, but it is the unopened flowerhead or 'choke' that is harvested for use.

Plants may be raised from seed sown outdoors in spring, but quality will vary and only the best plants should be saved for propagating from offsets (rooted suckers). Seedlings are planted out in early summer and will crop the following year or, exceptionally, late the same season. Plants are bought as offsets, which you can also take from your own plants in early spring by separating them with a trowel or spade from the side of the main crown.

Plant seedlings or offsets 90cm (3ft) apart in well-manured, free-draining soil, in a sunny position sheltered from cold winds. Mulch annually once soils warm up in spring and water freely in dry weather. In cold areas cover dormant crowns in winter with straw or dry litter for protection. Renew plants every 3–4 years with offsets taken from the best crowns.

For large chokes, thin branches at the tops of stems to the largest central head and 2–3 others. Cut chokes for use when they are plump and their scales still tight, starting with the main head; after the smaller lateral heads are harvested, prune the stems down to about half their height.

Globe artichokes need plenty of room for their large handsome foliage. Hardy cultivars tend to have prickly heads or inferior flavour, whereas choice, full-flavoured kinds such as 'Grand Camus de Bretagne' or 'Gros Vert de Laon' are more tender and some gardeners use handlights or a thick mulch for covering their dormant crowns in cooler gardens.

From mid-spring onwards, check asparagus beds every day or two as spears grow quickly and soon reach cutting size. Much asparagus is grown as a green crop, as here, but some gardeners prefer to blanch spears until they are white. To achieve this, earth up plants beneath smooth ridges of soil; these will start to crack when the spears are near the surface and ready to be harvested.

Asparagus

The asparagus beds that were once a prominent feature of every large kitchen garden were very wide, up to 1.5m (5ft), remade annually and raised up in gentle mounds for efficient drainage. This practice suggested that asparagus was a luxury vegetable, cropping for only 8 weeks in return for occupying large tracts of ground and consuming vast amounts of manure annually.

In fact these hardy perennials may be grown as single or double rows on level soil across the garden, or in blocks of shorter rows running across raised beds; in good soil they will be productive for 20 years or more. Some gardeners even grow plants in flower borders to enjoy their decorative fern-like foliage after cutting ceases at mid-summer.

Cultivars such as 'Connover's Colossal' in Britain and 'Martha Washington' or 'Mary Washington' in the USA are traditional market garden cultivars, now superseded in the eyes of many growers by all-male F_1 hybrids – female plants are less prolific and their berries may produce inferior self-sown seedlings to compete with the original plants. Hybrids have greater vigour and crop earlier in life (two years after planting or three from sowing), making them economical plants for the smaller garden. Most cultivars can be raised from seed, although non-hybrid kinds are variable and need careful selection to retain only the strongest seedlings.

Sites

Asparagus likes an open sunny position, sheltered from cold winds and late frosts; however, winters must be cool enough to allow several weeks' dormant rest. Most soils are suitable, providing they are not acid or waterlogged. Dig well before planting and mix in a good dressing of compost or manure. Remove all perennial weeds as asparagus resents deep cultivation near its roots. Plant replacement crops away from previous sites where soil-borne disease and dormant pests might persist.

Cultivation

Soak large seeds for 48 hours in water first. Sow outdoors on a seedbed, 2.5cm (1in) deep in late spring, spacing seeds or thinning seedlings 8cm (3in) apart; plant out the strongest the next spring. Hybrids sown in late winter in small pots for germination at 15°C (60°F) may be planted out in early summer for a light crop the following year.

Asparagus is normally planted in spring, using one year-old crowns, either bought or sown in a seedbed as above. Pot-grown asparagus may be planted in separate holes 10–15cm (4–6in) deep, but bare-root crowns are normally planted in a trench, dug about 10cm (8in) deep with soil heaped down the centre in a rounded ridge. Arrange the crowns centrally, spreading their roots down both sides of the ridge; cover with a little friable soil, and then earth up the stems as they grow until the ground is level once more.

Hand weed or hoe shallowly and water until plants are established. Remove any volunteer seedlings and berry-bearing female fronds as they appear, and cut down all the foliage almost to ground level when it turns yellow in autumn. Top-dress with a general fertilizer early in mid-spring and again when cutting ceases in summer.

When spears are about 15–20cm (6–8in) long, cut them at an angle with a knife about 5cm (2in) below soil level. One or two spears may be harvested from strong hybrids the first spring after planting, but other kinds should be left for a year to build up their strength. More may be gathered in the following year over a 6–week season, with a full crop the year after, harvesting for 8 weeks up to the longest day, after which plants are left to grow naturally. Resist cutting foliage from cropping plants for indoor decoration as this will weaken them.

Crop details Height: 1.2–1.5m (4–5ft). Spacing: 38–45cm (15–18in) in single or double rows 90cm (3ft) apart; allow 30cm (12in) between double rows. Season: late spring until mid-summer. Average yield: 10–20 spears, 225g (½lb) or more per mature plant.
Recommended cultivars Traditional: 'Connover's Colossal', 'Martha Washington'. F_1 hybrids: 'Accell', 'Boonlim', 'Cito', 'Franklim', 'Lucullus'.
Pests and diseases Asparagus beetles, slugs; root rots (see pages 76–7).

Rhubarb

Rhubarb is sometimes left to languish in a neglected corner of the garden but it deserves better treatment. Although strictly a stem vegetable, it is normally grown as the first home-produced fruit crop of the season, its tender pink or red leaf stalks ready to pull early in spring from open air plants, a few weeks sooner if forced outdoors, and even earlier from plants forced in warmth under glass. Strong plants can be harvested throughout the summer, but some cultivars become unpalatably acid late in the season and other fruit crops take over by then.

With their coloured stalks and dramatic palmate leaves, rhubarb plants are exceptionally decorative. Established crowns can reach 1.8m (6ft) across in full leaf and some gardeners treat them as ornamental plants, growing them beside pools to reflect their handsome foliage and allowing the stately 2.5m (8ft) stems of creamy white flowers to develop in summer. Provided these are cut down before they set seed, plants do not appear to suffer, although some authorities disapprove of letting rhubarb flower because of the increased risk in a wet season of rot affecting the hollow stem base.

Modern cultivars developed specifically for commercial forcing are valuable both for this and for early outdoor crops in gardens. There are numerous other classic cultivars, however, outstanding in quality; the only qualification against recommending them is that some stocks are hopelessly disabled by virus disease. Always buy crowns that are certified virus-free from reputable suppliers.

Sites

Most soils are suitable if well-drained and fortified with plenty of compost or manure dug in before planting. Choose a position that is open and warm in spring to encourage early growth but cool in summer because the plants do not like high temperatures.

Cultivation

Plants may be raised from seed, sown 2.5cm (1in) deep in a seedbed in spring; thin seedlings to 15cm (6in) apart and plant out at final spacings in autumn or the following spring. Seedlings vary considerably in quality, and only the strongest should be retained for cropping and possible propagation.

Established crowns are divided, in autumn or spring while dormant, by digging up the fleshy rootstocks and then slicing through vertically with a spade to separate healthy outer pieces or 'sets', each set with one or two large buds. The rootstock may then be replanted. Healthy crowns may be divided after several years if their leaf stalks become thin.

Plant dormant seedlings, sets or bought crowns in autumn on light soils or spring where the ground lies wet in winter, with the buds at or just below ground level. Water liberally in dry weather and mulch annually in autumn with decayed manure.

Harvest outdoor crops as soon as the stalks are long enough, lightly the first two years after planting and freely thereafter, continuing until quality starts to deteriorate in summer. Earlier crops can be forced by covering strong crowns in mid-winter with wooden boxes or forcing pots. Pack straw, hay or manure around the boxes for insulation; check if the crop is ready for use from early spring onwards.

Crop details Height: 60–75cm (2–2½ft). Spacing: 75 × 90cm (2½ × 3ft). Season: early spring to summer (forced 2–4 weeks earlier). Average yield: 2–2.5kg (4–5lb) per mature crown, much less forced.
Recommended cultivars 'Hawkes Champagne', 'Reed's Early Superb' (forcing), 'Stockbridge Arrow' (forcing), 'Stockbridge Harbinger' (forcing), 'Timperley Early' (forcing), 'Victoria'.
Pests and diseases Crown rot, honey fungus, viruses (see page 77).

Pest and symptoms	Principal vegetable crops affected	Prevention	Control
Asparagus beetle Tiny greyish grubs on foliage, and bright yellow-and-black beetles in summer and autumn.	Asparagus.	Crush beetles and black eggs attached vertically to stems.	Spray with derris, malathion or pirimiphos-methyl.
Bean seed fly Tiny white grubs on failed seeds and weak seedlings, especially in cold wet soils.	French and runner beans.	Rapid germination in warm soils, or sow under glass.	Dust drills with pirimiphos-methyl or gamma-HCH.
Birds Various kinds attack seedlings or mature plants.	Peas and beans, beetroot, brassicas, lettuce, sweet corn, tomatoes.	Cover seed drills with strands of black cotton stretched between sticks beside the rows or panels of wire netting; use plastic mesh netting for larger plants; humming tape and bird scaring devices are sometimes useful.	
Blackfly (black bean aphid) Colonies of small black flies, winged or wingless, on stems, pods and undersides of leaves in summer.	Broad, french and runner beans.	Pinch growing tips of broad bean plants when pods set.	Spray with derris, pyrethrum, systemic insecticide or insecticidal soap.
Cabbage mealy aphid Waxy greyish aphids on leaves and stems in summer; leaves curl and turn yellow.	Brassicas.	Dig and destroy old brassica stems promptly.	Spray with derris, pyrethrum, pirimicarb or insecticidal soap.
Cabbage root fly Small white grubs on the roots of seedlings and young plants.	Brassicas of all kinds.	Surround stems of young plants with felt collars; protect spring sowings under fleece or fine nets.	Sprinkle drills and planting sites with chlorophos or pirimiphos-methyl.
Cabbage white fly Slim white insects and tiny pale scales on undersides of leaves.	Leafy brassicas.	Clear exhausted brassicas promptly and keep down weeds (some weeds are also brassicas).	Spray with pyrethrum or pirimiphos-methyl.
Carrot fly Slim white grubs on seedling roots and in channels in mature roots.	Carrots, parsnips.	Sow thinly; sow in early spring or summer to miss attacks; lift maincrops in early autumn; enclose rows in barriers of plastic film 45cm (18in) high.	Dust drills with chlorophos or pirimiphos-methyl; water plants in late summer with pirimiphos-methyl.
Caterpillars Larvae of various moths and butterflies on leaves.	Brassicas.	Check plants regularly and crush any eggs on undersides of leaves.	Spray with derris, fenitrothion, permethrin, pyrethrum, pirimiphos-methyl or biological treatment *Bacillus thuringiensis*.
Celery leaf fly (leaf miner) Small white grubs at the end of tunnels in leaves.	Celery, parsnips.	Remove blistered leaves when planting and reject distorted seedlings.	Crush grubs in leaves; spray severe attacks with dimethoate or malathion.
Cutworms Large, thick, grey-green caterpillars in soil, eating plants at ground level and mining tubers.	Many plants including beetroot, cucumbers, lettuce, peppers, potatoes.	None.	Rake chlorophos or pirimiphos-methyl into soil before sowing or planting.
Eelworms Tiny threadlike creatures in onion bulbs and leaves, and round white or yellow cysts on potato roots; distorted, weak growth, rotting onions and leeks, and early death of potatoes and tomatoes.	One race affects onions and leeks, another potatoes and tomatoes.	Rotate susceptible crops, at least 4–6 years apart where infestations occur.	No treatment other than to destroy affected plants.
Flea beetles Tiny blue or black beetles, leaving small holes in seedling leaves.	All brassicas.	Sow early spring or summer to miss attacks; keep drills watered for fast germination and growth.	Spray seedlings with derris, gamma-HCH or pirimiphos-methyl.
Frit fly Tiny white grubs in the base of seedlings.	Sweet corn.	Grow in pots or under fine nets until 5–6 leaf stage.	Spray seedlings with fenitrothion or dust with gamma-HCH on emergence.
Greenfly (aphid) Colonies of small green or pinkish flies, winged and wingless, on the undersides of leaves, causing distortion.	Most crops are susceptible in varying degrees.	Crush or brush or hose off early infestations; grow, where appropriate, under fleece.	Spray with derris, pyrethrum, pirimicarb or insecticidal soap.
Leatherjackets Large, tough, greyish-brown grubs in the soil, eating stems at ground level.	Many young plants, especially lettuce.	Keep soil well-cultivated, especially where turf has been dug in.	Rake in chlorophos or pirimiphos-methyl before sowing and planting.
Mice	Pea, bean and sweet corn seeds and seedlings.	Some gardeners cover seeds with prickly holly leaves; otherwise set traps where inaccessible to birds and pets.	
Onion fly Small white grubs on the roots of seedlings and in the base of bulbs.	Onions, leeks, shallots.	Destroy thinnings and affected plants; firm soil after thinning; prepare seedbed at least a fortnight before sowing and destroy weeds.	Treat soil around seedlings with chlorophos or pirimiphos-methyl.
Pea moth Small white caterpillars or 'maggots' inside pods in mid-summer.	Peas.	Sow early spring before moths are on the wing.	Spray early to late summer with permethrin a week after first flowers open.
Pea thrips Narrow black or yellow flies on pods and foliage in summer, causing distorted and empty pods.	Peas.	None.	Spray with derris, pyrethrum, fenitrothion or dimethoate when seen.
Root aphids White powdery clusters of yellowish aphids on roots and in soil nearby.	Beans, carrots, lettuce, parsnips.	Clear finished crops promptly; use resistant cultivars; rotate crops.	Difficult; cull affected plants and/or water soil with pirimiphos-methyl.
Slugs and snails Soft-bodied molluscs, snails with shells, leaving a slimy trail and attacking leaves, stems, roots and tubers.	Most crops, especially while young or growing in moist soils.	Clear weeds and debris where they can hide.	Collect after dark and in wet weather, and destroy; spread pellets containing metaldehyde or methiocarb; water with aluminium sulphate.
Wireworms Shiny yellow wiry grubs, eating plants at ground level and mining roots and tubers.	Lettuces, potatoes and other roots.	Worst where turf has been freshly dug in, so avoid susceptible crops on these sites for 2–3 years, or strip turf and stack elsewhere.	Rake chlorophos or pirimiphos-methyl into soil before sowing and planting.

Disease and symptoms	Principal vegetable crops affected	Prevention	Control
Anthracnose Brown stripes on stems and spots on pods in cool wet summers.	French beans, runner beans.	Do not sow seeds with discoloured spots.	Destroy unhealthy seedlings, and spray adjacent plants with benomyl or copper fungicide.
Canker Cracked and discoloured rotting patches at tops of roots.	Parsnips.	Use resistant cultivars; rotate crops; avoid damaging roots when hoeing.	None.
Chocolate spot Brown spots and streaks on leaves and stems, especially in wet soils.	Broad beans.	Lime acid soils; check drainage; burn diseased plants after cropping.	Spray foliage with benomyl or carbendazim.
Clubroot Swollen distorted roots, discoloured leaves and wilting in hot weather.	All brassicas.	Lime soils; rotate crops; check drainage; dip transplant roots in benomyl or thiophanate-methyl solution.	Burn affected plants and do not grow brassicas there again for several years.
Common scab Rough crusted lesions on tubers.	Potatoes.	Avoid growing on alkaline and freshly limed soils; water crops in dry weather and grow drought-resistant cultivars on dry soils.	None.
Crown rot Soft brown decay of buds and crown with thin unthrifty stems and an unpleasant smell.	Rhubarb.	Do not plant too deeply or in soils where plants were previously affected.	Dig up and destroy.
Damping off Fungal infections of seedlings which collapse and die.	Beetroot, brassicas, lettuce, peas, tomatoes.	Sow thinly to avoid disease spreading; sow when temperatures are high enough for rapid growth as cold wet soils favour the disease.	Use a fungicidal seed dressing for early sowings; water seedlings with copper fungicide.
Downy mildew Pale or yellow markings on leaves, with affected areas becoming brown and dying.	Brassicas, lettuces, onions, peas.	Avoid overcrowding; rotate crops; remove affected leaves promptly; use resistant cultivars.	Spray with mancozeb.
Foot and root rot A wide range of fungal infections causing discoloured lower stems and black decaying roots.	Asparagus, beans, cucumbers, peas, tomatoes.	Use sterilized compost when sowing indoors; rotate susceptible crops; check soil drainage.	Destroy affected plants.
Fusarium wilt Black patches on leaves and stems, sometimes with pinkish-white fungal growth; black roots that eventually die.	Beans, lettuce, peas.	Rotate crops; grow resistant cultivars.	Destroy affected plants.
Grey mould *(Botrytis)* Brown patches on leaves and stems which eventually cause plants to break off at ground level; grey masses of mould on affected parts.	Lettuces.	Do not bury seedlings at planting time; allow enough room for air circulation; do not plant in cold wet soils.	Destroy affected plants and spray others with benomyl or thiophanate-methyl.
Halo blight Discoloured spots surrounded by pale 'halo' on young leaves which later darken and die; plants rarely grow well.	French beans, runner beans.	None.	Destroy affected plants; spray with benomyl or copper fungicide; do not save seeds from affected crops.
Honey fungus Dead brown areas with clear white streaks appear in crowns; honey-coloured toadstools appear around infected plants.	Rhubarb.	Do not grow near rotting tree stumps, especially of privet and rhododendrons.	Dig up and burn affected plants and roots.
Leaf and pod spots Brown spots, often sunken, on leaves, stems and pods.	Beetroot, celery, peas.	Rotate crops; use seed dressed with fungicide; where possible, avoid over-crowding.	Spray with benomyl or copper fungicide; burn plants after use.
Potato blight Brown patches on leaves in late summer, spreading to cause death of leaves; tomato fruits also affected.	Potatoes, tomatoes.	Only plant early cultivars in commercial potato growing areas; cut back diseased potato foliage in late summer and do not save infected tubers for storage; give preventive sprays of mancozeb or copper fungicide in mid-summer.	Spray with benomyl or copper fungicide; burn plants after use.
Powdery mildew White powdery spots and patches on leaves, eventually causing local collapse.	Cucumbers, peas, squashes.	Avoid overcrowding, especially with late sowings or in sheltered or dry positions.	Spray with benomyl or thiophanate-methyl; burn plants after use.
Rust Orange spots and blotches on leaves, and unthrifty growth.	Leeks, occasionally chives and other onions, mint.	Rotate crops; check drainage; do not over-feed with nitrogen; remake mint beds regularly on fresh soil.	Pick off affected leaves; burn seriously affected plants.
Stem rot Dirty yellow sunken lesions on base of stems.	Tomatoes.	Rotate crops and burn plants at the end of the season.	Pull up and destroy affected plants.
Viruses A wide range of disorders, caused by micro-organisms and often spread by aphids, soil pests and human contact; distorted or unthrifty growth, leaf mottling or streaking and reduced crops result.	Most crops are susceptible to one or several kinds of virus.	Always buy virus-free plants and seed potatoes; destroy affected plants before the condition can spread; control serious aphid infestations; wash or sterilize hands and tools after contact with infected material.	Dig up and burn affected plants.
White rot A serious disease producing fluffy white mould on base and roots of plants; leaves turn yellow.	Onions, leeks.	Rotate crops; water in hot dry summers.	Burn affected plants; do not grow onions in the same position again for at least 8 years.

FRUIT FROM THE GARDEN

Fruit should be grown in every kitchen garden. The joys of picking the first crisp early apple, sun-warmed strawberries by the basketful and peaches so ripe that the juice runs down your chin are ample rewards for their relatively undemanding care. Fruit trees and bushes are a permanent part of the garden landscape: some celebrate spring with breathtaking displays of blossom, but even in the depths of winter, long after their produce has been harvested and safely stored, their reassuring outlines offer continuity and the promise of future seasons.

Growing fruit on fences and walls can extend the potential cropping area of the kitchen garden. Many kinds of soft and top fruit are suitable for this purpose and look highly ornamental throughout the year. A tree such as this morello cherry fan offers masses of blossom in spring and heavy crops of fruit in late summer while its main branches arranged symmetrically like the ribs of a fan will embellish a sunlit or shaded wall even in the depths of winter.

Assessing the site

While vegetable crops that fail to do well can be resown later or in a different position without serious loss, fruit trees and bushes need permanent sites carefully matched to their special requirements. It may be several years before poor health or low yields indicate the wrong choice of position or aspect, so it is important to consider the various factors that affect growth at the outset.

Local climate will influence both the type of fruit likely to be happy in your garden and the choice of cultivars because these, too, often differ in suitability. Gooseberries, for example, prefer cool moist conditions in fairly light soils and can tolerate frost, whereas blackcurrants like rich heavy ground with shelter from frost and wind at flowering time. Pears flower earlier than apples and are therefore more at risk from spring frosts; some apple cultivars thrive in cold exposed gardens with short growing seasons, while others need a mild climate or a long warm autumn in which to ripen their fruits.

Hardiness and frost-protection

Hardiness is a vital consideration, not only for a plant's survival but, in the special case of fruit, for its chances of flowering and setting a crop without injury from frost.

Frost pockets should be avoided as sites for any fruits, but warm-climate crops such as greengages, peaches and many pears need special attention if they are to succeed in cool gardens. They may be trained on a warm sheltered wall or grown under glass in containers or soil borders, although it is sometimes possible to find one or two cultivars sufficiently robust to succeed in conditions that are less than ideal. These are often types that flower late and mature early, making them the best choice for gardens with short frost-free seasons.

A warm sunny position usually produces supreme quality and flavour but it is worth noting that excessive heat can adversely affect crops, especially deciduous fruits such as apples, pears and plums, together with many soft fruits. These need a distinct dormant period in winter, and absence of frost or of a prolonged period of chilling causes unhealthy growth and poor yields in very mild gardens, especially if these are also subjected to drought.

Rain and wind

Most fruits need well-drained but well-watered sites. This might seem a paradox but the good health of plants depends on their receiving the right amount of water at the right time. Good preparation before planting (see pages 84–5) can correct deficiencies such as inadequate drainage or the lack of humus in dry soils, while irrigation and mulching will help alleviate the effects of drought. In fact, most fruits prefer a dry climate provided they receive enough water at certain crucial stages; persistently wet weather encourages diseases and physiological disorders that are difficult to prevent or correct. In areas of heavy rainfall, always grow cultivars that have proved successful in the locality or choose less susceptible fruits – cooking apples rather than dessert storing apples, for example.

Shelter from strong winds is advisable for fruit crops, because pollinating insects are unable to work efficiently in turbulent conditions and branches laden with fruit are vulnerable to damage. In exposed positions you can provide windbreaks (see page 14), but make sure hedges and screens do not create frost pockets. Hardy fruits themselves often provide useful windbreaks for more susceptible crops and a large area of fruit may be protected by damson trees or a blackberry hedge, for example.

Aspect

Maximum sunlight is more important for some fruits than for others and this will help you to choose the best sites (see page 15). Warm-climate crops and dessert top fruit, especially late maturing cultivars and those intended for storage, need the most light and heat, whereas early cultivars and most soft fruits will tolerate shade for part of the day. Sites in heavy shade, especially beneath overhanging trees, or that receive uninterrupted sunlight for less than half the day on average are unlikely to be suitable.

Top fruit trained into simple formal shapes can be used to define, emphasize or decorate parts of the garden without sacrificing crop potential. These low espalier apple trees, trained horizontally along a single taut wire and complementing the dwarf box hedging, are an attractive feature, especially when they are flowering in spring and cropping in autumn.

Using the space

Provided their cultural needs are satisfied, fruit trees and bushes will adapt readily to various positions in the garden. Where there is space it might be best to gather all the plants together in a single plot for ease of maintenance and protection, especially if different types can be grouped together for convenience: taller trees may be sited where they cast little shade on adjacent crops, while bush fruits can be planted inside a fruit cage if birds are likely to be a problem. You will need to allow the full recommended distances between plants according to their type, but the intervening space can be used for growing a few vegetables during the first few years.

Where space is limited, fruits integrate successfully among other plants. Strawberries can be grown in the kitchen garden in rotation with other vegetables or as an edging to beds and borders. Fruit bushes and trees on dwarfing rootstocks make attractive features in flower beds and shrub borders, especially when trained ornamentally, but ensure you can tend, protect and, if necessary, spray the fruit without affecting flowering plants nearby. Larger fruit trees can be planted as specimens in borders or lawns, or trained as screens and divisions between different areas of the garden. Single espalier apple trees that have been trained about 38–45cm (15–18in) high like a horizontal cordon, sometimes known as 'step-over' trees, are ideal as edgings for borders and paths (see also page 91).

Providing support and protection

Various training methods, combined in some cases with an appropriate dwarfing rootstock, can be used to restrict the size and shape of many types of fruit and adapt them for growing in confined spaces. Walls and fences provide support and shelter for trained trees and soft fruits such as gooseberries and red currants; depending on the height of the wall these may be grown as large decorative fans and espaliers, or as cordons which take up much less space. House walls can be used to support fruit trees trained around windows and doors.

Select types of fruit to suit the aspect of the wall. Cultivars of the same fruit may be planted to mature in sequence according to the amount of heat and sunlight they will receive. Alternatively you can exploit the warmest walls for peaches and gages, planting apples, pears, plums, cherries and currants in cooler positions, reserving the shadiest walls for gooseberries, blackberries and acid cherries. Make sure structures are sound and arrange strong supports before planting: wooden trellis is adequate for soft fruit but the more substantial branches of top fruit will need tying to horizontal wires threaded through vine eyes or attached to wall nails.

Free-standing structures such as arches and pergolas are ideal for supporting trained fruit, but they must be strong enough to support heavy top growth. Arranging a series of arches to form a fruiting tunnel over a path creates an attractive and productive feature that occupies the minimum of space. A further advantage, shared by all forms of trained fruit, is that pruning (see pages 88–9 and under individual fruit entries) and other routine maintenance (see pages 86–7) can be carried out with relative ease, and with little disturbance to other plants.

Types of fruit

GROWING FRUIT
IN CONTAINERS
*All the fruits in this
book can be grown in
large pots or tubs, using
compact cultivars or tree
fruits on dwarfing
rootstocks. Use a good
soil-based compost and
make sure containers
drain efficiently. Plants
need careful and regular
feeding and watering,
together with annual
repotting in late
autumn, moving them
gradually into larger
pots – final size
38–50cm (15–20in).
Thin fruits to prevent
overcropping.*

The various fruit crops are usually grouped for convenience according to their growth habit and these distinctions are a useful guide when choosing which kinds to grow and where to site them.

Soft fruit includes those bush fruits such as gooseberries and currants (black, red or white) that grow naturally as shrubs, although many of them can be trained in restricted forms. Strawberries are herbaceous perennials, normally replaced every few years and moved around the kitchen garden as part of a rotation scheme. Cane fruits include raspberries, blackberries and hybrid berries, which fruit on one-year old stems that are then pruned out and replaced with new canes. Soft fruit plants can be expected to crop for 8–10 years or more.

Top fruits, those crops which grow naturally as trees with single stems or trunks, are productive for much longer than soft fruit. Examples described on the following pages are apples, pears, plums, peaches and cherries, the last three also being known as stone fruits because they contain a large seed or stone.

Since garden space is often limited, top fruits are usually grafted on dwarfing rootstocks that predetermine their ultimate size, whereas soft fruits are usually grown on their own roots. Pruning and training is used to shape both top and soft fruit.

Fruit forms

All fruits need pruning to ensure good health and high yields; the amount of pruning necessary depends on whether plants are to develop naturally or are grown as trained forms. Each method has its merits: a standard apple, for example, will make an attractive and spreading specimen tree that only needs pruning to remove dead or diseased branches. When the tree is mature, however, much of the fruit will develop on the outer branches and need picking from a ladder. A trained apple grown on a dwarfing rootstock, on the other hand, starts bearing much sooner and will be easier to maintain and harvest, but pruning in winter and summer may be essential, together with training on some system of support.

Spectacular spring blossom, such as that displayed by this espalier apple, is no guarantee of a good crop, which also depends on other factors such as the cultivar and the proximity of other compatible trees.

LEFT *Summer pruning exposes maturing fruit to the sun's warmth and also reveals the structure of these 'King of the Pippin' apple espaliers; behind, trained vertically against the wall, are ranks of single cordons. The amount of pruning needed to maintain these forms depends on the vigour of the rootstock that is used for grafting.*

Top fruits are grown as standards, half-standards and bushes according to the height of the trunk and the rootstock used. These are unrestricted forms that demand a lot of room, whereas trees trained as cordons, fans, espaliers and dwarf pyramids are restricted to size by pruning and therefore occupy less space. Because of the way they grow and bear their crops, stone fruits cannot be trained as cordons, but soft fruit such as gooseberries and red currants make attractive single, double or multiple cordons, fans, espaliers and even small standards when trained or grafted on tall main stems.

Vigour and rootstocks

Restricted forms of top fruits would need frequent and complex pruning to limit their size if they were grown on their own roots like soft fruit. By grafting a chosen cultivar on to a special rootstock of known vigour, however, the tree's growth rate can be predicted and the amount of pruning needed to maintain size is reduced. Further benefits include earlier fruiting, sometimes improved fruit quality and hardiness or disease-resistance.

Apples, pears, plums, peaches and cherries are grown on a number of rootstocks, and catalogues usually offer a range from which you can choose the most appropriate for your garden. Where size or yield is quoted, remember this is an estimate and in reality will be affected by the type of soil, the site's aspect and exposure, the form of the tree and the amount of pruning you do. Trees on very dwarfing rootstocks need fertile soil and firm support, often throughout their lives, and where soils are shallow or infertile a more vigorous rootstock is more likely to succeed, even though you might have to wait longer for maximum crops. Types of rootstock and their effects are listed in the separate fruit entries.

Pollination

The soft fruits described in this book will set fruit even where only a single plant is grown. Some top fruits also produce crops on their own, but many (especially plum and cherry cultivars) will not fruit in isolation because their flowers cannot be fertilized with their own pollen. Such cultivars are known as self-sterile; those that set fruit without needing pollen from other trees are known as self-fertile.

Obviously, if only one tree is to be grown, choose a self-fertile cultivar to ensure crops. A self-sterile tree must be grown near another different cultivar that flowers at the same time and is also compatible; not all cultivars fertilize each other equally well, for some produce very little pollen of their own, even though they might be fertilized readily by another tree. 'Triploid' cultivars are examples of poor pollen suppliers and these should be planted with two other compatible cultivars so that each is effectively fertilized. Some cultivars are notoriously cross-sterile and will not pollinate each other, while biennial bearers (cultivars flowering well only in alternate years) are not reliable as pollinators.

When choosing top fruit, therefore, it is wise to consult the catalogue of a reputable nursery to check that trees are either self-fertile or compatible with each other. Many apples can be grown on their own, although all crop more reliably if they are cross-fertilized with another cultivar. Peaches and acid cherries are self-fertile, whereas most sweet cherries, pears and plums are self-sterile.

Choosing and planting fruit

Wherever top fruit is to be grown, it is important to remove all weeds from the site and to keep it clear of competing plants for at least 3–4 years afterwards to ensure that there is no check to growth. Large trees on vigorous rootstocks may then be grassed down without harm, but smaller trees on dwarfing rootstocks, such as the young apple espaliers and pear bushes here, are best grown in clear soil for most of their lives.

Even after taking into account important factors such as local climate, type of soil, the size of tree required and its pollination needs, you will find there is a wide and often bewildering range of cultivars from which to make your choice.

If you have room for several plants, try to spread the selection evenly between early, mid-season and late maturing kinds to extend the supply over a long period. Remember that early top fruit crops do not store well and one or two trees will probably meet immediate needs, whereas fruit from long-keeping cultivars will stay in good condition for several months, sometimes until the following spring provided you are able to store the produce under ideal conditions. Surplus soft fruit may be frozen, bottled or otherwise preserved.

The fruit cultivars sold by greengrocers are not necessarily the best for garden cultivation; they are often popular more for their easy commercial management or long storage life than for their eating quality. Reliability is of course a prime virtue wherever space is limited, but if you have room it is worth exploring older or less familiar cultivars that might be noted for their flavour or some other quality. Many have regional origins which can be used as a guide to the growing conditions they

prefer: the apple 'Devonshire Quarrenden', for example, tolerates the high rainfall of the English west coast, whereas 'D'Arcy Spice' comes from the drought-prone east coast and needs hot dry summers in order to develop its full flavour.

Always buy fruit plants from a reputable supplier. Ordering is best done early in the season, and if possible go personally to discuss your choice and always select the best (see Selecting a healthy tree, right). Explain clearly the type of rootstock and the form you require: soft fruits such as gooseberries and currants are normally supplied as bushes unless you specify that you want cordons, standards or some other form. Top fruits can be bought as one-year-old maidens for you to do your own training – a maiden whip is a single stem grafted on a rootstock, while feathered maidens also have a few sideshoots. A two-year-old plant will have already been cut back by the nursery, with a start made to its training, while three-year-old plants have a basic trained framework of branches. Older plants are difficult to establish and should be avoided.

Fruit may be supplied bare-rooted (grown in a field and dug up while dormant) or container-grown in large pots for planting at any time (see Selecting a healthy tree, right). Bare-rooted fruit should be planted soon after delivery, but if this has to be delayed, plants must be heeled in to prevent the roots from drying out (see page 40). Various inspection schemes exist to check and guarantee the health status of the plants, and you should always confirm that the fruit is certified free from diseases.

Preparing the soil

The advice given earlier about soil structure (see pages 16–17) and fertility (see pages 18–19) applies to fruit as well as to vegetable crops. Most soils are suitable for fruit if they are well-drained but it might be necessary to improve the drainage of heavy clay. The soil should be deep enough for plants to root strongly: strawberries will grow in shallow soils but soft fruits need a soil depth of about 45cm (18in), top fruit at least 60cm (2ft).

SELECTING A
HEALTHY TREE
*Make sure bare-rooted
fruit trees have a
balanced and well-
developed root system
with no suckers growing
from the rootstock. The
main stem should be
straight with several
evenly spaced branches
with no signs of ill-
health. Check pots of
container-grown trees
are intact, with no thick
roots visible at the base
or surface of the compost.*

Slightly acid conditions are usually ideal, with pH levels between 6 and 7. Add lime to soils below pH6, but be careful not to over-compensate; making them too alkaline may result in deficiency symptoms such as chlorosis (leaves turning yellow prematurely), together with impaired yields or quality. Fruits such as pears and raspberries will not grow well on very chalky soil unless it is treated annually with sequestered (chelated) trace elements, which are easily absorbed, and regular top-dressings of sulphur or sulphate of ammonia to reduce the soil pH.

At least a month or two before planting, you will need to dig the site deeply and thoroughly, removing all perennial weeds and working in plenty of compost or decayed manure, especially if the soil is very sandy or heavy. Prepare planting sites about 90cm (3ft) across for individual trees and bushes or in a continuous strip for plants to be grown closely in rows. Soils already in good condition need only single digging or forking over just before planting.

How to plant

Accurate spacing is important to avoid problems in later years when plants develop. Mark out each planting position with a cane, then dig a hole about 1½ times the diameter of the plant's root system.

For tree fruit drive a stake into the bottom of the hole so that it is firm, vertical and about 8–10cm (3–4in) off-centre; the top of the stake should reach about half way up the main stem or trunk (see Planting a fruit tree, below). Soft fruit will not need staking although cane fruits, such as brambles, require a support structure.

When planting fruit for training on walls and fences, position the plant 23–30cm (9–12in) away from the base of the wall so that the roots are surrounded by good soil, and plant with the main stem leaning slightly towards its supports. Test all fruit in position before planting to allow for adjustments to the depth of the hole so that the surrounding soil matches the previous level at which the plant grew. This is indicated by the soil mark on the stem; resting a cane across the planting hole helps when checking this.

Spread out bare roots evenly and return the excavated soil in stages, carefully shaking the plant at first to settle soil between its roots and treading the surface gently once or twice while filling the hole. Finally loosen and level the surface all round. Where rabbits are a problem fit a spiral guard or cylinder of wire netting round the stem, secured to the stake with a cushioned tree tie.

Planting a fruit tree

Thorough soil preparation and unhurried planting are essential for success. Getting someone to help you may make it easier to ensure the tree is upright and at the right depth. Plant when soil conditions are suitable (neither frozen nor very wet), and drive in any support stakes before planting – a vertical stake about half the height of the main stem is usual, but an angled stake avoids damaging the roots of larger container-grown trees. Cover the soil after planting with a mulch or woven planting mat to suppress weeds.

Test the tree in the hole for size; check the old soil mark is at ground level.

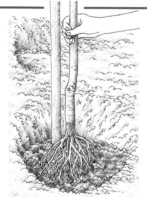

Drive in the stake, hold the tree upright and backfill around the roots.

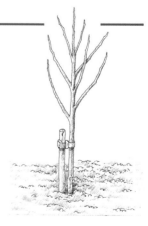

Firm and level the soil; secure the tree with one or more tree ties.

Routine care and maintenance

Birds and, in some districts, squirrels will quickly strip crops from bushes, especially red soft fruits such as strawberries, red currants and raspberries. A sturdy fruit cage can protect plants from plunder, and need not be plain or utilitarian, as this traditionally elaborate cage demonstrates.

The amount of care and attention needed by fruit trees and bushes varies according to the type of fruit and the particular season. Details are given in the separate fruit entries which follow, but a few basic principles can be outlined here.

Controlling weeds

Research has shown that keeping fruit trees free from weeds is one of the most effective ways to encourage rapid establishment, as this eliminates competition for water and nutrients. The importance of clearing perennial weeds from the site before planting has already been mentioned. Some gardeners surround new fruit with woven planting mats that suppress weeds but allow rainfall to penetrate through to the soil, while soft fruit cuttings are sometimes planted directly through black plastic sheeting to control weeds and stabilize soil moisture. You can use a weedkiller carefully, following the manufacturer's instructions, to keep the surrounding soil weed-free, hoe or hand weed as necessary, or mulch every spring with manure or compost for this purpose. Aim to keep a weed-free area about 90cm (3ft) across for at least the first 2–3 seasons after planting.

Watering and feeding

Adequate water supplies are also critical, especially during the first years of establishment: as a rough guide soft fruit will need watering in a dry spell during the first year after planting, top fruit for 1–2 years, particularly where soils are light and dry. Amounts vary and are specified in the crop entries, but you should always soak plants thoroughly, giving recently planted top fruit, for example, up to 22 litres per sq m (4gal per sq yd) every 7–10 days in dry weather; established trees can use twice this amount. Where large quantities have to be applied, it is often best to leave a hose-pipe gently trickling at the base of the tree for about half an hour.

Young top fruit and all soft fruit benefit from a spring mulch of compost or decayed manure spread around the stem. Established fruit, especially on light soils, should also be given a top-dressing of a balanced fertilizer (organic gardeners use blood, fish and bonemeal) in late winter or early spring, using about 105–140g per sq m (3–4oz per sq yd). Spread this evenly over the area of ground shaded by the branches so that all the roots can benefit. Mineral or trace element deficiencies may occur, especially on light soils, and should be identified and corrected, either with one of the treatments noted on pages 18 and 29 or with a top-dressing of seaweed meal at 135–200g per sq m (4–6oz per sq yd).

Thinning fruits

In a good year crops often set too heavily, so that the laden branches risk breakage and fruits are unable to reach their full size. Thinning reduces the number of fruits to sustainable levels and involves the removal of misshapen fruits and a proportion of those growing in clusters until the optimum number is left. Details for the different fruits are given in the individual entries.

Protection from birds

In many areas birds damage fruit plants by attacking the buds in late winter and early spring, and also the ripening fruit. Where this is prevalent, there is no alternative to covering plants, either with temporary veils of small-mesh plastic netting or with a permanent fruit cage where a number of fruits are grown together. Tree fruits such as cherries should be grown as small manageable trees or as fans against walls for ease of protection.

Harvest and storing

As a general rule, fruits are gathered when fully ripe for immediate use or storage. A whole crop seldom matures all at once, so you will need to go over trees or bushes several times to test which fruits are ripe before picking them. Young gooseberries may be gathered while immature as part of the thinning process so that the remainder can reach full size as dessert fruits, while some pear cultivars are picked when still hard to continue ripening in store.

Always harvest carefully to avoid damaging or bruising fruits, especially if intended for keeping, because only perfect fruit stores successfully. There are several ways to store or preserve surplus fruit and these are listed in the entries, as appropriate. All soft fruits, together with soft-fleshed top fruits such as peaches, plums and cherries, can be frozen, bottled or turned into cooked preserves. Apples and pears may be dried or frozen, but long-keeping cultivars are usually packed in boxes or perforated plastic bags and stored in a dark, cool and airy place.

Pests and diseases

The precautions and deterrent measures discussed on pages 32–3 apply to all fruits. Avoiding problems by growing resistant cultivars and by vigilance in checking for early symptoms is perhaps more important with fruit crops, because it is not practical simply to pull up a diseased specimen and usually a larger crop is at risk of being lost. Many gardeners follow preventive spray routines (sometimes the only way to stop fungal diseases from taking hold), but close attention to garden hygiene and simple precautions such as efficient pruning (see page 88) help foster a robust constitution, and are often the most effective measures. See also pages 110–11.

Good crops of fruit need to be picked over several times before their harvest is complete. Where taller trees are involved, such as this heavily laden half-standard pear, always work from a stable pair of steps, both for your own safety and also to avoid incidental damage to the tree and its crop.

Pruning fruit

To anyone growing fruit for the first time, pruning can seem a daunting and slightly arcane part of the cultural routine. Numerous methods have been developed for coaxing the maximum crop from the smallest manageable size of plant, starting at an early age and continuing regularly thereafter. All are based on a few essential principles, however, and any refinements can be introduced as you become familiar with the type of fruit or the peculiar habits of individual cultivars.

Reasons for pruning

In their natural state fruit plants are self-regulating and will achieve their own compromise between size, growth rate and crop yield. For this reason large, mature trees such as standard apples need little pruning after the first few years, during which the best number of evenly spaced branches are left to grow and form the tree.

In most gardens, though, space is precious and growth has to be restrained. Wise choice of rootstock where appropriate helps control size, but even the slowest growing tree will eventually become too large. Simply cutting back growth to limit size often removes 'fruiting wood', the term used to describe those parts of stems that bear fruit, so efficient

pruning tries to find a balance between restraining growth and encouraging good crops. The best fruits are often carried on young vigorous stems, and since cutting off shoots and branches usually stimulates more new growth, high quality produce can be the direct result of intelligent pruning.

It is also a valuable means of keeping a plant in good health. By thinning out branches, air is allowed to circulate freely through the tree or bush, preventing the occurrence of damp stagnant conditions that favour fungal diseases. More light is admitted, which helps ripen both the fruit crop and the young stems and buds that might otherwise be damaged by winter frosts. Dead, damaged and diseased shoots are cut out as part of the pruning routine, together with any that cross or rub against each other and might open vulnerable wounds, and these are further precautions against ailments.

When to prune

Pruning is a kind of creative interference and redirection of natural growth which depends for success on anticipating a plant's response to the removal of some or part of its shoots. Growth is stimulated by hormones, which tend to be concentrated at the apex of shoots, especially those growing vertically, while buds lower down the shoots are inhibited from growing so readily.

Cutting off the end of a shoot removes the dominant buds and diverts the growth hormones into those buds that are left, especially the ones at the end of the pruned shoot, and these now become dominant. This means that you can cut back to any bud, confident that this will now become the most active. If it is a slim leaf bud, it will produce a shoot growing in the direction in which the bud was pointing; if the bud is fat and rounded, it will produce flowers rather than new extension growth.

Vigour is an important consideration, because cutting out a strong shoot not only wastes a useful fruiting branch but can also stimulate too much new growth, whereas weak stems can be cut severely without causing a dramatic response. Balance is

Top fruit trees are a long-term investment, and it is important that every attention is paid to formative training in the early years and to maintenance pruning. A well-cared-for tree, such as this venerable espalier of pear 'Doyenné du Comice', will eventually become a cherished and impressive feature while retaining its ability to bear worthwhile crops.

PRUNING TERMS AND TOOLS

A main stem or branch is known as a *leader*, which will produce a number of *laterals* or *sideshoots*; these in turn produce *sub* or *secondary* laterals. Laterals and secondary laterals bear slim pointed *growth* or *leaf buds* and plump rounded *fruit buds*. Most pruning is done with sharp *secateurs*, together with a pruning *saw* or *loppers* for thicker stems.

essential, too, and under-pruning is as unwise as over-pruning, especially while a plant is young, when it is important to build up a sturdy framework that can sustain regular cropping.

Insufficient pruning in the early stages may mean major surgery later, with possible risk of disease. Any pruning leaves wounds that are open to infection, but the smaller they are, the sooner they heal. Major pruning is usually done in winter when plants are dormant, although stone fruits are pruned during growth when cuts heal more quickly. Trained fruits are pruned in summer as well as winter to control their vigour finely and encourage fruit production.

Always use sharp tools – secateurs for lighter pruning and loppers or a coarse-toothed saw for larger branches – and leave clean cuts. Prune just above a bud to avoid die-back of part of the shoot, and clear away all prunings.

Methods of pruning

The method used depends on the normal fruiting habit of the plant concerned and the reasons for pruning. Some fruits crop only (or best) on young stems and 'renewal pruning' concentrates on removing growth that has borne fruit for replacement by one-year-old stems; examples include raspberries,

blackberries, acid cherries and peaches. Blackcurrants crop best on shoots up to 3–4 years old, and renewal pruning aims to cut out about a third of the older branches each year to keep bushes vigorous. Apples, pears, gooseberries and red currants, on the other hand, fruit on short permanent sideshoots called 'spurs', produced on a permanent framework of older branches. Spur pruning consists of maintaining this system of sideshoots and cutting out all surplus growth, unless this is needed as replacement for old exhausted branches. Some cultivars of pears and apples (known as 'tip-bearers') crop on short spurs and at the end of long sideshoots and their care involves a combination of spur and renewal pruning (see Spur, tip and renewal pruning, below).

Maintenance or regulatory pruning is a continuous process that applies to the whole plant rather than its specific fruiting parts and aims to maintain shape, health and overall vigour. This kind of pruning starts with the early shaping of young plants and the formation of their branch structure, continuing with the removal of misplaced, diseased or exhausted growth and should be the first priority before turning to pruning for fruitfulness. Old neglected trees need 2–3 seasons of regulatory pruning to restore their shape and vigour.

Spur, tip and renewal pruning

It is important when pruning to distinguish between different growth habits – laterals on a spur-bearing apple, for example, need to be shortened annually, whereas this will render tip-bearers barren. Spur-bearing fruit crop on permanent sideshoots (1); tip-bearers fruit at the ends of short laterals formed the previous season (2); partial tip-bearers crop on both kinds of wood, but are pruned as spur-bearers. Renewal pruning (3) is for fruits that crop on one-year-old wood; spent stems cut out annually after harvest are replaced by new shoots.

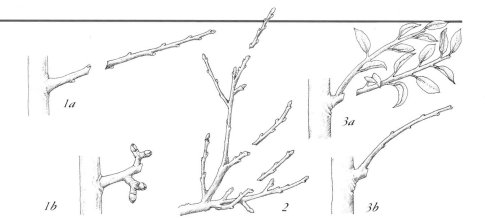

In winter shorten young laterals to 2 buds (1a) to form fruiting spurs (1b).

In winter cut tip-bearing laterals over 23cm (9in) long to 4 buds.

Remove the fruited shoot (3a) to replace with 1–2 new basal stems (3b).

Training fruit

All fruit needs training, at least in the early formative stages. Whether plants have been produced at home from hardwood cuttings, or bought as maidens or young bushes, training is as crucial as pruning during the first 3–4 years if a shapely and productive plant is to result. Pruning off the tip of a rooted cutting or shortening a maiden to the height of stem required will induce a number of sideshoots. Depending on the shape of tree wanted, remove these if they are not needed or in the wrong place, shorten them again to encourage branching, or leave them to grow longer in subsequent seasons.

Unrestricted forms

These include full-size standards, 5m (16ft) or more in height on trunks 1.5–2.2m (5–7ft) tall; they eventually bear the heaviest crops, but can spread to 6m (20ft) or more across. Half-standards have trunks 1–1.5m (3–5ft) high, grow almost as tall as standards and may need a similar amount of space. Both kinds are grown on vigorous rootstocks.

Bush trees have short stems, up to 90cm (3ft) high but only 45–75cm (18–30in) in the case of dwarf bushes, with a spread of about 4–4.5m (13–15ft). Both bushes and standards need careful early training to form a balanced head of permanent, evenly spaced branches, initially 3–4 growing near the top and at a wide angle with the main stem (see Forming a bush tree, below). In the second winter these are shortened by half to induce each to produce two sideshoots, so doubling the number of main branches; this is repeated the following winter to further double the framework of branches. Thereafter training consists of removing all surplus main shoots and shortening crowded sideshoots to about four buds; others can be left to flower and bear fruit.

Dwarf pyramids

The easiest free-standing trained form for gardens is the dwarf pyramid, useful for apples or pears and ideal for growing at close spacing because individual trees are seldom more than about 120cm (4ft) across at their widest point. More vigorous rootstocks, such as might be used for plums or cherries, will produce larger pyramids. Trees are decorative, with a tapering outline and a central main stem or 'leader'; this is shortened annually to encourage the formation of sideshoots until a final height of about 2.2m (7ft) is reached. Pyramids on dwarfing or semi-dwarfing rootstocks need staking for several years. Start where possible with a feathered maiden, cutting it back to about 50cm (20in) high after planting (see page 96).

Forming a bush tree

Bushes, standards and half-standards are all formed in the same way. Starting with a maiden whip or a feathered maiden, the aim is to shorten main stems (leaders) to stimulate branching and create a basic framework of branches that are widely and evenly spaced. Always cut to outward-facing buds to keep the structure open to admit plenty of light and air. This formative pruning is usually done in winter while plants are dormant and when temperatures are above freezing. Stone fruits should not be pruned until early spring.

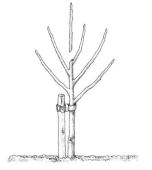

In the first winter cut back the leader to 3–5 strong buds or laterals at the required height.

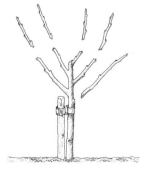

In the second winter remove unwanted branches; shorten the rest by about half.

In the third winter shorten the new leaders by half but leave any sideshoots unpruned.

Although most popular for plums and peaches, the fan is an ideal ornamental and productive form for training all top fruit and some soft fruit. Fans may be grown against walls and fences or on a system of posts and wires in the open garden, as here where a flowering apple fan reveals impressive symmetry, the result of meticulous attention to detail such as the use of canes to help train straight branches and a generous mulch to sustain uninterrupted growth.

Cordons

The most basic trained form is the single cordon, a straight stem up to 2m (6½ft) long, grown vertically or (preferably) at an angle and bearing fruit on short sideshoots or spurs. Single, double or multiple cordons are ideal for red currants and gooseberries, and for apples and pears on dwarfing rootstocks; planted close together, a large number can be grown in a limited space. They are simple to train (see page 92) and usually start cropping two years after planting. Cordons need some form of permanent support such as horizontal wires about 45cm (18in) apart and attached to a wall or fence about 1.8–2.5m (6–8ft) high or stretched between posts in the open. Choose well-feathered maidens when buying, that is maidens with plenty of sideshoots that can be pruned as fruiting spurs.

Fans

A fan has a number of long straight branches radiating from the top of a short trunk, the lowest branch arising about 45–60cm (18–24in) above the ground. Specimens two or three years old can be bought with the early stages of training already carried out; alternatively plant a feathered maiden and cut this back after planting to 2–3 buds or sideshoots at the required distance above the ground ready for subsequent training (see pages 98 and 101).

Espaliers

In its basic form an espalier has a number of horizontal branches (each behaving like a cordon) that extend sideways at regular intervals from a vertical main stem. There are normally 2, 3 or 4 tiers of branches, but more are acceptable on vigorous trees if the upper levels are accessible for picking and pruning; 'step-over' trees have only a single tier of horizontal branches or arms.

Espaliers are suitable for all fruits that produce spurs; tip-bearing apples and fruits such as peaches that need annual renewal pruning are difficult to train in this way. Like fans, espaliers must be grown on a supportive framework, either on walls at least 1.8m (6ft) high or as a decorative screen beside paths or across the garden. Pre-trained specimens are available, as for fans, or you can start with a feathered maiden, which is cut back to leave three good buds on a short trunk about 45cm (18in) high (see page 94 for further training).

Espaliers, fans and cordons grown at an angle are all productive forms because they involve lowering branches away from the vertical; this checks the rise of sap and slightly suppresses the rate of growth in favour of the development of fruit buds. Do not lower any branch too abruptly, though, as this can lead to breakage. When training an espalier, for example, arrange sideshoots first at 45 degrees and then lower them to the horizontal the following winter. If one arm develops more than another, lowering the stronger or raising the weaker branch will modify the growth rate until they are evenly matched. It often helps to attach a bamboo cane to the wires wherever a branch is to be trained, and to tie growth to this at frequent intervals until the branch is strong enough to remain in place unaided.

Top fruit

GROWING TOP FRUIT

Top fruit trees can take a long time to start bearing well, at least 4–5 years for cordons and up to 10 years for large standards, but they will then crop for many years if well-tended. Dwarfing rootstocks have made it possible to grow top fruit in the smallest garden, while their ease of cultivation and maintenance allows everyone to enjoy their own fruit trees in blossom and the chance to grow cultivars superior to those commercially available.

I have limited myself here to the most popular top fruits for the kitchen garden – apples, pears, plums, peaches and cherries. However, the adventurous gardener might want to explore more unusual fruits, such as mulberries, figs, quinces and apricots.

Apples

Of all top fruit, apples are the most popular and usually the easiest to grow anywhere except in very hot or wet districts, where pests and diseases can make their cultivation unprofitable. There are four main kinds: dessert, culinary or cooking, crab (see right) and cider apples, the last normally grown as large trees in fields and not therefore included here. Hundreds of cultivars are available, some of them regional specialities while others are noted for hardiness or for their tolerance of heavy, wet or poor soils.

Because of their wide variability it is advisable to check the credentials of any cultivar in a catalogue before buying: note whether the apple is spur- or tip-bearing (the latter is difficult to train in restricted forms), triploid (it will need two companions for effective pollination), disease-resistant and suitable for your soil and climate. Select the appropriate rootstock for the form you need, choosing a more vigorous type for infertile soils; in cold gardens, plant late flowering cultivars whose blossom is most likely to evade frost damage in spring.

Sites

A sunny position with shelter from cold winds and frosts at flowering time is ideal. Culinary apples tolerate light shade and also wetter soils than dessert cultivars, which prefer dry conditions when ripening; none will thrive in waterlogged ground, nor in very warm regions where winters are too mild to provide adequate chilling during dormancy. All soils should be deeply cultivated and manured well beforehand, and should be slightly acid (pH6.5).

Cultivation

Plant bare-root trees during dormancy, preferably in autumn while the soil is still warm, and container-grown trees at any time when the soil is workable. Stake free-standing trees securely and attach trained forms to supports.

Mulch newly planted and young trees in spring, spreading rotted manure 5cm (2in) deep over an area 90cm (3ft) across, but keep the material slightly away from the stem. Cropping trees may be mulched if you have enough manure or compost to cover the

Training a cordon apple

A cordon is simply a straight single stem closely pruned to develop a system of short fruiting sideshoots or spurs. It is an ideal form for small gardens and for any fruit that crops on spurs (note that tip-bearing apple cultivars are not suitable). Vertical cordons crop well, but planting at an oblique angle permits longer stems and needs less height. Multiple cordons with 2, 3 or more stems are formed by shortening the leader and training the required number of stems on parallel canes. Always tie in stems securely.

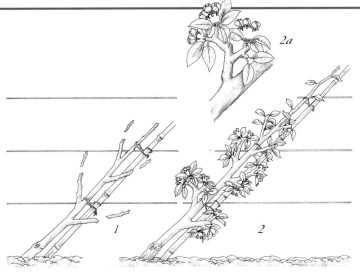

In the first winter (1) tie the unpruned leader to the cane and shorten all laterals to 4–5 buds. The next winter (2) continue tying in the leader and shorten new laterals. In spring pinch out blossom on the lower spurs (2a). Thereafter, allow spurs to fruit and prune only in summer; prune the leader when it reaches the top wire.

GROWING CRAB APPLES

Although often grown as ornamental spring-flowering trees, crab apples yield heavy crops of small, tart fruits used in wines and preserves. They are also widely planted as efficient pollinators for large-fruited apple trees – best for this purpose are the prolific cultivars 'Aldenhamensis', 'Golden Hornet' and 'Profusion'. 'John Downie' has large, well-flavoured fruits for preserves. Most kinds are self-fertile and trees crop well on their own. They are grafted on the same rootstocks as large apple cultivars, and may be similarly trained, although they are often grown as specimen trees with only basic winter pruning.

area that is shaded by the branches. Alternatively feed in early spring with a general fertilizer at a rate of 70g per sq m (2oz per sq yd) for dessert cultivars, half as much again for culinary apples; on light soils, especially where rainfall is high, dress with seaweed meal at a rate of 135g per sq m (4oz per sq yd) to restore trace element levels.

Water young trees whenever the soil is dry, applying about 22 litres per sq m (4gal per sq yd) every 7–10 days. Trees in bearing need about 45 litres per sq m (10gal per sq yd) every fortnight in mid- and late summer unless there is plenty of rain. Keep trees weed-free over an area about 90cm (3ft) across by hoeing, hand weeding or spraying with herbicide, until they are cropping regularly; grass can then be allowed to grow round trees on vigorous or semi-dwarfing rootstocks.

Thinning

A prolific set of fruit needs thinning to ensure large apples of good quality and also to prevent biennial cropping (when a light or barren season follows one with a heavy crop). On young trees thin clusters to leave just one or two fruits, pinching or snipping off the rest with scissors while they are still small. On older trees, wait until some of the fruits are shed

naturally in early summer (sometimes called the 'June drop') and then remove misshapen apples and any with holes in the skin (these contain moth grubs). One apple in the centre of clusters is usually larger than the others: if this 'king' fruit is distorted remove it, otherwise leave in place as this may be the best. Thin dessert fruits to about 10–15cm (4–6in) apart, culinary apples to 15–20cm (6–8in). Heavily laden branches should be propped up with forked poles or may be 'maypoled', that is supported with ropes attached to the top of a central stake.

Pruning

For the formative training and pruning necessary during the first four years, see page 90 (bushes, standards and half-standards, below (cordons), pages 94–5 (espaliers), pages 96–7 (dwarf pyramids), pages 98–9 (fans).

With established standard, half-standard and bush forms, prune in winter by first cutting out any dead, damaged and diseased wood, together with any shoot crossing the centre of the head or growing too close to another branch. No other pruning is usually necessary except where trees start to produce large crops of small fruit, when some of the spurs and sideshoots on spur-bearing cultivars can be thinned

3a

3

3b

In mid- to late summer shorten any new sideshoots growing on existing spurs back to one leaf beyond the basal rosette of leaves (3a). Shorten new laterals near the top of the young cordon to 4–5 leaves (3b) to encourage them to form spurs; when full length, prune the leader back to just above the base of its new growth.

Ripeness is all-important when picking apples, such as these 'Royal Gala', for storing – full, even colour is one indication, easy parting from the stem another. With their relatively short season of good quality, on the other hand, the harvesting of early apples often begins before they are fully ripe.

out; tip-bearing apples need some older shoots cut back to their base to leave an open network of young sideshoots with fruit buds at their tips.

After their fourth year, prune cordons in winter by cutting one-third from the leading shoot(s); in summer cut back new sideshoots to about 8cm (3in) long and secondary sideshoots to 2.5cm (1in). When the leader has reached its full height, prune only in summer by shortening both sideshoots and the new growth on the leader to about 2.5cm (1in) long. Prune fans and espaliers in the same way, treating each arm or branch like a cordon. On older cordons, fans and espaliers, congested or complicated spurs can be thinned by cutting out some spurs altogether and pruning others back to 2–3 fruit buds.

Continue pruning dwarf pyramids by cutting back the central leader in winter to leave about 23cm (9in) of new growth; remove any very vigorous new shoots and shorten lateral branches to buds facing downwards to encourage them to extend horizontally. In late summer shorten the leading shoots of side branches to about 23cm (9in) long, cut back sideshoots to 8cm (3in) and secondary sideshoots to 2.5cm (1in). When the tree has reached its full height, about 2.2–2.5m (7–8ft), cut back the leader to the base of its new growth late every spring and shorten all other vigorous shoots to 8cm (3in) in summer; in winter thin any overcrowded spurs and cut back complex ones to 2–3 flower buds.

Harvesting and storage

When gathering apples, test each for ripeness by lifting it gently in the palm of the hand – its stalk should part from the stem without the need for twisting or pulling. Check regularly for ripeness and discard any that show signs of decay. Early maturing cultivars do not remain in good condition for long, and you can start picking them when slightly under-ripe. Later maturing kinds should be fully ripe; for storage they should also be dry, unblemished and complete with their stalks. Use damaged fruit and crops from young trees for immediate consumption.

Keep apples in a cool but frost-free place, which should be fairly dry but not so dry that the fruit shrivels: 3–4°C (37–40°F) is the ideal temperature, in a shed where the floor can be damped down to prevent too dry an atmosphere. Here the fruit can be spread out on shelves or layered in boxes. Packing fruit in polythene bags, perforated with a few holes, will prevent moisture loss, or you can wrap the best specimens in grease-proof paper.

Crop details Season: mid-summer to late autumn (until mid-spring from store). Rootstocks: M27 (very dwarfing), M26 (dwarfing, for poorer soils), M9 (dwarfing), MM106 (semi-dwarfing), MM111 (vigorous). Forms: standard, half-standard, bush, dwarf pyramid, fan, espalier, cordon. Spacing: standard, half-standard 6–9m (20–30ft); bush

Training an espalier apple

Plant an unfeathered maiden in winter and cut back to the first wire, 38–60cm (15–24in) above ground. The next summer train the shoot from the topmost bud vertically, the next two at an oblique angle, and tie to canes. The second winter, lower the oblique stems to the horizontal, shorten other laterals to 2–3 buds to form spurs, and prune the vertical leader at the second wire. Repeat this sequence until the top tier is established. When fully formed, remove new growth at the ends of branches in early summer.

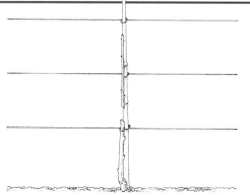

After planting a dormant maiden, tie the lower portion securely to an upright cane and prune the top back to the first wire.

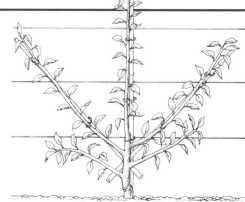

The next summer tie in the vertical leader as it grows, and tie the lower stems to canes attached to the wires at a 45-degree angle.

While trained fruit grafted on dwarfing rootstocks are the most appropriate for small gardens, standard and half-standard trees on more vigorous rootstocks can be accommodated in larger gardens, especially when pruned to an open structure to reduce the amount of shade cast on nearby plants.

1.8–5.5m (6–18ft); dwarf pyramid 1.5–2.2m (5–7ft); fan, espalier 3–5.5m (10–18ft); single cordon 75cm (30in) in rows 1.8m (6ft) apart. Average yield: standard 90–180kg (200–400lb); half-standard 45–90kg (100–200lb); bush 27–55kg (60–120lb); dwarf pyramid 4.5–6.5kg (10–14lb); fan, espalier 9–13.5kg (20–30lb); cordon 2.3–3.2kg (5–7lb).

Recommended cultivars in order of ripening; c=culinary, d=dual-purpose, t=triploid; numbers indicate relative flowering time on a scale from 1 (very early) to 8 (very late). All apples crop best when cross-pollinated by other cultivars with the same number, or the next number above or below. 'George Cave' 2, 'Katy' 3, 'Discovery' 3, 'Grenadier' (c) 3, '(Laxton's) Epicure' 3, 'Rev. W. Wilks' (c) 2, 'Merton Knave' 3, 'James Grieve' 3, 'Merton Charm' 3, 'St. Edmund Pippin' 2, '(Laxton's) Fortune' 3, 'Egremont Russet' 2, 'Golden Noble' (c) 4, 'Sunset' 3, 'Ribston Pippin' (t) 2, 'Suntan' (t), 'Blenheim Orange' (d,t) 3, 'Orleans Reinette' 4, 'Bramley's Seedling' (c,t) 3, 'Spartan' 3, 'Rosemary Russet' 3, 'Annie Elizabeth' (c) 4, 'Ashmead's Kernel' 4, 'Fiesta' 3, 'Edward VII' (c) 6, 'Tydeman's Late Orange' (t) 4, 'Pixie' 4, 'Sturmer Pippin' 3.

Common pests and diseases Aphids, birds, codling moth, wasps, winter moth; apple scab, bitter pit, brown rot, canker, powdery mildew (see pages 110–11).

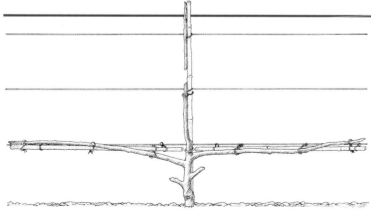

In the second winter retie the oblique stems to the first wire. Cut back the vertical leader to the second wire to repeat the first stage of training. Shorten other laterals on the main stem to 2 or 3 buds.

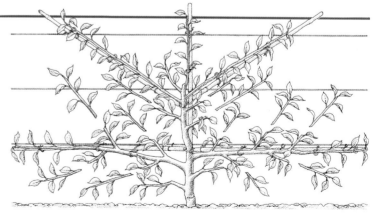

In summer encourage spurs to form by cutting back young laterals to 4–5 leaves. Training continues thus until all the branches are formed and aligned on the wires, after which each is pruned like a cordon.

Pears

Late-ripening fruits of 'Doyenné du Comice' warmed by the sun and beginning to turn colour.

France is generally regarded as the home of the classic pear, because fruits need long periods of warm sunny weather in summer to reach perfection. Planting in areas of high rainfall or cool summers is usually a gamble. Pears flower earlier than apples and in cooler gardens are often grown as wall-trained specimens to protect their unsurpassed displays of white blossom from spring frosts.

Dessert pears are the most popular for garden cultivation. A few cooking pears are available, producing hard fruits with little flavour until stewed. There are no very dwarfing rootstocks comparable to those used for apples so the choice is normally between Quince A, on which trees grow to a height of 3–6m (10–20ft), and the slightly less vigorous rootstock Quince C, which produces smaller trees but needs more fertile soil.

Sites

Pears have the same winter chilling requirements as apples, but as they flower 2–4 weeks earlier, protection from frost and cold winds at flowering time is even more crucial for good crops – avoid frost hollows and in exposed gardens plant in the shelter of a windbreak fence or hedge, or train them on a warm wall. Pears are also more prone to diseases such as scab in areas of high rainfall, but are less drought tolerant than apples and need plenty of humus in the ground, especially in light sandy soils. Work in heavy dressings of compost or decayed manure before planting, and lime soils that are below the preferred range of pH6–6.5.

Cultivation

Pears are planted, mulched and watered in the same way as for apples (see page 92). They need plenty of nitrogen in spring, so feed trees with a general fertilizer at the rate of 105g per sq m (3oz per sq yd) before spreading a mulch of compost or manure.

Thinning

A heavy set of fruit needs thinning in the same way as for apples (see page 93), although generally not so rigorously. Start after the natural drop in early summer and when the fruitlets have started to turn downwards; thin each cluster to two fruit, or one on younger and less leafy trees. Always gather up and destroy any fruitlets that fall prematurely, as these may contain pear midge larvae.

Pruning

For the formative pruning and training routines during the first four years, see page 90 (bushes, standards and half-standards), pages 92–3 (cordons), pages 94–5 (espaliers), below (dwarf pyramids), pages 98–9 (fans).

Training a dwarf pyramid pear

Aim to train a tapering tree with an open structure of nearly horizontal branches. Prune maidens 60cm (2ft) high to start, plums 120cm (4ft) high, and then prune each winter (to a bud opposite from the year before) to leave 23cm (9in) of new growth; cut main laterals similarly. In summer prune new growth on main laterals to 23cm (9in); leave shorter ones unpruned and cut their sideshoots to 8cm (3in) to form fruiting spurs. Shorten plum laterals by half in early spring, and summer-prune new growth to 6–8 leaves.

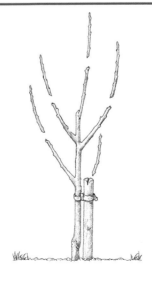

In the second winter cut back new leader growth to 23cm (9in). Cut back the laterals to the same length, to a downward facing bud (see left). The next summer prune main laterals to 23cm (9in). Shorten other sideshoots to 8cm (3in). Leave the leader unpruned (see right).

A group of fruits on the mid-season pear cultivar 'Seckle', showing the characteristic russetting.

When pruning cultivars with an upright form of growth, always cut back to just above an outward-facing bud to keep an open structure. You can encourage this by tying down young upright shoots, bending them gently outwards with lengths of string tied between the ends of the shoots and the main stem. Cultivars with a drooping habit are pruned to upward-facing buds to correct lax growth.

Annual maintenance pruning after forms have been trained is the same as for apples (see pages 93–4). A pear tree generally needs less pruning than an apple tree but will tolerate harder cutting back where necessary. Summer pruning can be carried out 1–2 weeks earlier than with apples.

Harvesting and storage

Timing is critical with pears, especially for early cultivars, because the fruits soon deteriorate if they are left on the tree for too long.

As soon as the skin colour of earlier pear cultivars starts to lighten in late summer or early autumn, you can test for near-ripeness by lifting a fruit in the palm of the hand and gently twisting its stalk, which should part fairly easily from the stem without tearing. Only a proportion of the crop reaches this stage of ripeness at a time, so it will be necessary to take several pickings from each tree. Gathered fruits can be laid out on a shelf in a cool shed, where they will keep for approximately 2–3 weeks; a few pears at

a time can be brought into warmth indoors for a day or two in order to finish ripening.

Late cultivars are left on the tree until nearly ripe and come away easily from the stem when tested. Store in single layers on shelves or in slatted boxes, in a shed or cupboard which, ideally, should be kept at 3–7°C (37–45°F). They will not all ripen together and may take days or several weeks before they are ready. Fruits should be checked regularly and when they start to colour or when the flesh near the stalk gives under slight pressure, bring them into warmth to mellow for a few days before eating.

Crop details Season: early to late autumn (until mid-winter from store). Rootstocks: Quince C (slightly dwarfing), Quince A (moderately vigorous), pear stock (very vigorous, for large trees only). Forms: standard, half-standard, bush, dwarf pyramid, fan, espalier, cordon. Spacing: standard, half-standard 6–9m (20–30ft); bush 3.7–4.5m (12–15ft); dwarf pyramid 1.5–2.2m (5–7ft); fan, espalier 4.5–5.5m (15–18ft); single cordon 75cm (30in) in rows 1.8m (6ft) apart. Average yield: standard 45–90kg (100–200lb); half-standard 22.5–55kg (50–120lb); bush 22.5–45kg (50–100lb); dwarf pyramid 3.5–5.5kg (8–12lb); fan, espalier 7–13.5kg (15–30lb); cordon 1.8–2.8kg (4–6lb).

Recommended cultivars In order of ripening; c=culinary, t=triploid; numbers indicate relative flowering time on a scale from 1 (very early) to 4 (late). 'Conference' and 'Seckle' are partly self-fertile, but all pears benefit from cross-pollination with one or more other cultivars with the same number or the next number above or below (check nursery catalogues for suitable partners, as even members of the same flowering group may be incompatible). 'Beth' 4, 'Williams' Bon Chrétien' 3, 'Merton Pride' (t) 3, 'Onward' 4, 'Beurré Superfin' 3, 'Louise Bonne of Jersey' 2, 'Beurré Hardy' 3, 'Conference' 3, 'Seckle' 2, 'Thompson's' 3, 'Doyenné du Comice' 4, 'Concorde' 4, 'Winter Nelis' 4, 'Joséphine de Malines' 3, 'Catillac' (c,t) 4.

Common pests and diseases Aphids, birds, pear midge, wasps, winter moth; brown rot, canker, fireblight, scab (see pages 110–11).

Thereafter, shorten the vertical leader each winter to leave 23cm (9in) of new growth. Summer-prune the upper laterals as in stage 2; prune the lower laterals to 5–6 leaves to limit their growth and promote fruiting sideshoots (spur or tip-bearing according to fruit type).

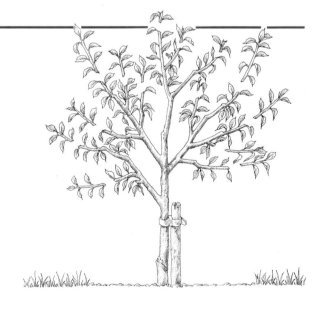

Plums

The variously coloured cultivars all have their devotees, but yellow plums were traditionally used for preserves.

Plums are popular and easily grown fruits. The many varied and worthwhile kinds differ from each other in their cultural needs and it would be difficult to grow an example of every kind in the same garden. Western European plums are a cool climate crop and include gages such as 'Jefferson', damsons (for example 'Prune') and the smaller bullaces and myrobalans, as well as conventional plums, some of which are sweet enough for dessert use while others are astringent and usually cooked.

Stone-fruits are pruned differently from 'pome' fruits like apples and pears, partly because of their vulnerability to disease and their tendency to heal wounds by exuding a gum that only appears in sufficient quantities when trees are actively growing. The available rootstocks are more vigorous than those of apples and pears, rendering plums unsuitable for intensive training as cordons and espaliers.

Sites

Plums need deep, moisture retentive soils and grow well on clay and slightly alkaline soils; they prefer a pH range of 6.5–7.2. As they flower early in spring, they need a sunny position with shelter from frost at flowering time so it is best to avoid exposed or low-lying sites. Gages need the most sun and should be trained as fans on warm walls in cooler gardens,

whereas damsons are very hardy and may be grown in boundary hedges or as windbreaks for less robust fruit. Make sure the site is weed-free because later deep cultivation can stimulate suckering, and add plenty of compost or manure to light soils.

Cultivation

Plant, water and mulch in the same way as for apples (see pages 92–3), and feed with extra nitrogen in early spring (see under Pears, page 96). Try to plant bare-rooted trees as early in the dormant season as possible to establish them well before their early flowering starts, and secure trees to stakes or supports with cushioned ties to avoid abrasions that might admit diseases.

Thinning

Crops need thinning early to avoid over-loading the brittle branches and to ensure good-sized fruits. Wait until after the natural drop in mid-summer and then use scissors to snip off the surplus to leave fruitlets about 5–8cm (2–3in) apart, slightly more for very large fruit.

Pruning

During the first four years, follow the formative training and pruning routines described on page 90 (bushes, standards and half-standards), pages 96–7 (dwarf pyramids) or below (fans), but carry out

---

Training a plum fan

Fix horizontal wires about 30cm (12in) apart. Cut the central leader from a feathered maiden to leave two strong branches. Tie in to 30-degree angle canes and shorten in early spring to 38cm (15in); continue tying in evenly spaced upward-growing sideshoots as they develop in summer, and remove all misplaced shoots. Early next spring shorten stems by one-third to encourage branching, and continue annually until all ribs are in place. Thin sideshoots to 15cm (6in) apart and tie in as fruiting shoots.

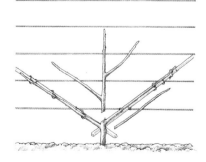

Prune to two good branches in early spring (apples and pears after planting) and tie in.

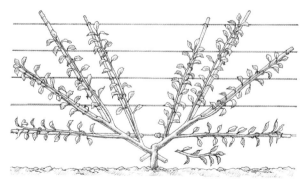

In summer the two original branches, which were shortened in spring to about 38cm (15in), produce strong shoots for training in as further ribs of the fan.

In a year when trees flower and set heavily, plums need to be thinned rigorously if dessert fruits are to achieve a good size.

winter pruning instructions in early spring to accelerate the healing of wounds. Larger cuts should be painted with a pruning compound as an insurance.

Keep pruning to a minimum on established bush, standard and half-standard trees. First remove any dead, diseased or broken branches in summer, then thin overcrowded branches. Continue pruning pyramids as described for apples (page 94) and fans as shown on page 101. Remove soil from around suckers and pull these off at their base (do not cut them as they will simply regrow more vigorously).

Overcropping and high winds may cause branches to break. Providing windbreaks, thinning heavy crops and supporting laden branches can reduce risks, but where injury does occur cut a broken branch back to its base or a strong fork, and protect cuts with wound paint.

Harvesting

Plums for cooking, freezing or bottling may be picked as soon as they develop a bloom. Leave all dessert fruits until they are fully ripe and soft to the touch; they will then part easily from the tree, gages and damson with their stalks and most plums without. Harvest several times, as the fruits do not all ripen together, but gather as many in as possible if heavy rain is forecast when they are nearly ripe, otherwise the skins may split. Use immediately or store for a few days in a cool dark place.

Crop details Season: late summer to mid-autumn. Rootstocks: Brompton (vigorous), Myrobalan B (vigorous), St Julien A (moderately vigorous), Pixy (semi-dwarfing). Forms: standard, half-standard, bush, pyramid, fan. Spacing: standard, half-standard, fan 4.5–6m (15–20ft); bush, pyramid 3–4m (10–13ft). Higher figures are for vigorous rootstocks. Average yield: standard 22.5–45kg (50–100lb); half-standard 13.5–27kg (30–60lb); bush, pyramid 13.5–22.5kg (30–50lb); fan 9–13.5kg (20–30lb).

Recommended cultivars In order of ripening: c=culinary, sf=self-fertile); numbers indicate relative flowering time on a scale from 1 (very early) to 5 (late). The pollination behaviour of cultivars varies widely: several are self-fertile, some partially self-fertile, but many are self-sterile. All benefit, however, from cross-pollination with another cultivar in the same or adjacent flowering group. Check catalogues for incompatibility between certain cultivars. 'Early Rivers' (c) 3, 'Czar' (c, sf) 3, 'Opal' (sf) 3, 'Pershore'/'Yellow Egg' (c,sf) 3, 'Oullin's Golden Gage' (sf) 4, 'Count Althann's Gage' 4, 'Early Transparent Gage' (sf) 4, 'Victoria' (sf) 3, 'Kirke's' 4, 'Jefferson' 1, 'Coe's Golden Drop' 2, 'Marjorie's Seedling' (c,sf) 5, '(Shropshire) Prune' (sf) 5.

Common pests and diseases Aphids, birds, wasps, codling moth, winter moth; bacterial canker, brown rot, silver leaf (see pages 110–11).

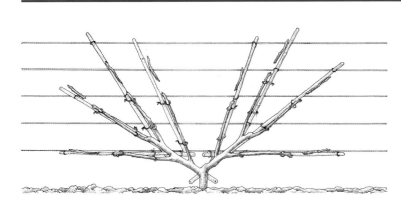

In spring of the next year shorten young branches as before, older ones by about one-third to a downward facing bud, to continue encouraging further branching to complete the framework.

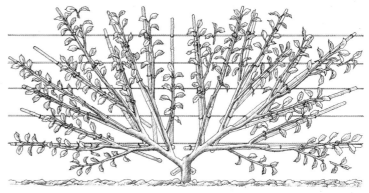

Late the same summer shorten to 45cm (18in) new extension growth and any other fruiting laterals on pruned branches. Spur-prune apple and pear fans as if each branch were a cordon.

Peaches

A choice fruit that needs cold winters, dry frost-free springs and warm sunny summers. In cool climates, plants are fan-trained on a warm wall for protection or grown in pots under glass. Nectarines, which are a slightly less hardy form of peach with smaller, smooth-skinned fruits, are grown in the same way.

Sites

As peaches flower very early, they need protection from early spring frosts and in cool gardens are usually grown on warm walls sheltered from cold winds. Most well-drained soils are suitable, if they are slightly acid (pH6.7–7). Manure sandy soils before planting; otherwise dig thoroughly and a week or so before planting dress with 105g per sq m (3oz per sq yd) of general fertilizer and half that amount of bonemeal.

Cultivation

Plant, water, mulch and feed as for apples (see pages 92–3). Water regularly before soils can dry out – this is especially important for plants growing on walls – and feed every fortnight with a high-potash liquid fertilizer as the fruits swell. Cover wall-trained trees with a polythene curtain or fine woven netting in winter and early spring to protect them from peach leaf curl and frost damage. In a cool season hand-pollinate by gently shaking the branches or dabbing the centres of open flowers with a soft thin paint brush or pad of cotton wool, every 2–3 days between bud-burst and the fall of petals.

Thinning

For large peaches, fruitlets need ruthless thinning, first to one per cluster when they are the size of hazelnuts and again when they are as large as walnuts to leave fruits 15–20cm (6–8in) apart; choose the closer spacing in warmer climates.

Pruning

For the first four years follow the formative training and pruning described for bushes (page 90) or fans (pages 98–9), and avoid winter pruning (see under Plum, pages 98–9).

Peaches fruit on young shoots produced the previous year. On established trees pinch out annually all new sideshoots on a fruiting stem when they have made 4–6 leaves, but leave one near its base to grow unchecked as a replacement shoot. Immediately the crop has been picked, prune out the fruited shoot to leave the replacement growing at its base.

Harvesting

When fruits feel soft near the base of the stalk, lift them in the palm of the hand and they will part freely from the stem if ripe. Take care not to bruise them or spoil their bloom. Fruit will keep for a week in a cool shed and surplus may be frozen or bottled.

Crop details Season: mid-summer to early autumn. Rootstocks: Brompton (vigorous), St Julien A (moderately vigorous); genetically dwarf plants are also available on their own roots for growing in pots. Forms: bush, fan. Spacing: bush 4.5–6m (15–20ft), fan 3.7–5.5m (12–18ft), higher figures for vigorous Brompton stocks. Average yield: bush 18–22.5kg (40–50lb), fan 9–13.5g (20–30lb).

Recommended cultivars In order of ripening (N= nectarine); cultivars are self-fertile, but hand-pollination may be necessary in a cold or wet season and is essential for plants grown under glass. 'Amsden June', 'Duke of York', 'Hale's Early', 'Early Rivers' (N), 'Peregrine', 'Lord Napier' (N), 'Redhaven', 'Humboldt' (N), 'Elruge' (N), 'Royal George', 'Saturne', 'Pineapple' (N), 'Bellegarde', 'Dymond'.

Common pests and diseases Aphids, birds, red spider mites; bacterial canker, grey mould, peach leaf curl (see pages 110–11).

Cherries

Modern dwarfing rootstocks allow cherry trees to be limited in height to about 3m (10ft). These are easier than large trees to protect from birds. Acid (pie or cooking) cherries are less attractive to predators and grow successfully on shady walls.

Sites

Deep well-drained soils with a pH of 6.7–7.5 are ideal; sandy soils should be well fortified with

The peach 'Peregrine' is one of the most successful cultivars for garden use, producing large fruits if ruthlessly thinned.

Because of their popularity with birds, cherries such as this 'Bigarreau Napoleon' have been difficult to grow profitably until the advent of modern dwarfing rootstocks.

compost or decayed manure during digging. Choose a sunny position for sweet cherries, sun or light shade for acid cultivars, with shelter from frost and cold wind at blossom time.

Cultivation

Plant, water and mulch in the same way as apples (see pages 92–3); do not wait until soils are dry before watering, as this may cause fruits to split. Thinning is unnecessary.

Pruning

Like peaches and plums, cherries are not spur-forming and, therefore, are not grown as cordons and espaliers, and only sweet cherries are grown as dwarf pyramids. For the first four years, follow the formative training and pruning routines described on page 90 (bushes, standards and half-standards), pages 96–7 (dwarf pyramids) or pages 98–9 (fans); avoid winter pruning (see under Plum, pages 98–9).

Established sweet cherries are pruned in the same way as plums (see pages 98–9 and Pruning an established fan, below), while acid cherries need renewal pruning as for peaches (see below).

Harvesting

Pick or cut the fruits with their stalks as soon as they are ripe and before they split. Use them immediately, or preserve by freezing or bottling.

Crop details Season: mid- and late summer. Rootstocks: Malling F12/1 (very vigorous), Colt (semi-dwarfing), Inmil (dwarfing), Camil (dwarfing). Forms: standard, half-standard, bush, pyramid, fan. Spacing on F12/1: standard, half-standard, bush 7.5–9m (25–30ft), fan 6m (20ft); spacing on Colt: bush 4.5m (15ft), pyramid 3.7m (12ft), fan 4.5m (15ft). Average yields: standard, half-standard 27–45kg (60–100lb); bush 13.5–22.5kg (30–50lb); pyramid, fan 9–13.5kg (20–30lb). Highest yields sweet cherries on F12/1, lowest acid cherries on Colt.

Recommended cultivars In order of ripening; a= acid, sf=self-fertile); numbers indicate relative flowering time on a scale from 1 (very early) to 6 (late). Only a few cultivars are self-fertile, while the majority have a complex pollination behaviour. These cultivars each need a partner that flowers at the same time but which belongs to a different compatibility group, so it is essential to select cherries from an informative catalogue that clearly identifies suitable pollinators. 'Early Rivers' 1, 'Roundel' 2, 'Merton Glory' 2, 'Merton Bigarreau' 3, 'Sunburst' (sf) 4, 'Bigarreau Gaucher' 5, 'Bradbourne Black' 5, 'Merton Favourite' 2, 'Stella' (sf) 4, 'Van' 3, 'Morello' (a, sf) 6, 'Nabella' (a, sf) 4.

Common pests and diseases Aphids (blackfly), birds, winter moth; bacterial canker, brown rot, silver leaf (see pages 110–11).

Pruning an established fan

Apple and pear fans are spur-pruned, each branch like a single cordon. Plums and sweet cherries fruit on old and new wood, and need only light pruning: in spring cut out new shoots growing away from or towards the wall, stop all other new shoots after 5–6 leaves in mid-summer and further shorten these to 3 leaves in early autumn. Peach and acid cherry shoots need annual renewal: cut out unwanted shoots in spring, leaving 1–2 to grow and replace the fruited shoots that were cut out after harvest.

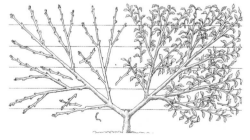

Early pruning   Late pruning
Plums and sweet cherries are first pruned at bud burst (left) when dead or diseased wood and misplaced shoots are removed. In mid-summer (right) stop new sideshoots at 5–6 leaves; shorten to 3 leaves post-harvest.

Early pruning   Late pruning
After flowering (left) prune peaches and acid cherries like plums; thin new sideshoots to leave 1–2 replacements, tying these in as they grow. Tidy misplaced shoots post-harvest (right); cut out spent stems; realign replacement shoots.

Soft fruit

GROWING SOFT FRUIT

Soft fruits are not difficult to look after and, unlike top fruits, do not require complicated pruning. Most crop early in life and stay a manageable size, making them easy to net or congregate in fruit cages as a deterrent against birds and squirrels.

Although the productive life of soft fruits is shorter than that of top fruits, they grow on their own roots and home propagation is simple provided plants are healthy and virus-free. Single specimens crop well on their own because most soft fruits are self-fertile, including those described here: strawberries, blackberries and hybrid berries, raspberries, blackcurrants, red and white currants and gooseberries.

Strawberries

Strawberries are short-term plants, usually rotated with vegetables in the kitchen garden. Summer-fruiting kinds yield their best crops the year after planting, but will bear for a further 2–3 seasons, in their last year producing small fruit ideal for jam-making. Some cultivars give a second, lighter crop in autumn. They are usually planted as rooted 'runners', plantlets that grow on long horizontal stems, but a few cultivars are grown from seed, sown in the same way as alpine strawberries.

Perpetual (everbearing or remontant) cultivars have a succession of small crops from mid-summer onwards, while alpine strawberries carry small, aromatic fruits on neat compact plants. Large-fruited kinds can be grown in pots under glass and may also be covered with cloches in spring to advance crops by 2–3 weeks (see Forcing strawberries, right). 'Day neutral' cultivars crop 12 weeks after planting if temperatures remain above 10°C (50°F).

Sites

A warm sunny position produces the best flavour and helps keep plants healthy; a little shade is acceptable for mid-season and late crops, but mould and mildew can be problems in a cool wet season. Shelter early crops from frost and cold winds. Most well-drained soils are suitable, except those that are very chalky (a slightly acid pH of 6–6.5 is ideal). Before planting dig in plenty of compost or decayed manure – allow about one large bucketful or 6.5kg per sq m (14lb per sq yd), and bury well below surface level. On poor soils you can also spread a dressing of general fertilizer at 105g per sq m (3oz per sq yd) just before planting.

Planting

Summer-fruiting cultivars must be planted in mid- or late summer to establish well and produce heavy crops the following year. Later plantings cannot sustain good crops in their first season and should be deblossomed in spring to conserve their vigour.

Propagating strawberries

Home propagation of strawberries is easy, but only worthwhile if plants are totally healthy; some gardeners maintain a stock bed of parent plants, sprayed regularly to keep them pest- and disease-free, and propagate from their runners. The first plantlets on runners make the strongest plants, for rooting either direct into the soil or in small pots of good compost set in the soil, as shown here. Plant well-rooted runners in fresh beds in late summer, or transfer to larger pots if they are to be used for forcing under glass in late winter.

Peg down runners with hoops of strong wire once the first plantlet develops.

Unless more plants are needed, pinch off runners beyond the first plantlet.

After a few weeks, sever rooted plantlets from their runners.

FORCING STRAWBERRIES

Pot-grown strawberry plants will fruit in the greenhouse in early spring (minimum temperature 7°C/45°F) or late spring without heat. In late summer root strong runners (see Propagating strawberries, below left) in 8cm (3in) pots, moving them on later into 15cm (6in) pots and stand outdoors in a sunny place. Water regularly and feed weekly until early autumn. House plants in batches from early winter onwards; keep them cool, damp down paths to maintain a humid atmosphere and give a high potash fertilizer weekly until flowers open. Keep the air dry during flowering and pollinate blooms by stroking their centres with a small soft brush; temperatures may now be raised to 15°C (60°F) for very early crops. Continue watering and feeding, and also damping down once the fruits appear. Keep in good light, and support fruit trusses with small sticks. Watch out for red spider mite, and ventilate freely to prevent mildew. Plant outdoors after fruiting.

Plant bare-rooted or pot-grown stock that is certified disease-free in soil where strawberries have not been grown during the previous 3–4 years. Plant firmly, with the base of the crown (the point where the leaves join the roots) at ground level, and water well immediately afterwards. Strawberries may be grown through black plastic to suppress weeds and conserve moisture: cut slits in the sheet at the required spacing and plant firmly, tucking the cut edges of the plastic around the crowns.

Water regularly, but avoid wetting fruits when they turn colour; plants in plastic mulches need watering only in very dry weather. When fruits first appear on plants grown in bare soil, tuck straw or strawberry mats round them to keep the fruits from touching the ground; do not mulch until the soil has warmed up. Remove all runners unless needed for propagation and protect ripening fruits with nets.

Harvesting

Pick fruits, complete with stalks, when they are fully coloured, and use immediately. Remove and destroy damaged fruits as these can attract fungal diseases. Check rows every 1–2 days as fruits ripen quickly, especially in hot weather. Surplus fruit can be bottled, made into jam or puréed for freezing.

As soon as a crop is cleared, cut down the foliage to about 5cm (2in) above the crowns using shears or a rotary mower for large areas. This, along with any weeds, runners and straw, should be composted, or burnt if there is any sign of disease. Feed plants with a general fertilizer, applied at the rate 105g per sq m (3oz per sq yd) and watered in if the weather is dry.

Propagation

A few new plants can be grown separately as stock plants to supply plantlets for future rows, or you can take strong plantlets from healthy cropping plants (see Propagating strawberries, left). The advantage of having dedicated stock plants is that they can be kept pest- and disease-free with a preventive spray routine. Where there is any doubt, however, buy fresh certified plants whenever you are making new

plantations. Only propagate from your own runners once or twice before restocking.

Leave plantlets to root naturally in the soil, or peg them down to root in small pots of compost – this is the best way to provide plants for forcing in the greenhouse. All healthy plantlets can be used, but the strongest crowns develop from the first plantlet on each runner, that is the one nearest the parent plant. Transfer to the new bed, well away from existing rows, as soon as plantlets are well-rooted.

Perpetuals and alpines

Perpetual strawberries are planted in autumn, winter or spring. Remove the first flush of flowers and then allow to crop, covering late fruit with cloches in cold areas. Replant every two years with runners or fresh stock. Alpines are best raised from seed, sown under glass at 18–21°C (65–70°F) in autumn or early spring, but healthy plants may also be divided and some cultivars produce runners. Water freely in dry weather and feed every fortnight with high-potash liquid fertilizer as soon as flowers appear.

Crop details Season: late spring to mid-summer (summer-fruiting); mid-summer to mid-autumn (perpetual, alpine). Spacing: summer, perpetual 45cm (18in) in rows 75cm (30in) apart; alpine 30cm (1ft) in rows 75cm (30in) apart, or 45cm (18in) square. Average yield: 225–675g (½–1½lb) per plant. Productive life: summer 3–4 years; alpine, perpetual 2 years. Propagation: rooted runners (summer, perpetual, some alpine), division (alpine), seed (alpine, some summer).

Recommended cultivars Summer-fruiting: early 'Cambridge Vigour', 'Elvira', 'Hedley', 'Honeoye'; mid-season 'Hapil', 'Providence', 'Royal Sovereign', 'Tamella', 'Tenira'; late 'Cambridge Late Pine', 'Domanil'. Perpetual: 'Aromel', 'Gento', 'Rapella'. Alpine: 'Alexandria', 'Baron Solemacher', 'Delicious', 'Fraises des Bois'.

Common pests and diseases Aphids, birds, red spider mite, slugs; grey mould, powdery mildew, viruses (see pages 110–11).

Most brambles mature over several weeks and so need harvesting regularly. These blackberry trusses are part-way through their season, with more berries ready for picking and others still ripening.

Brambles

Blackberries and hybrid berries are valuable for their late, heavy crops. Older kinds need plenty of room for their long arching canes that are often very spiny, although new compact cultivars can be trained like raspberries. Unarmed brambles may be trained on pillars and arches, but otherwise plants need training on a system of posts and wires (see Training blackberries, below); rampant cultivars make excellent hedges and windbreaks.

Sites

Plants flower late and so frost is rarely a problem. Hybrids need more warmth than blackberries, but both kinds thrive in full sun or light shade. Most soils are suitable if deeply dug and well-manured, with a pH in the range 6–6.5.

Cultivation

Plant firmly in winter or early spring, at the same depth as plants grew before, and shorten canes to about 23–25cm (9–10in) high. Spread a 75g (3oz) dressing of general fertilizer or bonemeal round each plant and rake in. In subsequent seasons mulch each plant in late winter with compost or decayed manure, or feed as at planting time. Water in very dry weather. Train canes evenly as they grow. Canes are produced one year and fruit the next, after which they are cut out at ground level to make way for new canes, in the same way as raspberries (see Training raspberries, below right).

Harvesting

Gather ripe fruits regularly, gently twisting them from their plugs. Surplus fruits may be frozen, bottled or made into preserves.

Propagation

Layer tips of healthy canes in summer, bending each one so that the end can be buried in a hole in the ground. Firm in place, and leave until rooted.

Crop details Season: hybrids mid- and late summer, blackberries late summer until the first frosts. Spacing: 1.2–4.5m (4–15ft). Average yield: 4.5–13.5kg (10–30lb). Productive life: up to 20 years.

Recommended cultivars c=compact, v=vigorous, th=thornless. Blackberries: early 'Black Satin', 'Waldo' (c); late 'Ashton Cross', 'Fantasia' (v), 'Himalaya Giant' (v), 'Loch Ness' (c), 'Oregon Thornless' (th). Hybrids: 'Boysenberry', 'King's Acre Berry', 'Loganberry', 'Marionberry' (v), 'Silvanberry' (v), 'Tayberry', 'Thornless Loganberry' (th), 'Thornless Youngberry' (th), 'Tummelberry'.

Common pests and diseases Aphids, birds, raspberry beetles; grey mould, viruses (see pages 110–11).

Training blackberries

Black- and hybrid berries crop on the previous year's stems; at the same time new canes are developing, which will bear the next year's fruit. For convenience, training systems keep these two generations apart until the fruit is harvested. There are several methods, all requiring the support of strong posts and wires, and some needing more space than others. The arrangement shown here is the best for smaller gardens, and confines the young canes in a central bundle, clear of the fruiting canes which are fanned out in a 'V'.

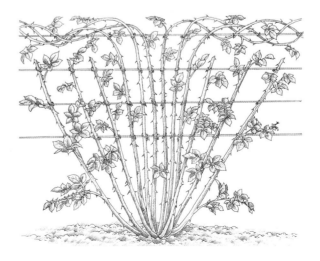

In the first autumn fan out and tie in the canes, cutting off their tips between the top two wires. The next summer train the new canes up the centre and along the top wire. Cut out the older, fruited canes and replace with the young canes, retied and trimmed to make a new fan.

Raspberries

There are two main kinds of raspberry, summer-fruiting which crop heavily in mid-summer and autumn-fruiting with a longer season from late summer until the first frosts. Yellow, black and purple cultivars are available with distinctive flavours. All kinds benefit from post-and-wire support (see Training raspberries, below).

Sites

Raspberries are a cool climate crop, growing in sunny or lightly shaded positions (the latter preferable in hot gardens). Soils should be slightly acid (pH6–7), well-drained but rich in humus, so dig in compost or decayed manure before planting.

Cultivation

Plant dormant canes, either bought or dug up as suckers from established rows, in autumn or early winter, a little deeper than the previous soil level mark, and firm. Cut back canes to about 23cm (9in) high and trim this stump to ground level once vigorous new growth appears. Mulch each spring with decayed manure or apply 105g per sq m (3oz per sq yd) of general fertilizer. Keep plants weed-free and pull up surplus canes more than 20cm (8in) away from the rows. Water freely in dry weather but not while the fruit is ripening.

Train in canes as they grow, spacing them about 10cm (4in) apart on the wires. Canes of summer-fruiting cultivars grow one year and fruit the next, after which exhausted canes are cut back to ground level for replacement by the current season's growth. Canes of autumn cultivars appear in spring and bear fruit the same year; exhausted canes are cut back in late winter just before new growth appears.

Harvesting

Pick fruits daily in the same way as for brambles.

Propagation

Dig up and replant suckers growing well away from the main rows, but only if they are healthy.

Crop details Season: mid-summer until the first frosts. Spacing: 45cm (18in) in rows 1.8m (6ft) apart. Average yield: 900g (2lb) per 30cm (1ft) run. Productive life: 10 years.

Recommended cultivars Summer-fruiting: 'Augusta', 'Glencoe' (purple), 'Glen Moy', 'Glen Prosen', 'Golden Everest' (yellow), 'Leo', 'Malling Jewel', 'Starlight' (black). Autumn-fruiting: 'Autumn Bliss', 'Fallgold' (yellow), 'Heritage', 'September'.

Common pests and diseases Aphids, birds, raspberry beetles; grey mould, spur blight/cane blight, viruses (see pages 110–11).

Ripening raspberries need checking frequently, daily in hot weather, as they do not stay in peak condition for long.

Training raspberries

As with blackberries, raspberries produce new canes while the previous season's are bearing fruit. This makes access difficult if canes are trained on a single row of posts and wires, whereas using two parallel rows allows the different generations of growth to be kept apart; plants are aligned down the central space between the rows. Fruiting canes are fanned out and trained on one row of wires, while the new stems are leaned against the other row and tied in as they grow, and in this way do not cause overcrowding.

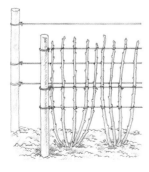

Remove exhausted canes in autumn, leaving a row of young stems fanned out and tied in.

Train the strongest new canes on the vacant row of wires; cut surplus canes to the ground.

After harvest prune fruited canes to the ground; continue tying in new rows of canes.

Blackcurrants

Blackcurrants prefer cool climates, although some cultivars flower very early and may be damaged by frosts unless protected by windbreaks or a fine net cover at blossom time. They make sturdy, robust bushes and are greedy feeders, but repay lavish conditions with heavy crops of fruit. Their main disorder is reversion virus which is transmitted by the big bud mite; yields from affected bushes dwindle gradually, and most bushes succumb to this unless replaced with certified stock every 8–10 years (see page 110 for prevention and control).

While producing some of the largest fruits, the blackcurrant 'Laxton's Giant' has lax growth that requires careful pruning to encourage a more upright habit.

Sites

A sunny position sheltered from frost and cold winds is best; plants tolerate shade but do not crop so heavily. Most soils are suitable if deeply dug, well manured and slightly acid (pH6.5). Make sure the ground is weed-free, because the multi-stemmed bushes are difficult to weed once established.

Cultivation

Choose two-year-old bushes that are certified free from disease and with at least three strong stems, and set them about 5cm (2in) deeper than the previous soil level mark. Plant firmly, taking care with the lower buds, then cut down shoots to 5cm (2in) high. Top-dress each bush annually in early spring with 115g (4oz) of general fertilizer and mulch with compost or decayed manure about 8cm (3in) deep. In dry weather give 23 litres (5gal) of water every 10 days to each bush, except when the fruit is ripening.

Pruning

The best fruit is borne on stems that were produced the previous year (see Pruning blackcurrants, below). Cutting back after planting will produce several strong stems which will fruit the following year. The second winter after planting cut out any weak stems and from the third winter onwards cut out one-quarter to one-third of the older (and darker) fruited stems. This, combined with annual heavy feeding, will maintain a succession of young growth to keep bushes vigorous. Ideally, no stems that are over four years old should be retained.

Harvesting

Gather complete bunches when ripe, about a week after the currants turn blue-black. Some cultivars retain fruit longer than others but most early kinds need prompt harvest. Surplus fruit can be frozen, bottled, dried or turned into juice and preserves.

Propagation

Take hardwood cuttings in autumn (see Taking hardwood cuttings, page 109), retaining all the buds to induce shoots to grow from below ground.

Pruning blackcurrants

Bushes will crop on both old and young stems, but the latter bear best quality fruit. Pruning aims to keep bushes rejuvenated by replacing some old wood each year with vigorous new growth. Start with a multi-stemmed bush, cutting it back after planting to encourage renewal from the base and feeding this growth lavishly each spring. In later years prune out after harvest about one-third of dark, old stems in favour of new, paler ones, cutting them either to ground level or to a low young sideshoot.

Plant new bushes a little deeper than previously and prune 2.5cm (1in) above ground; cut out any weak low shoots.

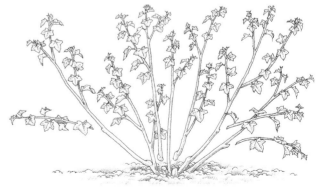

Prune mature bushes after harvest, cutting out low, thin or damaged shoots, together with a quarter to one-third of older stems.

White currants such as 'White Versailles' are colour variants of red currants and are treated in the same way, but they possess a distinctive flavour of their own.

Crop details Season: mid- to late summer. Spacing: 1.2–1.8m (4–6ft) each way, according to vigour. Average yield: 4.5–7kg (10–15lb). Productive life: 10 years.

Recommended cultivars 'Baldwin', 'Ben More', 'Ben Nevis', 'Ben Sarek', 'Blackdown', 'Goliath', 'Jet' 'Laxton's Giant', 'Seabrook's Black', 'The Raven', 'Wellington XXX'.

Common pests and diseases Aphids, big bud mite, birds, winter moth; grey mould, powdery mildew, viruses (see pages 110–11).

Red and white currants

Red and white currants are simple, reliable crops to grow and, unlike the closely related blackcurrants whose stems are progressively renewed, plants develop a permanent framework of branches that may be trained ornamentally as cordons, standards and fans, as well as open-centred bushes.

Sites

A warm position in full sun or light shade is suitable, with protection from high winds which damage the brittle branches. Frosty sites are best avoided, although bushes are very hardy and grow successfully on cool shaded walls. Any fertile, well-drained soil is acceptable, but light sandy soils should be fortified with plenty of compost or manure, together with a dressing of rock potash at 135g per sq m (4oz per sq yd). Aim for a slightly acid pH of 6.7–7.

Cultivation

Choose plants with a clear single stem or 'leg' about 10–15cm (4–6in high) and 3–5 evenly spaced shoots above this height; standards should have a clear leg 90–108cm (3–3½ft) high. Remove any suckers present at planting time or that appear later. Plant firmly in autumn or early winter, staking standards and tying other trained forms to support wires. Dress with potassium sulphate or rock potash, 50g (2oz) per bush, in late winter and mulch in spring with compost or manure. Water well in dry weather.

Pruning

For the first few years, follow the formative training and pruning routines described on page 90 (bushes and standards), pages 98–9 (fans), page 108 (cordons). Prune established bushes and standards as below, cordons and fans as described on page 109. The fruit develops on short spurs produced by cutting back sideshoots, in summer to about 4–5 leaves and again in winter, shortening to 1–2 buds.

Harvesting

Gather and use ripe fruits as for blackcurrants. Some cultivars retain their ripe fruit for several weeks, especially where grown on shady walls.

Pruning red and white currants

Red and white currants grown as bushes are trained and pruned to maintain an open-centred arrangement of evenly spaced branches. Prune bushes in winter, but if birds tend to attack the buds, wait until healthy buds are about to burst and can be distinguished from any that are damaged. Always remove completely any low-growing sideshoots within 10–15cm (4–6in) of the ground to keep the main stem clean, and prune other branches to an outward facing bud to preserve the open centre of the bush.

Immediately after planting a bush shorten all stems by about half their length.

In winter prune main stems by half their new growth, shorter sideshoots to one bud.

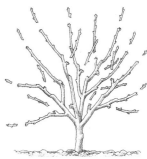

Shorten each established main stem by 5–8cm (2–3in), and sideshoots to one bud.

107

Propagation

Take hardwood cuttings in autumn (see Taking hardwood cuttings, below), removing all but the top 3–4 buds at planting time to ensure a clear leg.

Crop details Season: mid- to late summer. Forms: bush, dwarf standard, fan, cordon. Spacing: bush, standard 1.2–1.5m (4–5ft); fan 1.8m (6ft); single cordon 30cm (1ft). Average yield: bush, standard, fan 2.8–4.5kg (6–10lb); single cordon 900g (2lb). Productive life: 15–20 years.

Recommended cultivars Red: 'Fay's Prolific', 'Jonkheer van Tets', 'Laxton's No 1', 'Red Lake', 'Redstart', 'Rondom', 'Stanza'. White: 'White Grape', 'White Pearl'/'White Transparent', 'White Versailles'.

Common pests and diseases Aphids, birds, sawfly larvae; coral spot, grey mould (see pages 110–11).

Gooseberries

When their immature berries are thinned and used for cooking, gooseberries supply the first soft fruits of the season. They revel in cool moist surroundings, although they also need sunshine to produce their full flavour, which varies according to the colour. Fruits are smooth or hairy and red, yellow, green or white according to cultivar. Connoisseurs distinguish differences between the hundreds of heritage cultivars, a legacy of former competitive breeding and cultivation for shows. Most kinds have vicious spines, but firm open pruning can reduce discomfort at harvest time.

Sites

Gooseberries prefer a sunny position, but will tolerate light shade and may be grown on a cool wall. Shelter from strong winds will prevent injury to young shoots. Soil requirements and preparation are similar to those for red currants.

Cultivation

Always choose plants with a clear leg about 10–15cm (4–6in) high, as stools (multi-stemmed plants) are difficult to weed and prune without injury from the thorns. Plant, water and feed in the same way as red currants. Gooseberries need high potash levels, and scorching of leaf margins is a common indication of deficiency. Mulching helps to keep soils moist, an important precaution against mildew, and suppresses weeds. Do not water heavily when the fruit is nearly ripe as this can cause the skins to split.

Thinning

Fruits often set heavily, and these should be thinned if you want large dessert gooseberries. From late spring onwards remove alternate fruits and thin clusters to single berries; use the unripe thinnings for

Training a cordon gooseberry

Cordon gooseberries produce high quality fruit on space-saving plants that are pruned in winter and summer to restrain growth to a single stem with short fruiting spurs. Tie in the central leader as it develops and keep the bottom 10–15cm (4–6in) clear of sideshoots. The leader is shortened to about 15cm (6in) of new growth each winter until full grown, when it is cut back to a single bud. After the first year new sideshoots are pruned each summer to 4–5 leaves and further shortened in winter to 2.5cm (1in), just beyond a bud.

After planting cut the leader by half, sideshoots to 2.5cm (1in).

Every summer tie in the leader; prune new sideshoots to 4–5 leaves.

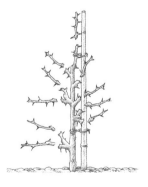

In winter cut sideshoots as in year 1; prune the leader according to height.

Powdery mildew annually affects gooseberry bushes in many gardens, but the cultivar 'Invicta' is disease-resistant and therefore a sensible choice wherever the problem recurs.

cooking. Fruit on young vigorous stems can be thinned more severely to leave specimens 5–8cm (2–3in) apart for the largest dessert berries.

Harvesting

Net the ripening fruits as they are very popular with birds. Gather fruits when they are fully coloured and slightly soft to the touch; you will need to go over plants several times as fruits do not all mature together. Surplus fruits may be frozen, bottled or made into preserves.

Pruning

To reduce the risks of mildew (encouraged by congested growth) and also facilitate picking among the thorny stems, it is important to maintain a well-spaced framework of branches, especially on bushes – traditional wisdom recommends keeping an open centre in which a gardener's wide-brimmed hat may be rested comfortably. Some cultivars have a very lax habit and their stems should always be pruned to an upward-facing bud to counter this.

For formative training and pruning, see page 90 (bushes and standards), pages 98–9 (fans) or page 108 (cordons). Thereafter cordons and fans are spur-pruned in summer and winter in the same way as red currants. The simplest way to maintain bushes and standards is to prune immediately after harvest, first cutting out dead, diseased or over-crowded main stems and any that are too low or cross the centre of the bush. Long sideshoots are shortened to about five leaves, while old branches can be cut out for replacement by strong young stems.

Propagation

Root hardwood cuttings as for red currants, but take a few extra as success rates are not always high (see Taking hardwood cuttings, below).

Crop details Season: mid- to late summer (unripe fruit for cooking late spring to early summer). Forms: bush, dwarf standard, fan, cordon. Spacing: bush, standard 1.2–1.5m (4–5ft); fan 1.8m (6ft); single cordon 45cm (18in). Average yield: bush, standard, fan 2.3–2.5kg (5–6lb); single cordon 450–900g (1–2lb). Productive life: 15–20 years.

Recommended cultivars g=green, r=red, w=white, y=yellow, M=partial mildew resistance. 'Broom Girl' (y), 'Crown Bob' (r, M), 'Early Sulphur' (y), 'Golden Drop' (y), 'Gunner' (g), 'Hino Red' (r, M), 'Hino Yellow' (y, M), 'Invicta' (g, M), 'Jubilee' (y) 'Keepsake' (g), 'Lancashire Lad' (r, M), 'Lancer' (g), 'Langley Gage' (w), 'Leveller' (y), 'London' (r), 'Lord Derby' (r), 'May Duke' (r), 'Whinham's Industry' (r), 'White Lion' (w), 'Whitesmith' (w).

Common pests and diseases Aphids, birds, sawfly larvae; powdery mildew, leaf spot (see pages 110–11).

Taking hardwood cuttings

Soft fruits such as gooseberries and black-, red and white currants grow readily from hardwood cuttings prepared in early or mid-autumn from well-ripened shoots. Cut off the top at an angle above a bud and trim the cutting to about 23–30cm (9–12in) long with a straight cut at the bottom. Leave all buds intact to aid rooting, but trim any buds or shoots from the lower three-quarters of rooted gooseberry, red currant or white currant cuttings when lifted the following autumn; this will ensure a clear leg on future plants.

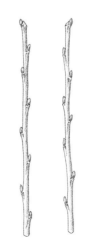

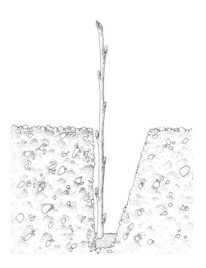

Use a spade to dig a narrow, V-shaped trench about 15cm (6in) deep in a sheltered, well-drained bed; on heavy soils spread sharp sand in the bottom. Stand cuttings upright in the trench to half their length and tread the soil firm around them. Cuttings will be rooted and ready to transplant by the next autumn.

Pest and symptoms	Principal fruit crops affected	Prevention	Control
Big bud mite (currant gall mite) Abnormally large buds that fail to open and contain minute grubs which spread reversion virus.	Blackcurrants.	Pick off and burn affected buds in winter and early spring.	Spray with derris or carbendazim 3 times at 14–day intervals starting at budburst, to kill migrating mites.
Birds Various kinds attack both buds and ripening fruit.	All fruits.	Net individual plants or group inside a fruit cage.	
Blackfly (black bean aphid) Colonies of small black flies, winged or wingless, on the undersides of leaves.	Cherries.	Grow flowers that attract hoverflies, their chief predators.	Spray with derris, insecticidal soap, pyrethrum or pirimicarb.
Codling moth Small white caterpillars burrowing to the centre of fruits where they feed.	Apples, plums, occasionally pears.	Suspend proprietary pheromone traps in trees in late spring.	Spray with pyrethrum or fenitrothion in early summer and again 3 weeks later.
Greenfly (aphid) Colonies of small green or pink flies, winged and wingless, on the undersides of leaves, causing distortion and spreading viruses.	All fruit crops are vulnerable.	As for blackfly.	As for blackfly.
Pear midge Small grubs in blackened fruitlets falling in mid-summer.	Pears.	Collect and burn affected fruits promptly.	Spray with fenitrothion or pirimiphos-methyl when buds show white colour.
Raspberry beetle Small white grubs inside ripening fruits.	Raspberries, brambles.	None.	Spray with derris, pyrethrum or fenitrothion, brambles when flowers first open, raspberries when first fruits turn pink.
Red spider mite Microscopic insects causing yellowing leaves and fine webs; common in dry seasons.	Most fruits, especially strawberries and top fruit.	Occasionally spray foliage forcefully with water during drought.	Difficult, owing to resistance. Spray with derris, insecticidal soap or pirimiphos-methyl, 3–4 times at 5–day intervals.
Sawfly Small spotted caterpillars feeding on leaves, rapidly causing defoliation if unchecked.	Gooseberries, red currants.	Encourage insectivorous birds into the garden.	Check plants regularly between mid-spring and late summer; pick off caterpillars by hand or spray with derris, pyrethrum, fenitrothion or pirimiphos-methyl.
Slugs Soft-bodied molluscs, leaving a slimy trail and attacking all parts of plants, especially fruits.	Strawberries.	Clear away weeds and mulching material after cropping.	Spread pellets containing metaldehyde or methiocarb before laying straw or mats round plants.
Wasps Black-and-yellow flying insects that attack ripening fruit.	Most top fruits.	Trap by hanging jars of sweetened water in tree branches; enclose choice fruits in paper, net or muslin bags.	Track down the nests and destroy colonies.
Winter moth Pale green caterpillars feeding on leaves, blossom and fruitlets in spring.	Top fruits.	Attach grease bands to tree trunks and stakes between autumn and spring to trap female moths.	Spray caterpillars with derris, pyrethrum, pirimiphos-methyl or the bacterial agent *Bacillus thuringiensis*.
Woolly aphids Colonies of small flies covered with a fluffy white waxy coating, chiefly on bark and young shoots.	Apples.	None.	Scrape off local colonies or paint with methylated spirits; spray forcefully with derris, dimethoate or pirimicarb.

Disease and symptoms	Principal fruit crops affected	Prevention	Control
Bacterial canker Round spots on leaves develop into holes; elongated cankers on stems ooze droplets of liquid; leaves and flowers wither.	Apple, cherries, peaches, plums.	None.	Cut out cankered branches, treat wounds with canker paint and burn diseased material; spray foliage with copper fungicide in late summer and twice more at monthly intervals.
Bitter pit Sunken pits on surface, with small brown patches scattered through flesh, and a bitter taste; a symptom of calcium deficiency, often on young leaves.	Apples.	Water regularly in dry weather and mulch trees; maintain suitable pH levels.	Trees may be sprayed with calcium nitrate every 10 days in summer and autumn, but condition is usually seasonal and disappears if preventive treatment is followed.
Brown rot Soft brown areas of decay on fruits, eventually spreading with concentric rings of creamy white pustules.	Top fruit.	Remove and burn wizened fruit left on trees after harvest, together with all fallen fruit and leaves.	Pick off and burn affected fruits at first signs.
Canker Sunken discoloured patches on stems surrounded by rings of loose flaky bark; encircled shoots die back.	Apples, pears.	Control woolly aphids and avoid leaving ragged pruning wounds.	Cut affected areas back to clean wood; treat wounds with canker paint and burn diseased material.
Coral spot Shoots die back and develop bright pink pustules.	Red currants.	Clear away all prunings.	Cut back affected stems to clean wood and burn.
Fireblight Leaves and shoots wilt and turn brown as if scorched; affected shoots ooze in spring.	Pears, occasionally apples.	Check hawthorn hedges in rural areas as these are prime hosts of the disease.	Prune locally affected stems back to clean wood that shows no internal discoloration, dipping tools in disinfectant before, during and after use to prevent spread of disease; badly affected plants must be dug up and burned.
Grey mould *(Botrytis)* Flowers or ripening fruits rot and become covered with a greyish-brown fluffy fungal growth; often more prevalent in a cool wet season.	Most soft fruits and peaches.	Pick off damaged fruits and clear away any that have fallen prematurely; prune to ensure good air circulation; avoid wetting ripening fruit when watering.	Clear and burn affected fruits; spraying fruits is not advisable but other affected parts may be treated with carbendazim or thiophanate-methyl.

Disease and symptoms	Principal fruit crops affected	Prevention	Control
Leaf spot Dark brown spots, eventually spreading to whole leaf which then falls off; causes diminished yields.	Most fruits, especially gooseberries and currants.	Avoid wetting foliage when watering, and keep plants well-fed and in good health.	Pick off and burn affected leaves; spray with copper fungicide at 10–day intervals and feed plants on poor soils.
Peach leaf curl Red blisters on leaves that later turn powdery white and fall prematurely.	Peaches.	Shelter fan-trained trees with polythene sheeting in winter to prevent spores landing; give routine sprays of copper fungicide in mid-winter and again a fortnight later and also in autumn just before leaf fall.	Pick off infected leaves before they turn white and spray as for leaf spot.
Powdery mildew Greyish-white powdery fungal patches on fruits and leaves; affected shoots are often stunted and may die back.	Apples, pears, blackcurrants, gooseberries, strawberries.	Water and mulch to prevent drought at the roots; avoid growing susceptible plants on dry sites or grow resistant cultivars of fruits such as gooseberries; apply precautionary sprays of systemic fungicide.	Prune out and burn affected shoots; spray with a suitable fungicide according to type of fruit.
Scab Dark spots on leaves and fruit, spreading to form ugly patches; affected leaves fall prematurely.	Apples, pears.	Encourage good air circulation by avoiding overcrowded stems; gather and burn fallen leaves in autumn.	Remove cracked and scabbed shoots or fruits, and spotted leaves, and burn; spray with benomyl, carbendazim or thiophanate-methyl every 2 weeks from budburst until mid-summer.
Silver leaf Leaves assume silvery hue and then turn brown, starting usually on a single branch which eventually dies, leaving the infection to spread; infected wood shows central dark stain when cut.	Plums, cherries, occasionally other top fruits, currants, gooseberries.	Prune stone fruits during the growing season when wounds heal quickly, and seal cuts with pruning paint; avoid wounding or pruning plants unnecessarily; clear and burn all dead wood and prunings.	Cut back affected shoots to clean wood at least 15cm (6in) beyond stained tissues, paint the wounds and disinfect tools; dig up and burn plants if bracket fungi grow on the stems.
Spur blight/cane blight Dark patches around leaf nodes or just above ground level, eventually turning silver-grey and causing die-back.	Raspberries, occasionally some hybrid berries.	Feed and water plants to maintain strong healthy growth; prune to reduce over-crowding.	Cut out and burn diseased growth, and spray with copper fungicide.
Viruses A wide range of disorders, caused by micro-organisms and spread by various insect pests or human contact; symptoms are distorted growth, leaf mottling or streaking, and reduced yields.	Most crops are susceptible, especially strawberries, raspberries and blackcurrants.	Plant certified stocks and tolerant or resistant cultivars; propagate only from healthy plants; replace regularly with new certified stock; do not replant on the same site; control insect pests.	Dig up and burn affected plants and disinfect all tools used.

Care with routine preventive measures and a prompt response where trouble occurs are crucial to the successful cultivation and cropping of fruit plants. It is important here, for example, to control the red spider mite affecting the marrow plants trained on the tunnel nearby and to remove their dead leaves, as these problems can also threaten the health of the espalier apple trees.

HERBS IN THE KITCHEN GARDEN

Herbs enhance our lives in numerous ways, their leaves, flowers or roots supplying us with unique flavours, perfumes and medicinal remedies. The range and diversity of herbal species are so vast that complete gardens are often dedicated to their cultivation as both ornamental and practical plants. Culinary herbs have been grown for centuries – used for flavouring, preserving and garnishing food – and many of them merit space in the kitchen garden, planted either as a decorative and aromatic border or as crops among the vegetables.

Whether grown with other crops or gathered together in a garden of their own, herbs are attractive plants, especially when in flower. Here, lavender edges the gravel paths, while prostrate cultivars of thyme and marjoram produce mats of dense foliage and flowers. Fragrant standard roses stand like sentinels around a young olive tree in its terracotta pot.

113

Using culinary herbs

Cooks generally agree that culinary herbs such as mint, sage and thyme have the best aroma and flavour when freshly gathered, so including them in the kitchen garden makes good sense. Happily, most are ornamental garden plants, especially those cultivars selected for outstanding colour or habit. As their needs are modest, too, a basic collection will provide both aesthetic appeal and essential ingredients in return for simple routine attention.

Although they are often grouped together, every herb grows best in situations resembling its native habitat. Plants may be annual, biennial or perennial, some are aromatic woody shrubs requiring hot sunshine and light well-drained soils, while others are fast-growing leafy plants needing plenty of water and nourishment, and often tolerating light shade. Few can survive in water-logged soils or heavily shaded positions, however.

Provided their basic requirements are satisfied, where to grow the herbs is a matter for personal choice. They may be planted in ornamental pots, gathered together in a bed near the kitchen door, or integrated into flower borders. In the kitchen garden perennials are best given a border to themselves, edged with a compact herb such as thyme, while annuals may be sown in the same way as vegetables.

Preparing the soil

The site must be free from perennial weeds, for these are difficult to remove once herbs are in place. Fork out all weed fragments or spray with a suitable herbicide, and then dig over the site, at the same time adding plenty of garden compost (but not manure, which may be too rich). Free drainage is essential for most herbs, so make any necessary improvements at this stage (see page 16); on heavy clay soils you could create a raised herb bed. There is no need to add fertilizers, but the soil should be raked to a fine, level tilth before planting.

Sowing and planting

Although most herb species can be started from seed, perennials are normally bought as container-grown specimens for planting at any time, but preferably in spring. Arrange the potted plants on the soil first to ensure adequate distances between them and to check the overall appearance. Water the pots and allow them to drain before planting, and water the whole bed afterwards to settle the soil.

Seeds may be sown in drills outdoors, small amounts in a separate seedbed and larger quantities of popular herbs such as parsley in rows among the vegetables, or they can be started under glass. This is

Propagating herbs

Many perennial herbs can be propagated from the soft tips of shoots, prepared as short cuttings. Trim the cutting just below a leaf node and remove the lower leaves. Insert in a pot of moist cutting compost and keep warm inside a plastic bag to maintain humidity. Woody perennials can be propagated by mound layering. In spring, heap moist, well-broken soil over the crown of the plant to cover all but the ends of the branches. These will root as layers by the autumn and may be detached for potting up or transplanting.

Use strong healthy tips, cut to length just before inserting in compost.

Earth up woody perennials with moist soil in spring.

In autumn scrape off the soil, sever rooted branches and pot up or transplant.

Routine care

Keep herbs weed-free, either by hoeing and hand-weeding, or by mulching. An organic mulch of compost or bark is ideal for moisture-loving species and on very light soils. On heavy ground, herbs sensitive to wet conditions, particularly grey-leaved kinds and those of Mediterranean origin, are better mulched with gravel or grit to aid drainage.

Aromatic woody perennials and seed-bearing herbs such as dill do not normally need watering and feeding, unlike leafy perennials such as lovage and angelica, and those that are constantly cropped – parsley, basil and chives, for example. These should be watered regularly and fed occasionally, as must all herbs in containers.

Pruning and cutting back are important routines. Perennials are lightly pinched back after planting to encourage bushy growth, followed by an annual trim after flowering. Heavily cropped herbs may be cut back hard once or twice during the season to stimulate plenty of young foliage, and all should be deadheaded after flowering unless seeds are required.

Herbs are seldom troubled by pests and diseases, although aphids, red spider mite and scale may be minor local problems, and rust can seriously disable mint. Clear away all dead growth in autumn, and bring tender herbs indoors or protect them where they grow – hardiness often depends on good drainage and shelter from cold winds.

Harvesting herbs

Leaves and shoots are picked as needed, but as many culinary herbs develop maximum flavour just before or during flowering, that is the best time to gather them for drying, freezing or some other form of preservation, such as infusion in oil or vinegar. Harvest materials on a dry morning, and use the opportunity to tidy plants, gathering outer leaves or straggly shoots to leave plants neat and shapely. Keep different cultivars and species separate when gathering and processing, as their flavours are often subtly different, and dry leaves and stems away from bright sunlight to preserve their natural qualities.

At the height of the season, a well-tended herb garden is filled with plants ready for harvest, as above, where sage, marjoram, thyme and other culinary herbs are in peak condition. Regular propagation by cuttings, division or sowing is essential to maintain their health and vigour.

the ideal method for raising early seedlings or perennials where only a few plants are needed, and also tender herbs such as basil which need warmth at all stages of growth.

The best time to sow is spring, as soon as the soil is warm enough. Some fast-growing herbs – chervil, coriander and dill, for example – are sown again every 3–4 weeks to maintain supplies, while a second sowing at mid-summer of other herbs such as parsley provides young plants for winter cropping. Biennials and perennials (except cultivars, which must be propagated from layers or cuttings, see Propagating herbs, left) are sown in a seedbed in early summer for transplanting in autumn. Woody perennials, such as rosemary, can be propagated by mounding (see Propagating herbs, left).

Ten key culinary herbs

Chives (*Allium* species)

Common chives (*Allium schoenoprasum*) are clump-forming perennial bulbs with hollow, grassy herbaceous leaves, and small heads of mauve flowers. The leaves, which have a subtle, mild onion flavour, are the part normally used, although the flowers make a pretty and edible garnish. Chinese or garlic chives (*A. tuberosum*) have white flowers and a mild garlic flavour; welsh or bunching onions (*A. fistulosum*) are larger with evergreen leaves and a stronger flavour.

Cultivation Sow in spring in seedtrays or modules, or divide existing clumps in spring or autumn. Plant in small groups 23cm (9in) apart, in moist fertile soil in full sun or light shade. Cut leaves and flowers as required; leaves for freezing, or drying at low temperatures, are best gathered before flowering. Cut back once or twice during the season to encourage young foliage, and divide clumps for replanting every few years. Cloche for early use, and pot up in autumn for winter supplies under glass.

Tarragon, french (*Artemisia dracunculus*)

It is the leafy stem tips of this tall aromatic herbaceous perennial with spreading rhizomatous roots that are used, fresh as required or gathered as flowering begins for freezing or drying. Russian tarragon (*A. dracunculus dracunculoides*) is a coarser plant, hardier, but considered inferior in flavour.

Cultivation Divide roots into small handfuls in spring, or make cuttings from shoot tips in summer. Plant 60cm (2ft) apart in fairly dry well-drained soil, in a sunny position sheltered from cold winds. Cut down dead stems after the first frosts and protect the slightly tender roots with a mulch of leaves or straw. A few roots may be dug up and replanted in a frame or cool greenhouse for winter use.

Bay (*Laurus nobilis*)

Easily grown in large containers, this evergreen shrub or tree with glossy leathery leaves may be clipped into simple topiary or pruned as an ornamental tree. It is slightly tender in cold districts, especially while young.

Chives

French tarragon

Bay

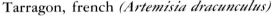

Mint

Basil

Cultivation Plant in early autumn or spring in rich well-drained soil, in full sun but sheltered from frost and cold winds; shield young plants with a windbreak or protect foliage until established. Move containers under glass in winter or insulate. Pick leaves as needed, or gather in summer for drying in darkness. Trim trees in summer, and propagate in early autumn from semi-ripe cuttings with a 'heel' (piece of older wood retained at the base of a cutting when it is pulled from the stem), or by layering.

Mint (*Mentha* species)

Nearly two dozen species and many more cultivars exist, mainly aromatic herbaceous perennials with spreading roots that may become invasive. The commonest mints used for flavouring include apple or round-leaved mint (*M. suaveolens*), spearmint (*M. spicata*) and peppermint (*M. × piperita*). Variegated cultivars such as pineapple mint (*M. suaveolens* 'Variegata') make attractive ornamental plants.

Cultivation Divide the long branching roots in autumn or spring, and plant horizontally 5cm (2in) deep and 15–30cm (6–12in) apart, in moist soil that has been well-dug and manured or composted. Choose a position that is cool or lightly shaded in summer, and keep plants watered in dry weather. Harvest leaves as required – just before flowering for freezing, drying or infusing. Cut some stems nearly to ground level in summer to ensure young leaves in autumn. Roots may be planted in boxes of compost in autumn to force early growth. Dig up clumps every 3–4 years, divide and replant in fresh soil.

Basil (*Ocimum basilicum*)

The leaves of this tender bushy annual are fragile and warmly aromatic. Several cultivars have coloured or decorative leaves; the hardier dwarf bush basil (*O. minimum*) has a bitter-resinous flavour. In cold districts grow under cloches or in pots indoors.

Cultivation Sow in warmth during spring, potting up seedlings individually and hardening off for planting out after the last frosts, 15cm (6in) apart in moist fertile soil, in full sun and sheltered from cold winds. Sow again in mid-summer for autumn and early winter use in pots. Water freely when dry, but avoid splashing the sensitive leaves. Pick these as needed and preserve by freezing or infusing; drying changes the flavour dramatically. Pinch out flowering tips to prolong the life of plants.

Marjoram *(Origanum* species*)*

The spicy lingering flavours of these bushy perennials need sun and warmth to develop fully. Chief amongst the numerous decorative cultivars and species are sweet marjoram *(O. marjorana)*, usually treated as an annual in cool climates; pot marjoram *(O. onites)*, the hardiest kind; and wild marjoram or oregano *(O. vulgare)*, the most pungent.

Cultivation Sow under glass in early spring or outdoors a month later, and thin or transplant 25–30cm (10–12in) apart in light well-drained soil in full sun. Perennial plants may also be divided in autumn or spring, or soft cuttings taken in summer. Pick leaves as needed during the growing season, or just before flowering for freezing or drying in shade.

Parsley *(Petroselinum crispum)*

The rich green leaves of this hardy biennial or short-lived perennial are usually tightly curled but can be flattened in vigorous plain-leaved forms. Popular for flavouring and garnishing, this herb may be grown as a decorative edging or pot plant.

Cultivation Sow outdoors or in seedtrays under glass in spring, and again in mid-summer for winter use under cloches or in pots indoors. Germination is often very slow, but soaking seeds overnight in warm water or flooding seed drills with hot water often hastens emergence. Thin or transplant to 15cm (6in) apart in moist fertile soil, in full sun or light shade. Cut leaves before flowering as needed, and preserve by freezing. Plain-leaved kinds also dry successfully.

Rosemary *(Rosmarinus officinalis)*

Hardy in warmer gardens, this perennial evergreen shrub has dense needle-like foliage and blue flowers in late spring. It is a popular medicinal, cosmetic

Marjoram

Parsley

Rosemary

Sage

Thyme

and culinary herb, with numerous ornamental cultivars, some dwarf or prostrate and others suitable for hedging or training on a warm wall.

Cultivation Sow seeds under glass in spring, layer in autumn or take semi-ripe cuttings in late summer; plant in well-drained fertile soil, in full sun with shelter from cold winds. Less hardy kinds should be grown in pots, or in a warm position outdoors with protection in winter. Clip or prune to shape after flowering. Pick young shoots for immediate use at any time, or at flowering time for drying in shade.

Sage *(Salvia officinalis)*

In its common form, which is hardier and better-flavoured than other kinds, this bushy evergreen perennial has grey-green pebbly leaves, but there are many ornamental red, purple, gold and variegated cultivars. Pineapple sage *(S. rutilans)* is a tender species with scarlet flowers in winter and fruit-flavoured leaves for summer drinks and desserts.

Cultivation Take soft cuttings in summer or semi-ripe cuttings in autumn, or sow seeds in spring; plant out 60cm (2ft) apart in fertile well-drained soil, in full sun with shelter from cold winds. Pinch out growing tips, especially after flowering, to keep plants bushy, and replace 4–5 year old bushes when lower stems become bare. Use leaves fresh as needed, or pick just before flowering for drying in shade.

Thyme *(Thymus* species*)*

Common thyme *(T. vulgaris)*, with low-growing mounds of tiny evergreen leaves, is the usual culinary form, but there are many other desirable species and cultivars, including the mat-forming wild thyme *(T. serpyllum)* and lemon thyme *(T. × citriodorus)*.

Cultivation Sow seeds or divide plants in spring, take semi-ripe cuttings in summer or layer older bushes in autumn, and plant out 15–30cm (6–12in) apart according to the cultivar in very well-drained soil in full sun. Clip with shears after flowering, and replace plants when 4–5 years old. Gather leaves and tips of shoots as required, during flowering for drying or infusions.

THROUGH THE SEASONS

Plant growth is affected by a number of influences such as temperature and day length. Seeds germinate, fruit trees bloom and vegetables mature only when conditions are just right, and the timing of these critical moments depends not on the calendar but on local factors such as climate, altitude, the garden's aspect and exposure, or the likelihood of frosts. Rather than give exact dates, you will find on the following pages a guide to the most important seasonal activities for you to interpret and adapt to your own kitchen garden.

Forward planning ensures unbroken supplies from the kitchen garden, especially with crops such as these cabbages, leeks and other winter vegetables that need a long season of growth. Sown in spring under glass or in a seedbed outdoors, they are planted out finally in early summer. They must then make rapid growth, as here, before cool autumn days harden them off and prepare them to withstand winter conditions.

Spring

Life returns to the garden in this busy season and with so much to do it is tempting to make an early start. Soils must be warm enough to stimulate prompt germination, however, and one or two warm sunny days may not raise temperatures sufficiently. So resist sowing too early unless you can cover beds with cloches or similar protection. Alternatively, many crops can be started early in the greenhouse or cold frame. You can cultivate the soil throughout the season as long as the ground is not frozen or so wet that it sticks to your boots.

Early spring

- Clear exhausted crops and weeds before digging light soils or forking over clay that has been broken down by frost.
- In a cold spring cover areas with cloches, polythene or woven fleece to warm the ground ready for sowing.
- Feed over-wintered vegetables such as spring cabbage and sprouting broccoli.
- Plant first early potatoes and onion sets in a warm bed, together with perennial vegetables and herbs; early crops started under glass and fully hardened off may be planted out, under cloches if necessary.
- Remake mint beds and start dividing perennial herbs.
- Sow bulbing onions, spinach, broad beans, beetroot, early peas, carrots and other early crops. In cool gardens it may be better to wait a further 3–4 weeks.
- Make successional sowings of radishes, turnips, spring onions and lettuce in frames, or outdoors if warm enough, together with summer cauliflowers, calabrese, early brussels sprouts and leeks for transplanting later.
- Sow celery, herbs and outdoor tomatoes in the greenhouse.
- Feed soft fruit and cover against birds.

Tulips and pear blossom celebrate spring, and polythene warms the soil ready for sowing.

- Protect early blossom on fruits such as wall-trained peaches.
- Finish winter pruning and planting fruit as soon as possible, and start pruning fan-trained cherries and plums.
- Plant strawberry runners if not done late the previous summer.

Mid-spring

In a cool season much of early spring's routine may be delayed until mid-spring, but temperatures are gradually rising and it should be possible to complete the work now.

- Make further successional sowings of salad crops outdoors, repeating at 3–4 week intervals until mid-summer.
- Make a last sowing of broad beans (later ones would overlap with french and runner beans); any bean seeds left over can be sown for digging in as green manure.
- Sow carrots, beetroot, early peas, parsnips, annual herbs, spinach and autumn and winter brassicas.

- Start squashes, outdoor cucumbers, french and runner beans in pots under glass.
- Sow sweet corn in pots, or outdoors under cloches in warmer gardens.
- Earth up first early potatoes and plant other kinds.
- Plant asparagus and globe artichokes.
- Harden off early greenhouse sowings in a cold frame ready for planting.
- Dig out a celery trench, sowing lettuces on the ridges of excavated soil.
- Rake down a fine seedbed for maincrop roots, leave for a fortnight for weed seedlings to germinate, hoe these off and then sow at the end of this period.
- Propagate older perennial herbs by mounding (see page 114).
- Start thinning the tiny fruits on peaches.
- Spray gooseberries prone to mildew, blackcurrants against big bud mite, and apples and pears if scab is a problem.

Late spring

As growth accelerates, hoeing and hand weeding become important routine tasks. Watering may be necessary, too, on light soils. Watch for the first signs of pests and diseases, and take preventive steps where appropriate.

- There are many sowings to make now: outdoors most crops can be started, including sweet corn, french and runner beans, chicory, spinach and annual herbs. Make two sowings of maincrop peas, one early in the season, the other 3 weeks later.
- Thin earlier outdoor sowings, and start to transfer those made under glass to the cold frame for hardening off. The earliest sowings such as onions and leeks can be planted out, under cloches if necessary, together with outdoor tomatoes in warmer gardens.
- Plant new hardy herbs.
- Continue earthing up potatoes, especially if frost threatens.

- Transplant brassicas to their permanent positions.
- Erect poles for climbing beans.
- In the fruit garden untie grease bands (sticky collars of grease-impregnated material which trap insects) from trees and burn; thin young raspberry canes to leave the strongest and tuck straw around strawberry plants as soon as trusses of fruitlets start to arch over. Thin young gooseberries and check the bushes for mildew.
- Mulch all kinds of fruit.

Summer

The first fruits of your labours should soon be ready, offering the prospect of a feast of young vegetables. There is harvesting and increased watering to do now, as well as further sowing and planting. It is tempting to relax once the main crops are in, but there will be gaps in supplies later unless you continue sowing; the longest day is approaching and with it the deadline for the last sowings of some ve-getables. Pests and diseases may seem serious now, but think twice before spraying because natural predators are also increasing in number. As crops begin to fill the garden, flaws in your original cropping plans may become apparent, and this is often a time for the cunning use of catch crops and intercrops.

Early summer

- Continue hoeing and mulching to prevent weeds from taking hold.
- Plant out tender crops such as tomatoes, marrows and runner beans after hardening off. Celery may be planted out, winter brassicas and leeks transplanted from nursery beds.
- Check the stability of supports; train in cucumbers, climbing beans and blackberries.
- Sow successional vegetables and salad crops, in light shade in a hot season; sow

As trained fruit ripens in the summer sunshine, globe artichokes approach flowering time.

lettuce *in situ* or in pots to avoid any check after transplanting.
- Sow an early carrot, together with an early pea, at the start of this period followed by another near the end.
- Make a last sowing of dwarf beans for covering with cloches in early autumn.
- Sow chinese cabbage and a second batch of parsley.
- Earth up maincrop potatoes, and check first earlies as they should be ready to use.
- Finish cutting asparagus.
- Start lifting over-wintered onions for immediate use.
- Net raspberries and spray if the grubs of raspberry beetles are usually a problem; spray gooseberries if sawfly caterpillars have appeared.
- Thin young fruits on apples and pears.
- Summer-prune trained forms of gooseberries and currants.
- Remove runners from strawberry plants unless needed for propagation.

Mid-summer

There may be a crisis now if you have not kept on top of weeds, so hoe frequently and mulch after watering, which should be targeted on the neediest plants.
- Continue successional sowings of early crops, especially where the first crops have finished and been cleared.
- Make a last sowing of early carrots at the start of this period, together with winter radishes, and spring cabbage in a seedbed.
- Finish transplanting winter crops.
- Start blanching leeks grown on the surface, and earth up potatoes for the last time – check their foliage from now on for blight.
- Train outdoor tomatoes and pinch out the growing tips when they have set 3–4 trusses.
- Harvest shallots, garlic and over-wintered onions, and dry before storing.
- Many herbs will now be ready to gather for preserving; cut down part of mint beds to encourage a new crop of young foliage.
- Continue thinning top fruit after they have shed their excess fruits, and support heavily laden branches, especially on plum trees.
- Summer-prune soft fruit, moving on to trained pears and then apples.
- Gather ripe blackcurrants; prune bushes.
- After fruiting clear older strawberry plants; cut the foliage from those to be kept and peg down runners for future plants.

Late summer

- There is still time to sow summer radishes outdoors, together with turnips, lettuces and other salad crops that can be cloched later or transplanted to a frame in cool districts.
- Sow an early carrot variety in a cold frame.
- Outdoors sow a second batch of spring cabbage, perpetual or winter spinach, bulbing onions and a hardy strain of spring onion, both for over-wintering.
- Water and mulch runner beans.

- Dig up second early potatoes and large beetroots for storing, and start lifting and drying maincrop onions.
- Earth up early celery and water liberally in dry weather.
- Continue gathering herbs.
- Pick soft fruit, especially raspberries whose fruited canes can be pruned.
- Start summer-pruning fan plums and cherries.
- Make new strawberry beds and pot up a few runners to keep outdoors until forced in late winter.
- Pick the earliest apples and pears.
- Stay alert for pests and diseases, especially wasps on ripening fruit.
- Order fruit plants for autumn delivery.

Autumn

The first frosts may be imminent now, together with shorter days and cool damp nights, and it is important to gather in and store all tender crops, and to keep cloches ready to cover those left outdoors. Fungal diseases become more of a threat as temperatures drop, so clear away dead or decaying leaves and plants to reduce the risks. On heavy soils you can start winter cultivation, adding lime, manure or compost as required. Sites for new fruit should be prepared well in advance of delivery. Some gardeners prefer to postpone digging light soils until the late winter and to sow instead a green manure cover crop (see page 17) such as winter beans.

Early autumn
- Clear outdoor tomatoes and cucumbers.
- Start lifting roots such as maincrop carrots and potatoes for storing; marrows and winter squashes should also be dried and stored.
- Continue earthing up celery and surface-grown leeks.
- Check brassicas for caterpillars.

Autumn is harvest-time, when onions are laid out and dried ready for storing.

- Finish transplanting spring cabbage, but keep back a few plants as an insurance against losses.
- Thin late vegetable sowings and transplant thinnings to a cold frame.
- Plant autumn onion sets.
- Sow winter lettuces outdoors or in a frame, together with other salad crops under cover.
- Sow summer cauliflowers for early use next year and keep in a frame over winter.
- Finish all summer pruning; prune blackberries as they complete fruiting.
- Cut out fruited shoots from peaches and acid cherries and tie in replacements.
- Fix grease bands on fruit trees and their stakes.
- Take hardwood cuttings of soft fruit for rooting in a sheltered spot outdoors.

Mid-autumn
- Check all supports and tree ties before the autumn winds arrive and clean sticks and canes for storing in a dry place.

- Use a soil testing kit to assess where lime and essential nutrients may be needed.
- Continue clearing exhausted crops, especially brassica stumps, but leave the roots of peas and beans to rot in the ground.
- Finally earth up celery and leeks, banking the soil to shed rain.
- Earth up or stake winter brassicas; protect late cauliflowers by bending leaves over their curds.
- Cut down artichokes; clear asparagus fern and cover crowns with rotted manure.
- Dig up and store chicory roots, and force a first batch under cover.
- Plant garlic now, outdoors or in pots in a frame in cold districts.
- Sow spinach and hardy broad beans.
- Under cover sow an early carrot variety, greenhouse lettuces and radishes, and salad crops for cutting as seedlings; cover outdoor crops if the weather deteriorates.
- Dig up mint roots for boxing and forcing under cover, and pot up other herbs such as chives and parsley; cover parsley and chervil outdoors with cloches. Mulch or remove indoors doubtfully hardy herbs and clear autumn leaves from prostrate woody perennials such as thyme.
- Pick and store all fruit.
- Finish pruning blackberries; start winter pruning soft fruit as soon as the leaves fall; there is still time to take hardwood cuttings.

Late autumn
- Empty hosepipes and sprinklers, and store.
- Dig heavy ground except when wet.
- Finish storing root crops; start checking regularly the condition of stored produce.
- Cover globe artichokes and outdoor root crops with straw or leaves and cover rhubarb crowns with a mulch of decayed manure.
- Stake brussels sprouts disturbed by high winds and net all brassicas against birds.

- Sow hardy peas and broad beans outdoors in a warm sheltered bed or under cloches.
- Ventilate crops in frames carefully as they need plenty of air as well as insulation from cold.
- Protect young bay trees from hard frost and insulate containers left outdoors.
- On light soils divide and replant perennial herbs.
- Start planting bush and tree fruit, but heel plants in or store under cover if the weather is not suitable.
- Continue winter-pruning soft fruit, followed by top fruit (but not stone fruit).
- Net soft fruit trees if birds are a problem – remove small-mesh fruit cage roofs if heavy snow is forecast.

Winter

Everything should have been stored or protected from the elements by now and you can assess the results of your work and make plans for next year. Seeds need choosing and ordering. Cultivation and fruit pruning are the main winter tasks, as is the construction or repair of paths, fences and tools. From mid-winter the first sowings of the year may be made under cover if you can provide enough warmth.

Early winter
- Check windbreaks and supports and ensure plants have not been disturbed by wind and frost.
- Note where puddles linger after heavy rain and correct any drainage problems (see page 16).
- Manure deep beds and construct new ones; finish winter digging on heavy soils, but keep off the ground if it is wet.
- Ventilate crops in frames and greenhouses, when possible, but insulate against hard frost.
- In severe weather protect celery, parsnips

Although the garden seems dormant in winter, rhubarb is already stirring under forcing pots.

and leeks with straw, and cover chicory and turnips with straw or leaves to force and blanch early growth. Chicory and rhubarb can be forced in a shed or greenhouse.
- Plant shallots after the shortest day.
- Pots of herbs can be brought in succession from a frame to crop indoors.
- Continue winter pruning fruit plants.
- Remove any shrivelled fruits from trees to prevent diseases carrying over.
- Pick swollen blackcurrant buds that will contain big bud mites.

Mid-winter
- Lime soils manured in the autumn; when the ground is frozen, spread manure or compost on the surface ready for turning in later.
- Cover rhubarb crowns to force early stems.
- Order seeds and seed potatoes, and chit on arrival. Cabbages and whole stems of brussels sprouts can be pulled up for suspending upside down in a cool shed (see page 53).

- In a heated greenhouse or a warm place indoors, sow bulbing onions and lettuces, and tomatoes for growing under warm glass.
- In mild sheltered districts sow hardy peas and broad beans in the open or under cloches.
- Press on with any delayed pruning and planting of fruit plants.
- Spray fruit trees and bushes with a winter wash if pests were a problem last season.

Late winter
The first real signs of revival appear now, although it may still be too soon to sow.
- Break down soil that was dug in the autumn, covering areas with polythene sheets, if necessary, to keep the soil dry for early preparations, and start digging lighter soils.
- In a warm greenhouse sow lettuces, onions, leeks, celery and tomatoes, and continue forcing chicory and rhubarb.
- Outdoors, in frames or under cloches, sow early carrots, broad beans, peas, beetroot, turnips, parsnips and salad crops.
- Harden off cauliflowers sown in autumn, ready for planting in early spring.
- Feed spring cabbage, and cover spare plants with cloches to force early heads.
- Plant rhubarb, jerusalem artichokes, garlic if not started in autumn, and onion sets and shallots in warmer gardens.
- Divide clumps of chives for replanting; and sow parsley in pots for an early crop.
- Drape polythene sheeting or fine net over early fruit blossom on walls.
- Cover or spray peaches against leaf curl.
- Cut autumn raspberries to ground level.
- Cover a row or two of strawberries with cloches and bring potted strawberry plants indoors for forcing.
- Start feeding soft fruit towards the end of this period.
- Check stocks of seeds, pots, trays, compost and fertilizers for early spring sowings.

Index

Page numbers in *italics* refer to illustrations.

acid cherries
  growing 100
  pollination 83
  pruning 89
acid soils
  weeds 31
acidity
  soils 18
alfalfa 17
Allium see chives
alpine strawberries 103
altitude 15
american cress 67
ammonia sulphate 19
annual weeds 31
anthracnose 77
aphids 32, 76, 110
apple mint 116
apples
  climate 80
  espaliers 81, *81, 83, 94–5*
  growing 92–5
  harvesting 94
  pruning 89, 93–4
  regional cultivars 84
  ripeness 94, *94*
  storage 94
  thinning 93
  training *9, 11*, 90, 91, *91*
arches
  fruit support 81
Artemisia dracunculus see
  tarragon
artichokes
  growing *25*, 73
asparagus
  growing 74
asparagus beetles 32, 76
aspect 15, 80
autumn
  maintenance tasks 122–3

baby beetroot *59*
baby corn 65
bacterial canker 110
bare-rooted fruit 84, 85, *85*
bark mulch 30
barn cloches 23
base dressings 29, 40
basil 115, 116–17
bay 116
bean seed fly 76

beans
  see also broad beans; french
    beans; runner beans
  sowing 38
  supports 45, *45*
beds
  types 15
beetroot
  cultivars *59*
  growing *10, 57*, 59
  sowing *59*
belgian chicory 67
Bibb lettuce 65
biennial bearers 83
biennial herbs 115
big bud mite 110
biological control 32
bird chillies 69
birds 32, 76, *86*, 87, 110
bitter lupins 17
bitter pit 110
black bean aphid 76, 110
blackberries
  climate 80
  growing 104
  pruning 89
  training *104*
blackcurrants
  cultivars *106*
  growing 106–7, *106*
  harvesting 106
  propagation 106
  pruning 89, 106, *106*
blackflies 32, 76, 110
blanching
  asparagus *74*
  leeks 63
blossom *83*
boron 29
Botrytis 77, 110
box hedges *7, 9*
brambles
  growing 104
  harvesting 104
  propagation 104
brassicas
  growing *7, 8*, 49–55
  intercropping 22
  soil 17
  transplanting 40
broad beans
  cultivars *46*
  growing *11, 19*, 46–7
broccoli
  see also brassicas

calabrese distinction 51
  growing 52
broccoli spears 51
brown rot 110
brussels sprouts
  see also brassicas
  diseases *53*
  growing *7*, 52–3
bulbing onions
  growing 60–1
bunching onions 116
bush beans 44
bush tomatoes *11*
bush trees 90, *90*
butterflies
  caterpillars 32, 76

cabbage mealy aphid 76
cabbage root fly 76
cabbage white fly 76
cabbages
  see also brassicas
  growing *9*, 49, *119*
  red *25*
  spacing 21, 41
  successional sowing 22
calabrese
  see also brassicas
  cultivars *51*
  growing 51
  hybrid cultivars 51, *51*
  successional sowing 22
calcium 18
cane blight 111
cane fruits 82
cankers 33, 56, 77, 110
Capsicum
  C. annuum see sweet
    peppers
  C. frutescens see hot
    peppers
carrot flies 32, *33*, 56, 76
carrots
  cloches 23
  companion planting *33*
  cottage gardens *35*
  growing *11, 19, 25*, 56, *57*
  sowing *37*, 38
catch crops 22, *37*
caterpillars 32, 76
catmint *33*
cauliflowers
  see also brassicas
  growing 50–1, *50*
cayenne peppers 69

celery
  growing 72
celery leaf fly 76
centipedes 32
chalky soils
  fruit 85
  weeds 31
chard *11, 25*
chemicals 19
cherries
  see also acid cherries;
    morello cherries
  cultivars *101*
  fans *79*, 87, *101*
  growing 100–1
  harvesting 101
  pollination 83
  pruning 101
  training 90
chervil 115
chicory
  forcing 67, *67*
  growing 67
  red 67
chinese chives 116
chitted seeds 36, 42
chives 115, 116
chlorosis 85
chocolate spot 77
chou palmier 7
clay soils 16, 17, 26
climate
  fruit 80
cloches 23
  barn 23
  glass 23
  hardening off 43
  plastic 23
  polycarbonate 23
  soil warming 39
  tent 23
  tunnel 23
clubroot 49, 77
codling moth 110
cold frames 23, 43
common scab 77
common thyme 117
compact varieties 21
companion planting *33*
compost
  ammonia sulphate 19
  garden *10, 17*, 18
  making 19
  mulches 30
  types 18

contact insecticides 32
containers
  fruit growing *82*, 84
  vegetables 39
continuous cropping 22
cooking apples 92
cooking pears 96
copper 29
coral spot 110
cordons
  apples *83, 92–3*
  fruit 83, 91
  gooseberries *108*
coriander 115
corn salad 67, *67*
cos lettuces 65, 66
courgettes 71
crab apples
  growing 92, 93
cress 67
crisphead lettuce 65
crop covers 23
crop rotation 20–1, *20–1*, 33
crown rot 77
cuckoo spit 32
cucumbers 70, *70*
culinary herbs 114–17
cultivars
  see also individual species
  seed selection 36
currants
  growing 106–8
  harvesting 107
  propagation 106, *106*, 108
  pruning 106, 107, *107*
cuttings
  hardwood *109*
cutworms 76

damping off 77
density *see* spacing
dessert apples 92
dessert pears 96
digging
  double *26*, 27
  hints 27
  single 27
  vegetable plots 26
dill 115
diseases
  brussels sprouts *53*
  fruit 87, 110–11
  herbs 115
  prevention 33
  vegetables 77

double digging *26*, 27
downy mildew 77
drainage
  herbs 114
  soil assessment 16
drills
  preparation *38*
  sowing 37–9
dwarf bush basil 116
dwarf pyramids
  pears *96–7*
  pruning 94
  training 90
dwarf varieties 21
dwarfing rootstocks 81, 82, 83, 92

eelworms 76
elephant garlic 62
espaliers
  apples 81, *81*, 83, *94–5*
  fruit 83
  pears *88*
  training 91
everbearing strawberries 102

F₁ hybrids
  brussels sprouts 52
  calabrese 51
  spinach 64
  vegetables 36
fans
  cherries 87, *101*
  fruit 83
  morello cherry *79*
  plums *98–9*
  tomatoes *68*
  training *68*, 91, *91*
farmyard manure 18
feathered maidens 84
feeding
  fruit 86
  routine 29
fences
  fruit *79*, 81, 85
  protection 32
  shelter 14
fenugreek 17
fertile soils
  creation 18–19
fertilizers
  fruit 86
  NPK value 29
  organic 19
field beans 17

fireblight 110
flageolet beans 44
flea beetles 76
floating mulches 23, 32
flocculation 17
foliar feeds 29
foot rot 77
forcing
  chicory 67, *67*
  rhubarb *75*
  strawberries 103
forking 27
french beans
  growing *25*, 44
  hedges *11*
french tarragon 116
frit fly 76
froghoppers 32
frost-protection 14, 80
fruit 79–111
  see also individual species;
    soft fruit; top fruit
  choice 84
  maintenance 86–7
  planting 85
  pruning 82–3, 88–9
  site assessment 80–1
  siting 20, 81
  spacing 21
  thinning 86–7
  training 81, 82–3, 90–1
  types 82–3
  watering 28, 86
fruit buds 89
fruit cages *86*, 87
fruit trees
  bird-protection 87
  planting 85, *85*
  pruning *88*
  selection *85*
  soil improvement 17
  weed control 86
fruiting wood 88
fungicides 33
fusarium wilt 77

garden compost 10, *17*, 18
garden peas
  growing 47–8, *47*, *48*
garlic
  drying *62*
  growing 61–2
garlic chives 116
glass cloches 23
globe artichokes 73, *73*

glyphosate 26
gooseberries
  climate 80
  cordons *108*
  cultivars *109*
  growing 108–9
  harvesting 109
  propagation 109
  pruning 89, 109
  thinning 108–9
  training 91
grafting 83
green manure
  bitter lupin 17
  fenugreek 17
  lucerne 17
  mustard 17
  winter beans 17
greenflies 32, 76, 110
greengages 80
greenhouses
  sowing vegetables 42–3
grey mealy aphids 32
grey mould 77, 110
ground preparation *see* soil
  preparation
growbags 39
growth buds 89

half-standards 90
halo blight 77
hardening off 43
hardiness
  fruit 80
hardwood cuttings
  soft fruits *109*
haricot beans 44
harvesting
  apples 94
  beetroot 59
  blackcurrants 106
  brambles 104
  broad beans 47
  broccoli 52
  brussels sprouts 53
  cabbages 49
  calabrese 51
  carrots 56
  cherries 101
  currants 107
  french beans 44
  fruit 87
  gooseberries 109
  herbs 115
  leeks 63

lettuce 66
onions 60
peaches 100
pears 97
peas 48
peppers 69
plums 99
potatoes 58
radishes 54
raspberries 105
runner beans 46
strawberries 103
sweetcorn 65
tomatoes 69
turnips 55
heading lettuces 65
hearted lettuces 65
hedges 14, 80
heeling in 40
herbicides 26, 31
herbs 113–17
  harvesting 115
  intercropping 20
  planting 114–15
  propagation *114*
  pruning 115
  sowing 114–15
honey fungus 77
hot peppers
  growing 69, *69*
hoverflies 32
humus 16, 28
husbandry 25–33
hybrids
  brussels sprouts 52
  calabrese 51, *51*
  seeds 36
  spinach 64

iceberg lettuce 65
infertile soils
  improvement 16–17
insecticides 32
intercropping 20, 22, 32
iron 29
irrigation *see* watering

japanese radishes 54
jerusalem artichokes 14, 73

kale *7*

lacewings 32
ladybirds 32
lamb's lettuce 67

land cress 67
laterals 89
Laurus nobilis see bay
lavender *113*
leaders 89
leaf buds 89
leaf lettuce 66
leaf miner 76
leaf spinach 64
leaf spots 77, 111
leatherjackets 32, 76
leaves
  compost 17
leeks
  cultivars *63*
  growing *8*, 63, *119*
  small gardens *25*
legumes
  see also beans; peas
  growing 44–8
lemon thyme 117
lettuces
  see also loose leaf lettuce
  cloches 23
  cultivars *66*
  growing *10*, *11*, *19*, 65–6
  intercropping 22
  leaf 66
  red *25*
  sowing *22*, 37, *66*
  spacing 21
  successional sowing *22*
  transplanting 40
light 14, 80
lime 16, 17, *20*, 85
loams 16, 31
loose leaf lettuce *14*, 38, 41, 65
loppers 89
lucerne 17

magnesium 18
maiden whip 84
maintenance
  pruning 89
  routine 25–33
  seasonal 119–23
manganese 29
mangetout 47
manures
  green 17
  types 18
  use of 18–19
marjoram *113*, *115*, 117
marrows *25*, 36, 71, *71*

melons
  seeds 36
Mentha see mint
mesclun 66
mice 76
mildews 33, 77, 111
millipedes 32
minerals 86
mint 114, 116
modules
  sowing 43, *43*
molybdenum 29
mooli radishes 54
morello cherries *79*
moths
  caterpillars 32, 76
moulds 32, 77, 110
mounding/mound layering *114*,
  115
mulches 30
  bark 30
  cardboard 30
  carpets 26, 30
  compost 30
  evaporation 28
  floating 23, 32
  herbs 115
  plastic film 30
  soil improvement 17
mushroom compost 18
mustard 17

nectarines 100
netting 32, *33*
new potatoes 58
nitrogen 18, 29
nitrogen-fixing bacteria 44
no-dig vegetable plot 26
NPK fertilizers 29
nursery seedbeds 37, 39
nutrients 18–19

Ocimum basilicum see basil
onion fly 76
onions
  bulbing 60–1
  cottage gardens *35*
  small gardens *25*
  sowing *37*
  spring 61
  transplanting 40
open-pollinated seeds 36
oregano 117
organic gardening 19
Origanum see marjoram

palm tree cabbages *7*
parsley *10*, 39, 114, 115, 117
parsnips
  cottage gardens *35*
  growing 56–7
  seeds 36
  sowing 38
  watering 39
paths *7, 8, 10*, 20
pea moths 76
pea thrips 76
peaches
  cultivars *100*
  growing 100
  harvesting 100
  pollination 83
  pruning 89, 100
  thinning 100
peach leaf curl 111
pear midge 110
pears
  climate 80
  cultivars *96*, 97
  growing 96–7
  harvesting *87*, 97
  pollination 83
  pruning *88*, 89, 96–7
  soil 85
  storage 97
  thinning 96
  training 90, 91
peas
  growing *11*, 44, 47–8, *47, 48*
  shelter *8*
  sowing 38
pelleted seeds 36, 38, 39
peppermint 116
peppers
  growing 69
perennials
  cauliflowers 52
  crops 73
  herbs 115
  weeds 31, 86
pergolas
  fruit support 81
perpetual spinach 64
perpetual strawberries 102, 103
pests
  biological control 32
  brussels sprouts *53*
  control 32
  fruit 87, 110
  herbs 115
  vegetables 76

petits pois 47
Petroselinum crispum see
  parsley
pH
  fruit 85
phosphorus 18, 29
pinching out
  beans *46*
pineapple mint 116
pineapple sage 117
pioneer crops 17
planning 13–23
planting
  companion *33*
  fruit 85, *85*
  herbs 114–15
  vegetables 40–1
plastic cloches 23
plastic film 30, *33*, 39
plastic sheeting 86
plums
  cultivars *99*
  fans *98–9*
  growing 98–9
  harvesting 99
  pollination 83
  pruning 98–9
  thinning 98
  training 90
pod spots 77
pole beans 44
pollination
  fruit 83
polycarbonate cloches 23
polythene sheeting 23, 26, 30,
  31
pot leeks 63
pot marjoram 117
potash 18, 29
potassium 18, 29
potato blight 77
potatoes
  black plastic 30
  cultivars *58*
  growing *57*, 58
  soil improvement 17
poultry manure 18
powdery mildew 77, 111
pre-germinated seeds 36, 42
pricking out
  seedlings 42, *42*
pricking over 27
propagation
  blackcurrants 106
  brambles 104

currants 108
  gooseberries 109
  herbs *114*
  raspberries 105
  strawberries *102*, 103
protection
  fences 32
  frost 14, 80
  fruit 81, *86*, 87
pruning
  apples 93–4
  blackcurrants 106, *106*
  cherries 101
  currants 107, *107*
  espaliers *83*
  fans *101*
  fruit 82–3, 88–9
  gooseberries 109
  herbs 115
  methods 89
  peaches 100
  pears 96–7
  plums 98–9
  timing 88–9
pruning saws 89
pumpkins 71
purple sage *51*
pyramids
  pears *96–7*
  training fruit 90

rabbit manure 18
radicchio 67
radishes
  see also brassicas
  cultivars *55*
  growing *10*, 54
  sowing 38
rain
  fruit 80
raised beds 15
raspberries
  growing 105, *105*
  harvesting 105
  propagation 105
  protection *86*
  pruning 89
  soil 85
  training *105*
raspberry beetle 110
red cabbages *25*
red chicory 67
red currants
  growing 107–8
  harvesting 107

protection *86*
pruning 89, 107, *107*
training 91
red lettuces *25*
red spider mite 110
regulatory pruning 89
remontant strawberries 102
renewal pruning *89*
resistant cultivars 32, 33
rhubarb
  forcing *75*
  growing 75
ripeness
  apples 94, *94*
  pears 97
  sweetcorn 65
romaine lettuce 65
root aphids 76
root crops
  growing 56–63
  soil 17
  transplanting 40
root rot 77
rootstocks 81, 82, 83, 92
rosemary 115, 117
Rosmarinus officinalis see
  rosemary
rot 33, 77, 110
rotation
  crops 20–1, *20–1*, 33
rotavation 26
round-leaved mint 116
rove beetles 32
ruby chard *25*
runner beans
  growing 45–6
  screens *11*
  training *8*
russian tarragon 116
rusts 33, 77

sage *51*, 114, *115*, 117
salad crops *10*
salad leaf crops 41
salad potatoes 58
Salvia officinalis see sage
sandy soils 16, 26–7
savoy cabbages *48*
sawfly larvae 32, 110
scabs 33, 111
screens
  carrot root flies 32
  peas 47, *47*
  runner beans *11*
  shelter 80

season
  extension 23, 40
seasonal maintenance 119–23
secateurs 89
secondary laterals 89
seed drills
  preparation *38*
  sowing 37–9
seedbeds
  preparation *37*
  sowing 37
seedlings
  pricking out 42, *42*
  thinning 39
  watering 28
seed packets
  storage 36
seeds
  herbs 114–15
  vegetables 36
  weeds 31
seep hoses 28, *28*
self-fertile fruits 83
self-sterile fruits 83
sewage sludge 18
shade 14
shallots
  growing 62
shelter 14, *14*, 80
sideshoots 89
silty soils 16
silver leaf 111
single digging 27
site assessment 80–1
sloping ground 15, *15*
slugs *30*, 32, 76, 110
snails *30*, 32, 76
snow peas 47
soft fruit 82
  see also fruit; individual
  species
  growing 102–9
  hardwood cuttings *109*
  pollination 83
  protection *86*
  soil 84
  storage 87
soil blocks 43
soils
  acidity 18
  assessment 16–17
  improvement 16–19
  moisture 39
  preparation 26–7, 84–5, 114
  temperature 39

sooty mould 32
sowing
  beetroot *59*
  density 37–8
  drills 37–9, *38*
  herbs 114–15
  lettuces *66*
  method 42
  outdoors 37–9
  seedbeds 37, *37*
  successional *11*, 22, 40
spacing
  cauliflowers *50*
  crops 21, *21*
  garden peas *48*
  vegetables 40–1
spearmint 116
spinach
  growing 64
  stress *30*
spinach beet 64
spray lines *28*
spring
  maintenance tasks 120–1
spring onions
  growing 61
sprinklers 28
sprouting broccoli
  see also brassicas
  growing 52
spur blight 111
spur pruning 89, *89*
squash
  growing 71
squirrels *86*
standards
  apples 82
  fruit plants 90
stem rot 77
step-over trees 81
stone fruits 82, 89
storage
  apples 87, 94
  fruit 87
  pears 87, 97
  seed packets 36
strawberries
  black plastic *31*
  forcing 103
  growing *7*, *9*, 82, 84, 102–3
  harvesting 103
  propagation *102*, 103
  protection *86*
  siting 81
strip cropping 23

sublaterals 89
subsoil 16
successional sowing *11*, 22, 40
sugar loaf chicory 67
sugar peas 47
sugar snap peas 47
sulphur 18
summer
  maintenance tasks 121–2
summer cabbages
  spacing 41
sunlight 14, 80
support
  beans 22, 45, *45*
  fruit 81
  peas 47, *47*
swedes
  see also brassicas
  growing 55
sweet cherries
  pollination 83
sweet corn
  growing 64–5
  intercropping 22
  ripeness *65*
  shade *39*
  shelter 14
sweet marjoram 117
sweet peppers
  growing 69

tarragon 116
tent cloches 23
terracing *9*, 15, *15*
thinning
  apples 93
  fruit 86–7
  gooseberries 108–9
  peaches 100
  pears 96
  plums 98
  seedlings 39
thyme *113*, 114, *115*, 117
Thymus see thyme
tip pruning *89*
tip-bearers 89
tomatoes
  bush *11*
  fans *68*
  growing 68–9
top-dressings 29, 86
top fruit
  see also fruit; individual
  species
  choice 84

growing 82, 92–101
  maidens 84
  pollination 83
  pruning *88*
  site preparation 84, *84*
  soil 84
  training *11*, 83
  watering 86
trace elements 29, 86
training 68, 91, *91*
  apples *9*, *11*, 81, *81*
  blackberries *104*
  bush trees *90*
  cherries 90
  cordons 91, *92–3*
  dwarf pyramids 90, *96–7*
  espaliers 81, *81*, *83*, *88*, 91,
    94–5
  fans 91, *98–9*, *101*
  fruit 81, 82–3, 90–1
  gooseberries 91, *108*
  pears 90, 91
  plums 90, *98–9*
  raspberries *105*
  red currants 91
  runner beans *8*
  tomato fans *68*
  vegetables *9*
transplanting
  vegetables 40–1
trees
  see also fruit trees; individual
  species
  leaves, compost *17*
  soil fertility *19*
trelliswork *15*, 81
trench celery *72*
trenching 27
triploid cultivars 83
tunnel cloches 23
turk's cap gourds 71
turnip tops 54
turnips
  see also brassicas
  growing 54–5, *57*

unhearted lettuce 65

vegetables
  see also individual crops
  diseases 77
  growing 35–77
  pests 76
  planting 40–1
  seeds 36

sowing 37–9, 42–3
  spacing 40–1
  transplanting 40–1
viruses 77, 111

walled gardens 14, *14*, 28
walls
  fruit *79*, 81, 85
wasps 110
watering
  see also individual species
  fruit 28, 86
  routine 28
waterlogged soil 16
Webbs lettuce 65
weedkillers 26, 31, 86
weeds
  annual 31
  control 86
  herbs 114, 115
  mulches 30
  onions 60
  perennial 31, 86
  removal 26, 31
  vegetables 41
welsh onions 116
white currants
  cultivars *107*
  growing 107–8
  harvesting 107
  pruning 107, *107*
white rot 60, 77
whiteflies 76
wild marjoram 117
wild thyme 117
wilts 33
windbreaks 14, *47*, 80
winter
  maintenance tasks 123
winter beans 17, 122
winter moth 110
wireworms 32, 76
witloof chicory 67
woody perennials *114*, 115
woolly aphids 110

zinc 29

Acknowledgments

Author's acknowledgments

A number of invaluable people helped create this book. In particular, the author thanks those who taught him the craft of the kitchen garden or provided the opportunity to find out the hard way; and also the talented team at Conran Octopus who have made producing the book a memorable pleasure.

Publisher's acknowledgments

The publisher would like to thank the following photographers and organizations for their kind permission to reproduce the photographs in this book:

1 John Glover (Preen Manor, Shropshire); 2–3 Arnaud Descat/MAP; 4–5 Juliette Wade (Dr and Mrs A.J. Cox, Woodpeckers, Warwickshire); 6–7 Clay Perry (Barnsley House, Gloucestershire); 8 Eric Crichton (designer: Duchess of Devonshire, Chatsworth); 9 above Georges Lévêque; 9 below Clive Nichols (Barnsley House Garden, Gloucestershire); 9 left Gary Moyes/BBC Gardeners' World Magazine; 10 Boys Syndication; 11 Brigitte Thomas; 12–13 Jerry Harpur (designer: Michael Balston, Rofford Manor); 15 Karen Bussolini (Governor's Place, Williamsburg VA); 17 above Tim Sandall; 17 below Eric Crichton; 18 Eric Crichton (Mr and Mrs D. Hodges, Brook Cottage, Oxfordshire); 19 Eric Crichton; 21 Eric Crichton (Hunstrete House Hotel, Avon); 22 Brigitte Thomas; 23 Neil Campbell-Sharp/National Trust Photographic Library (Barrington Court, Somerset); 24–5 Clive Nichols (Hadspen Gardens, Somerset); 27 Jerry Harpur (designer: Michael Balston); 29 Georges Lévêque (Château de Quincize); 30 Eric Crichton; 31 Brigitte Thomas; 32–3 Boys Syndication; 34–5 Eric Crichton (Mrs E. Pedder, Yeomans); 36 Brigitte Thomas; 37 Michèle Lamontagne (Barnsley House Garden, Gloucestershire); 38 Clive Nichols (Ivy Cottage, Dorset); 41 Christian Sarramon (Miromesil); 43 Michael Howes/Garden Picture Library; 46 J.C. Mayer/G. Le Scanff/Garden Picture Library; 47 Clive Nichols (Ivy Cottage, Dorset), 49 Derek St. Romaine; 51 Eric Crichton; 53 J.C. Mayer/G. Le Scanff; 55 Eric Crichton; 57 Tessa Traegar; 58 Photos Horticultural; 59 Michèle Lamontagne; 61 Brigitte Thomas; 62 Eric Crichton; 63 J.C. Mayer/G. Le Scanff; 65 John Heseltine; 66 Brigitte Thomas; 67 Michèle Lamontagne; 69 above Neil Campbell-Sharp; 69 below Jacqui Hurst (Suffolk Herbs); 70 Reed Consumer Books; 71–3 Elizabeth Whiting & Associates; 74 Derek Fell; 75 Marianne Majerus; 78–9 Reed Consumer Books; 81 Steven Wooster/Garden Picture Library (designer: Rosemary Verey; Mr and Mrs Huntingdon, Old Rectory, Sudborough); 82 John Glover (Hri Hatton Fruit Garden, Kent); 83 Neil Campbell-Sharp (Barrington Court); 84 N. and P. Mioulane/MAP; 86 C. Pemberton-Piggott/Garden Picture Library (West Green, Hampshire); 87 Lucy Mason; 88 J.C. Mayer/G. Le Scanff; 91 Michèle Lamontagne; 94 N. and P. Mioulane/MAP; 95 John Glover (Cokes Barn, Sussex); 96 Eric Crichton; 97 Derek Fell; 98 John Heseltine; 99 Lucy Mason; 100 Tania Midgley; 101 Andrew Lawson; 104 Eric Crichton; 105 Neil Campbell-Sharp; 106–7 Eric Crichton; 109 Photos Horticultural; 111 Hugh Palmer (Barnsley House Garden, Gloucestershire); 112–13 Clive Nichols (Le Manoir Aux Quat' Saisons); 115 Georges Lévêque (Parc du Belvédére, Laeken, Belgium); 118–19 Clay Perry (Barnsley House, Gloucestershire); 120 MAP; 121 Juliette Wade (Dr and Mrs A.J. Cox, Woodpeckers, Warwickshire); 122 Georges Lévêque; 123 Clive Nichols (The Old Rectory, Berkshire).

The publisher also thanks Jackie Matthews, Barbara Nash and Janet Smy.

Index compiled by Indexing Specialists, Hove, East Sussex BN3 2DJ.